# *SHAW'S CHAMPIONS*

# SHAW'S CHAMPIONS

*G.B.S. & Prizefighting*
*from Cashel Byron to Gene Tunney*

## BENNY GREEN

ELM TREE BOOKS · LONDON

To Mike Molloy

First published in Great Britain 1978
by Elm Tree Books/Hamish Hamilton Limited
90 Great Russell Street, London WC1B 3PT

Copyright © 1978 by Benny Green

**British Library Cataloguing in Publication Data**

Green, Benny
    Shaw's champions.
        1. Shaw, Bernard – Friends and associates
        2. Corbett, James John    3. Tunney, Gene
        I. Title
        822'.9'12        PR5366
        ISBN 0-241-89735-1

Printed in Great Britain by
The Camelot Press Ltd, Southampton

# CONTENTS

# ILLUSTRATIONS

# ACKNOWLEDGEMENTS

I would like to thank Miss Susan Jeffreys for so resolutely hunting down reviews in long-since defunct American newspapers. Also, Mr Michael Holroyd for his selfless devotion to the cause of my duty in drawing my attention to correspondence between Bernard Shaw and Gene Tunney.

The author and publishers also wish to thank the following for permission to reproduce copyright material in this volume. For photographs: The Historical Picture Service, Gilbert Odd Esq. and The Radio Times Hulton Picture Library. All extracts from works and correspondence of Bernard Shaw are reproduced by permission of The Society of Authors on behalf of the Bernard Shaw Estate. For extracts from *Bernard Shaw, His Life and Personality* by Hesketh Pearson by permission of Michael Holroyd Esq., literary executor to the late Hesketh Pearson; from *Bernard Shaw, Man of the Century* by Archibald Henderson by permission of Da Capo Press Inc.; from *Conversations With Max* by S. N. Behrman by permission of the estate of the late S. N. Behrman and Brandt and Brandt; from *A Man Must Fight* by Gene Tunney (reprinted in *The Aspirin Age* edited by Isabel Leighton, *The Boxing Companion* edited by Denzil Batchelor and *The Noble Art* edited by T. B. Shepherd) by permission of Houghton Mifflin Company; from an article by Norman Clark reprinted from the *New York Post*; from *The Roar of the Crowd* by James Corbett (reprinted in *The American Reader* edited by P. M. Angle) by permission of G. P. Putnam's Sons, © 1925 by James J. Corbett; from *Thirty Years with G.B.S.* by Blanche Patch by permission of Victor Gollancz Ltd; from *Very Ordinary Sportsman* by J. P. Mallalieu by permission of the author.

Every effort has been made to trace the copyright holders of the quoted material. Should there be any omissions in this respect, we apologise and shall be pleased to make the appropriate acknowledgement in future editions.

# INTRODUCTION

The idea that Bernard Shaw could ever have been interested in prizefighting is so uncongenial to most of his readers that they either ignore it altogether or shrug it off as just one more instance of an old man's disconcerting tendency to buffoonery. Clearly the Vegetarians, the Fabian Socialists, the Anti-Vivisectionists, the Ibsenists and the Wagnerites are all confused by this juxtaposition of their hero with prizefighting because it disrupts all Shavian systems and upsets all Shavian ethics. Indeed, the only aspect about it which is never questioned is its incongruity. How could this dedicated humanitarian – who boasted that his funeral cortège would consist of all the animals he had never eaten, who advised the revolutionary theorist to hide under the bed until the shooting was over and who described the spectators at the Colosseum games as 'the vilest of voluptuaries' – possibly have relished the spectacle of two hired hands trying to punch each other into the nearest infirmary? Admittedly there are a few scattered hints to be found among the reminiscences of the late Victorians, but on first sight these read more like biographical licence than cold fact. It has been claimed, for instance, that Edith Nesbit would sometimes 'induce her husband and Shaw to put on gloves and spar together',[1] but as both Miss Nesbit and her husband, the Fabian Hubert Bland, appear in their differing ways to have been such incorrigible romancers, it is tempting to dismiss the anecdote as so much period colour. It is, in fact, the kind of situation too contradictory even for Shaw, the arch-dialectitian, to justify. And so it is only natural that the self-appointed apologist should try to justify it for him.

There is one very inviting method of resolving the contradiction. In his own lifetime Shaw referred more than one biographer to a fictitious character called G.B.S., a pantomime

ostrich[2] who waited to see what the world expected of it and then
did the opposite, with the object of attracting attention to the
serious thinker hiding behind the feathers. Shavians opposed to
prizefighting might be excused for putting the whole thing down
to the ostrich and thinking no more about it. Unfortunately, the
theory will not support itself. There is no avoiding the fact that
prizefighting exercised a fascination over Shaw long after he
needed or desired self-advertisement, and that as late as his
ninety-third year he was still eagerly seeking eye-witness
accounts of championship contests. In any case, ostriches, even
Shavian ostriches, cannot write, and Shaw wrote about
prizefighting at sufficient length and with sufficient persistence
to leave no doubt in the reader's mind that the sport held
something very much like a hypnotic attraction for him.

The other apparent escape from the impasse is to dismiss
Shaw as a hypocrite who adopted peaceful postures in his work
only because they were fashionable, at least among other
intellectuals, or because the general context of his thought
seemed to demand them. To do this is not only to be unfair to
Shaw but to overlook the fact that prizefighting, so far from
being a contradiction in his life, was a highly promising if
unexpected area in which to demonstrate the viability of the life
force, the 'march onward and upward', the triumph of mind
over matter, the mystical belief in a benign biological force
which was pushing ignoble Man towards Godhead despite
himself. Taking for a moment the viewpoint of Shaw the
demagogue who ran before the truncheons of the Metropolitan
Police in Trafalgar Square on Bloody Sunday, it becomes quite
clear what it was about prizefighting which first intrigued Shaw
as a very young man and continued to do so for the rest of his
life.

The aspect of physical combat which troubles the layman
most of all is the question of courage. To the average man who
would run a mile to avoid a punch on the nose, there is
something unspeakably morbid about a profession based on the
act of punching other people and being punched in return. So
alien is it to the normal cowardly instincts of the sedentary male
that he begins to tell himself that perhaps boxing has nothing to
do with courage at all. Perhaps the boxing ring too has its

cowards, and a jab in the eye from a fourteen-stone antagonist does not hurt at all once you have become used to the idea of it not hurting. It is a comforting theory which would be even more comforting if there were any way of corroborating it.

At first sight this does not seem too difficult a thing to do. There is the obvious tactic of asking a prizefighter. He should know if anyone does. But there is an insurmountable difficulty here. Prizefighters as a class happen to be so doggedly inarticulate that, as Shaw realised even in his twenties, the novelist has only to graft on to the character of a professional pugilist the manners of an exquisite to unearth a rich vein of social comedy. Even if the average prizefighter wanted to give away trade secrets, which is doubtful, he would find it almost impossible to do so. It is pointless asking a man of limited sensibilities whether limited sensibility precludes the worst excesses of fear, which is why it is virtually impossible for the outsider to know what it must really be like to be a fighter, and why also the intellectual thrashes around in search of a rational explanation for what appears to be the most irrational of instincts.

But the intellectual will stop and listen if the talk is of mind over muscle, of science over brute strength. The concept is one which he can grasp without leaving the sanctuary of his desk. Besides, he finds it gratifying to build a bridge, however tenuous, between the killer instinct which must baffle him, and the art of ratiocination which he flatters himself he possesses. This is especially the case if he happens to believe, as Shaw evidently did, that the human will is itself a muscle which can be made to influence the rate of growth of all the others. This kind of interest by the thinker in the man of action, is commonplace enough, but in the unique case of Shaw as the author of *Cashel Byron's Profession*, the process reverses itself to form a remarkable case history, the only one in which, instead of the philosopher being utterly captivated by the prizefighter, the prizefighter becomes utterly captivated by the philosopher.

# PART ONE

# *WRITING*

'In boxing my interest is purely scientific: I have no
sympathy with either party. I hate the sight of blood.'
George Bernard Shaw

By the time he completed *Cashel Byron's Profession* in 1883, Shaw was already a failed Victorian novelist with at least three rejected manuscripts being nibbled by the mice in Fitzroy Square. The themes he had selected for these earlier books had been respectively the Great Painter, the Great Musician and a study of Rationalism and Materialism. If, in this context, prizefighting as a theme for a novel sounds unlikely, the events surrounding it appear quite unbelievable. One of the first friends Shaw made on his arrival in London in 1876 was a man called Pakenham Beatty, 'an Irish dilettante with a penchant for Swinburnean poetry, educated at Harrow and Bonn, living on an inheritance which he rapidly squandered',[1] and later to be satirised as Chichester Erskine in Shaw's *An Unsocial Socialist*. Beatty was on terms with several people in the pugilistic world, among them Ned Donnelly, Professor of Boxing to the London Athletic Club. Before long Donnelly was giving Beatty's penniless young friend lessons in the noble art of self-defence, and it is not hard to see what it was about Donnelly which appealed so strongly to men like Shaw and Beatty.

If Shaw's early flirtation with the prize-ring is to be understood, then it must be understood also what kind of establishment Donnelly ran. The gymnasium at 18 Panton Street, a few paces from the Haymarket Theatre, was a school for gentlemen, with the accent on self-defence rather than licensed assault. Shaw, the distant connection of an Irish baronet, would have been the first to appreciate the subtle social differences between Donnelly's ultra-respectable establishment and the public-house backyards of the paid professional. Even more to the point, the noble art as Donnelly understood it, was a precise science in which a legitimate parry existed for every possible offensive move. Around the time he and Shaw first met,

Donnelly published a small manual on the art of boxing,[2] and its pages reveal how utterly he believed that comprehensive skills could be acquired simply by swotting up the text. Donnelly was, in fact, a pugilistic crammer, and his methods must have been a revelation to any timid young man with a firm belief in the power of his own intelligence.

There was something else about Donnelly likely to have a strong appeal to Shaw, and that was his evident pretension to some sort of literary style. This curious quirk in Donnelly's nature lifted him for the most part no higher than the stilted phraseology of the sporting journalism of the period. In his attempt to convince the reader that the impulse to strike your fellow-man is respectably primeval, Donnelly could write, 'Even the Jews did not wholly eschew the art of smiting', and in trying to find a good word for a defeated veteran featherweight in the Amateur Boxing Association Championships of 1884, he remarks, 'We do not mean to infer that the veteran did not rub out a chalk or two in the wind-up.'

But there are moments in Donnelly's text when he escapes these limitations and soars into unembarrassed metaphor. Analysing the left-hand counter to the head, and in describing the effect of an unexpected blow full in the face, he writes:

> It opens a spacious firmament to the bewildered eyes, wherein you discover more planets in a second than the most distinguished astronomers observe in a lifetime.

But Donnelly can do much better than this. On his very first page he flies directly in the face of received Shavian dogma with 'He would teach who first must have learned', evidently being unable to anticipate the birth of that maxim for revolutionaries, 'Those who can, do; those who can't, teach', still lying deep in the womb of time, as Shaw might have put it.

At the front of Donnelly's slim volume is a list of subscribers. They include three peers of the realm, one elder son, a naval captain, and three army officers. In attending the gymnasium in Panton Street, where Donnelly was on call from ten o'clock in the morning till one, and from four till eight daily, Shaw was hardly slipping down the social scale, although it is doubtful whether he or Beatty went so far as to follow their tutor's instructions for toughening the skin:

> Take a pint of whisky, a pint of vinegar, some horse-radish, rock-salt and about five lemons. Squeeze in the above, put in a pot, and boil it well. When cold put in a quart bottle. Rub yourself with it three times a day.

But the unquestioned rectitude of Donnelly's establishment cannot alter the fact that once inside it, men were taught to strike each other, and it is this which must make Shaw's behaviour seem incomprehensible to so many Shavians. Worse, however, was to come, although how much worse remains uncertain. In an autobiographical fragment published in 1901 Shaw gives the following account of his one-time boxing connections:

> Twenty years ago a poet friend of mine, who, like all poets, delighted in combats, insisted on my sharing his interest in pugilism, and took me about to all the boxing competitions of the day. I was nothing loth; for, my own share of original sin apart, anyone with a sense of comedy must find the arts of self-defence delightful (for a time) through their pedantry, their quackery, and their action and reaction between amateur romantic illusion and professional eye to business . . . at all events, it was the boxing world that came under my notice; and as I was amused and sceptically observant, whilst the true amateurs about me were, for the most part, merely excited and duped, my evidence may have a certain value when the question comes up again for legislative considerations, as it assuredly will some day.
>
> The first competitions I attended were at the beginning of the eighties, at Lillie Bridge, for the Queensberry championships. There were but few competitors, including a fair number of gentlemen; and the style of boxing aimed at was the 'science' bequeathed from the old prize-ring by Ned Donnelly, a pupil of Nat Langham.[3]

Now the implication here is clear that Shaw attended these boxing tournaments in a mood of most un-Shavian compliance only because of the enthusiasm of his 'poet friend' (equally clearly Pakenham Beatty) and perfectly clear also that Shaw is describing his experiences as a spectator, an impression borne out by the following paragraph from a letter sent by Shaw to Beatty's son, Mazzini, in December 1899. In offering to subsidise young Beatty's educational expenses, Shaw had evidently encountered pangs of pride and conscience on the young man's part. In his attempt to explain that in helping the son he was only discharging a long-standing debt to the father, Shaw wrote:

> When I plunged into London, it took me nine years of preying on my mother and father and anybody else who, like your father, would stand me a dinner or a stall at a boxing competition, before I got on my legs as a journalist. Those nine years were my apprenticeship; I did a lot of work in them – wrote five novels and dozens of articles, lectured and ranted, and picked up all sorts of efficiencies.[4]

By 1946 either Shaw's recollection of his own youth had become confused, or the euphoria of reaching the age of ninety was tempting him to disclose the plain unvarnished Shavian truth. In a typescript preface added to the manuscript of *Cashel Byron's Profession* donated to the National Library of Ireland, Shaw gave this amended account of his pugilistic past:

> An intimate acquaintance of mine in 1882 was Pakenham Beatty, a minor poet and amateur pugilist, both of which tastes an independent income enabled him to gratify to the utmost of his powers. He insisted on my accompanying him to all the boxing exhibitions, meeting his teachers, and finally putting on the gloves and acting as his sparring partner after studying an instruction book by Ned Donnelly, who is sketched in the resultant novel as Ned Skene. In this way I became observant of professional boxing; but it attracted me first on its economic side by the comedy of the contrast between the visionary prizefighter as romantic warrior hero and the matter-of-fact trader in fisticuffs at certain weights and prices and odds. There are, besides, no sports which bring out the difference of character more dramatically than boxing, wrestling and fencing. I acquired a taste for them (as a

spectator) that I retain to this day, and that enabled me to add a few articles on boxing to my more becoming and expected achievements in criticism, and to write the . . . novel . . . I soon got an imaginary reputation in my little circle as a boxer; and as I looked credibly like a tall man with a straight left and had in fact picked up some notion of how to defend myself, I was never attacked with bodily violence nor troubled by any fear of it from political opponents.[5]

However, a very different, and altogether more extraordinary picture begins to emerge when turning to Dan H. Laurence's annotations to Shaw's *Collected Letters*, where one finds this in the thumbnail sketch of Pakenham Beatty:

On 17th March, 1883, Beatty and Shaw actually applied for participation in the Amateur Boxing Championship at Lillie Bridge Grounds (Shaw, who weighed barely 10 stone, or 140 pounds, entered both Middle and Heavyweight classes), but though their names appeared on the official programme, they were not chosen for competition.[6]

Perhaps the rebuff was unimportant, because by now Shaw had sublimated his interest in boxing by writing a novel about it. Conjuring up his hero by mixing in equal parts the personalities of the flamboyant Beatty and a famous pugilist of the day called Jack Burke, and drawing heavily on Donnelly for his portrait of the trainer Ned Skene, Shaw had, on 12 April 1882, settled down to his self-imposed task of five foolscap pages a day. Byron, the unloved son of a successful actress, runs away from boarding school after indulging in the standard schoolboy fantasy of pole-axing his mathematics master with one perfect right-hander. He then works his passage to Australia and is there befriended by Ned Skene, who quickly recognises his boxing genius. The action then jumps forward several years: Byron, now a highly successful prizefighter, seeks a place in London society and falls wildly in love with the impossibly Shavian Lydia Carew. She, after savouring at some leisure the paradox of a society which excludes prizefighters, who maim their fellow citizens one at a time, in favour of generals who butcher theirs by the thousand, finally agrees to marry Byron. The champion, prepared to make the sacrifice of relinquishing his profession, has one last fight with the brutal William Paradise which he wins easily, inherits a large estate and settles down to a life of happy parasitism as the local Conservative member – although it is not very long before the delightful originality of his thought causes him to leave the party and continue as an Independent.

By the time of his rejection as a pugilist at Lillie Bridge, Shaw was already beginning to experience further rejections as the author of *Cashel Byron's Profession*, completed a month before the escapade at the Amateur championships. Indeed, the year 1882 was something of a watershed in Shaw's life, for it provided at least two of the cornerstones on which the classic Shavian edifice was eventually to rest: Socialism and Vegetarianism. On 5 September 1882, by which time *Cashel Byron's Profession* must have been half-completed, he attended a debate at the Non-conformist Memorial Hall in Farringdon Street to hear an address by Henry George, the apostle of Land Nationalisation and Single Tax. Shaw said he could tell that George was an American, not only from his accent, but also because he 'spoke of Liberty, Justice, Truth, Natural Law, and other strange eighteenth-century superstitions; and because he explained with great simplicity and sincerity the views of the Creator, who had gone completely out of fashion in London in the previous decade and had not been heard of since.'[7] It was George who first fired Shaw's interest in economics, and whose eloquence led him first to Henry Hyndman's Marxist Democratic Federation and at last to Marx himself.

Not long before the George lecture, in 1881, Shaw had fallen a victim to the London smallpox epidemic and been placed on a diet, over which he had no control, and which breached the vegetarian code he had only just begun to embrace. In October 1881, completely cured, he returned to his vegetarian diet and remained staunch to it for the sixty-nine remaining years of his life; 1882, the year of the composition of *Cashel Byron's Profession*, was therefore George Bernard Shaw's first as a dedicated socialist-vegetarian.

There was something else which occurred in 1882 which gives us a convenient insight into the working methods which Shaw was applying to his composition of the novel. On 24 July, while

scrutinising that day's edition of the *Daily News* for possible
sources of employment, Shaw noticed this:

Wanted, a copyist, to copy MS of a novel. State terms per
folio, and number of words. Miss Southam, Windermere.

In offering to perform the chore for ten guineas, Shaw made
the following comprehensive, and perhaps a little too
comprehensive, offer:

I will reproduce the novel in a fit state for the printers' hands,
I will co-operate with the author to make the work as perfect
as possible without interfering with his authorship. If there
are any solecisms in the use of titles, blunders in allusions of
the fine arts, impossible legal disputes, or such other slips as
are common in fiction, I will correct them, and if it is desired,
give a critical opinion of the work.[8]

Miss Southam must have responded to this bombardment
with a request for Shaw's credentials, because on 28 July, he
wrote to her that 'there are certain considerations which make it
difficult for me to satisfy by means of reference my competence
to assist you. Your own judgement will serve you better than that
of those who are strangers to you, and personal friends of mine.'
The maddeningly infallible logic of these instructions did not
quite win over Miss Southam, and on 31 July Shaw answered her
once again, this time explaining why it was impossible for him to
revise Volume One without knowing what happened in Volume
Three. Fortunately for posterity, Shaw added something else to
this third communication. Unable to resist the pedagogic
inclinations of his own literary soul, Shaw used the letter as an
excuse to deliver an address on the art of writing effective
narrative fiction, into which category, no doubt, he considered
*Cashel Byron's Profession* to belong:

Do not be too much afraid of tautology. The work of a novice
often owes much of its awkwardness to efforts to avoid
repeating the same word twice on a page. This is especially the
case in dialogue. For instance, if you invent a conversation
between Mrs Smith and Mrs Jones, you need not study such

alternatives to 'Said Mrs S' as 'replied Mrs Jones', 'observed Mrs Smith', 'rejoined', 'remarked', 'answered', and so on. Also, call your hero by his name as often as you have occasion to mention him. Do not ring changes on him as 'the impassioned youth', 'the young artist', 'our hero', and the like. The tendency to do these things is stronger than your good taste will let you suppose at present. Try to make the dialogue describe itself. For instance:

'The church seems such an odd profession for Harry to choose,' said Mrs Smith.
Mrs Jones started and looked incredulously at her visitor, as she said, 'I thought he was going into the army.'
This is very bad. I would correct it as follows:
'The church seems an odd profession for Harry to choose.'
'The church! I thought he was going into the army.'

Shaw then goes on to chat pleasantly about Shakspere [*sic*] and Molière, insists that neither Milton nor Byron possessed the faculty of character drawing, which item of information Miss Southam must have found invaluable in her own quest for literary fluency, and then resumes the lecture:

Never use an adjective or adverb unless it is absolutely necessary to the sense or rhythm of the sentence. Let the hero love the heroine and not be passionately devoted to her, let the heroine suffer pain, and not poignant anguish, let the villain make efforts, and not desperate struggling. When you do use an adverb, do not put 'very' before it. And do not qualify facts or thoughts which are too impressive in themselves to need your assistance, as I once heard a German tragedian do in this fashion: 'To be or not to be, that is the awful question'.
If you wish your adjectives to be effective, you must not cheapen them by scattering them broadcast on trivial occasions. Do not pet and dandle your favourite characters. This is one of the commonest and most objectionable habits of lady novelists.

Only in the closing sentence of this letter does Shaw betray the vulnerability of the budding author; no doubt with his mother and his sister Lucy in mind, he tells Miss Southam not to show her manuscript to just anybody:

> If a rule can be said to exist for such a matter, it is that an author's friends flatter, and her family ridicules her work.[9]

With which instructions Ethel Southam disappears from the annals of literary history, except that when Dan Laurence went to the British Museum catalogue in the hope of discovering her novel, all he found listed under her name was a book written in collaboration with one Gertrude Southam, entitled *Hors de Combat, or Three Weeks in a Hospital*, published by Cassell in 1891. Whether she ever took Shaw's advice must remain a mystery, but there certainly came a time when Shaw himself spurned it. In 1921, writing a reminiscent preface to the belated edition of his first novel, *Immaturity*, he explains:

> I did set up one condition in my early days. I resolved that I would write nothing that should not be intelligible to a foreigner with a dictionary, like the French of Voltaire; and I therefore avoided idiom. (Later on I came to seek idiom as being the most highly vitalised form of language.)

Of all five of Shaw's 'novels of my nonage', *Cashel Byron's Profession* came closest to commercial acceptance, a fact which later drew from its creator the observation, 'I never think of *Cashel Byron's Profession* without a shudder at the narrowness of my escape from becoming a successful novelist at the age of twenty-six.'[10] While engaged in the composition of the novel, Shaw appears to have been under no illusions as to its profundity, and even suggested, to no less a person than the publisher to whom he had been trying to sell the book, Richard Bentley, that the low tone of the novel was calculated. Bentley had been interested enough in the manuscript to pay for three independent readers' reports on it, but had eventually decided that the subject-matter was not sufficiently elevated, an opinion with which Shaw, already long familiar with Bentley's rejections of his work, thoroughly concurred:

> You are quite right as to the horrible blackguardism of the book, but pray remember that I have tried science and the

finer arts as subjects in vain, and that the lower I go, the better I seem to please.[11]

As the 1880s passed and his ambitions as a novelist slowly withered, Shaw grew progressively less charitable towards poor Byron, his coolness towards his brain-child modulating swiftly from indifference to irritation and finally to positive contempt. Having insulated himself to an almost inhuman degree from the sting of rejection by publishers, he could afford to laugh at the very idea of being stung by rejection from himself, and it seems doubtful that his off-hand detachment about a book whose writing had occupied him every day for fourteen months was altogether affectation. In a letter to the actress-poet Alma Murray in October 1886, he dismissed his prizefighting novel as 'a shilling shocker', although a few lines later he was canny enough to add that he considered it 'one of the cleverest books I know, although I wrote it when an infant, comparatively speaking.'[12] Two years later he actually congratulated the publisher T. Fisher Unwin on having had the perspicacity to reject the book: 'Your repudiation of *Cashel Byron's Profession* is a positive relief to me; for I hate the book from my soul.'[13] By January 1891, he was acknowledging to his friend of boyhood, Matthew McNulty, the justice of the frankly absurd charge that the big fight scene in the novel is based on the wrestling match in *As You Like It*. And by January 1905, Shaw had plainly had enough of the whole business; in priming his future biographer Archibald Henderson, he found himself obliged to say something about the literary judgment of W. E. Henley. In March 1886, Henley had written a letter to William Archer in which he proceeded to praise *Cashel Byron's Profession* rather too fulsomely:

> Who the deuce is Bernard Shaw? And where these many years has he been dissembling his talent? I like his book immensely; it has vigour, humour, originality and wit; it makes me hopeful of fiction. I read the book with astonishment and delight.[14]

The generosity of the tribute was something Shaw could never forgive, and he wrote to Henderson:

Henley admired *Cashel Byron's Profession* – I have always considered this the mark of a fool, by the way.[15]

If Shaw is right about this, then the literary world must have been even more generously stocked with fools than is usually the case; in analysing the reactions to *Cashel Byron*, it appears that almost everyone except those publishers and publishers' readers who withheld the accolade of publication, sensed something unusually powerful and attractive about the book. One of these enthusiasts was Robert Louis Stevenson, who reacted with amused approval when the story belatedly appeared as a serial in the mid-1880s. In a letter to Shaw's oldest journalistic ally William Archer, who must eventually have become disenchanted with the voluminous mail which the novel inspired, Stevenson attempted, not very perceptively as it happens, to break Shaw's prose style down into its component parts, a gesture much too candid for the delicate sensibilities of Sir Sidney Colvin, one of that comical band of literary sharepushers who tried so hard to inflate Stevenson's posthumous market price. In editing his hero's letters, Colvin took great care to leave out Stevenson's recipe for a Shavian tract; fortunately for posterity, Shaw took even greater care to put it back again in the 1901 edition of *Cashel Byron's Profession*:

| | |
|---|---:|
| Charles Reade . . . . . . . | 1 part |
| Henry James or some kindred author, badly assimilated . . . . . . . | 1 part |
| Disraeli (perhaps unconscious) . . . . | $\frac{1}{2}$ part |
| Struggling, overlaid original talent . . . | $1\frac{1}{2}$ part |
| Blooming gaseous folly . . . . . | 1 part |

That is the equation as it stands. What it may become, I don't know, nor any other man. Vixere fortes – O, let him remember that – let him beware of his damned century: his gifts of insane chivalry and animated narration are just those that might be slain and thrown out like an untimely birth by the Daemon of the Epoch. And if he only knew how I had enjoyed his chivalry! Over Bashville the footman I howled with derision and delight. I dote on Bashville: I could read him for ever: de Bashville je suis le fervent: there is only one

Bashville: and I am his devoted slave: Bashville est magnifique; mais il n'est guere possible. Bashville – O Bashville. J'en chortle! (Which is finely polyglot.). . . . What am I to say? I have read your friend's book with singular relish. If he has written any other, I beg you will let me see it; and if he has not, I beg him to lose no time in supplying the deficiency. It is full of promise, but I should like to know his age. There are things in it that are very clever, to which I attached small importance; it is the shape of the age. And there are passages, particularly the rally in presence of the Zulu King, that show genuine and remarkable narrative talent – a talent that few will have the wit to understand, a talent of strength, spirit, capacity, sufficient vision, and sufficient self-sacrifice, which last is the chief point in a narrator. It is all mad, mad and deliriously delightful: the author has a taste in chivalry like Walter Scott's or Dumas's, and then he daubs in little bits of socialism; he soars away on the wings of the romantic griffin – even the griffin, as he cleaves air, shouting with laughter at the nature of the quest – and I believe in his heart he thinks he is labouring in a quarry of solid granite realism. . . . It is *horrid fun*. All I ask is more of it. Thank you for the pleasure you gave us, and tell me more of the inimitable author.

Stevenson was being extremely acute in his perception of the un-Victorian nature of Shaw's novel-writing style, although it is very possible that he was influenced in his judgement by a very different kind of reaction to the book inside his own family. In October 1950, on the eve of his fatal accident, in composing the last piece of writing he was ever to finish, Shaw was still speculating on the curious genesis of this book he had professed, long ago, to hate from his soul, and recalled the revulsion felt towards his shilling shocker by Mrs Robert Louis Stevenson, who was so disgusted by Byron's remark, 'I hate my mother' that 'she shut the book with a bang and flung it away. All heroes in 1882 had to love their mothers and in due degree the rest of their relatives.'[16]

Another literary professional who commended *Cashel Byron's Profession* was Archer himself, who reviewed it favourably in *The*

*Pall Mall Gazette* for 8 March 1886, although in resorting in his
opening line to the drawing of a Gilbertian parallel, he no doubt
exasperated Shaw beyond measure. Eight years later, when
Archer performed the same parlour trick in reviewing *Arms and
the Man*, he drew down on his head a fearful outburst of
intellectual Shavian wrath, in which Shaw bellowed that the
typically Gilbertian hero 'is ridiculous through the breakdown
of his ideals, not odious from his falling short of them. As
Gilbert sees, they don't work, but what Gilbert does not see is
that there is something else that does work, and that in that
something else there is a completely satisfactory asylum for the
affections.'[17] Perhaps the violence of Shaw's reaction to Archer's
innocent critical chatter was due in part to the fact that not only
was he sticking the Gilbertian label on Shaw's best comedy to
date, but also he had already tried to stick it on to Shaw's best
novel; at any event, Shaw went quietly on the occasion of the
Byron review which read:

'I don't think much of our profession,' says Mr Gilbert's
Pirate King, 'but contrasted with respectability it is
comparatively honest.' Mr Shaw might have printed this
saying on the title-page of *Cashel Byron's Profession*. Cashel
Byron does not think much of his calling, which is that of
pugilism, but contrasted with many other professions and
pursuits of the highest respectability, he holds it to be
comparatively honest, useful and humane. The matter of the
story consists in the conversion of Miss Lydia Carew, an
heiress and a 'phoenix' among women, to this method of
thinking. As Cashel himself would put it, the book describes
his victorious fight, in some ten or a dozen rounds, against the
one prejudice which degrades Miss Carew to the level of our
common humanity. It is a paradox in action, a reduction to
absurdity of many of our egoisms, sentimentalisms and
hypocrisies, a social or sociological satire in the guise of a
Cymon-and-Iphigenia love story. Mr Shaw is an *a priori*
novelist. He scorns the patient art of the modern realist. Lydia
Carew is as fabulous an animal as the phoenix to whom she
laughingly compares herself, and, psychologically, Cashel
Byron is scarcely less impossible. It is true that the author's

knowledge of the prize-ring and all that appertains to it is extensive and peculiar; that some of his minor characters, such as Ned Skene and his wife, Mellish, Lucian Webber, and Alice Goff, are sketched with humorous felicity yet without caricature; and that an occasional touch every here and there reveals a really profound insight into the springs of human action. Yet on the whole *Cashel Byron's Profession* is not a work of observation and analysis but a pure exercise in satiric logic. Its wit, its thoughtfulness, and its unconventionality fascinate the reader: he is neither carried away on the wings of passion nor thrilled with the conviction of reality. Whatever may have been Mr Shaw's intention, his book, as a whole, produces the effect of a piece of brilliant persiflage; but brilliant it is – of that there can be no doubt.

Almost every chapter in the story may be said to constitute a scene of subtle comedy. In the early chapters, indeed, Mr Shaw once or twice slips into farce, through attributing to his encyclopaedic heroine a preternatural obtuseness as to the real nature of the 'profession' exercised by her athletic acquaintance. Such a passage as the following, for example, is somewhat overcharged.

Lydia: 'I begin to hold the clue to you. Idiosyncrasy. You have attached yourself to the modern doctrine of a struggle for existence, and look on life as a perpetual combat.'

Cashel: 'A fight? Just so. What is life but a fight? The curs forfeit or get beaten; the rogues sell the fight and lose the confidence of their backers; the game ones and the clever ones win the stakes, and have to hand over the lion's share of them to the loafers; and luck plays the devil with them all in turn. That's not the way they describe life in books, but that's what it is.' This passage occurs in one of the most delicious scenes in the book, where Cashel, at Mrs Hoskyn's aesthetic tea, illustrates an extempore lecture on the necessity of 'executive power' by sending the dignified Lucian Webber spinning half-way across the room at a tap of his open hand, and dropping him into an easy chair with the bland remark, 'It's like pocketing a billiard ball!' Better still, however, is the great dialogue between Cashel and Lydia immediately after her discovery of the nature of his 'profession'. Here Mr Shaw is quite at his best, both as a humorist and, if we may coin an expression, as a paradoxical psychologist. Cashel's summing up of the irony of his fate in the phrase 'It's a lonely thing to be a champion' comes in with irresistibly comic effect, and the little passage of arms with the footman Bashville, in which he relieves his exultation at the close of the interview, is really inimitable. Mr Shaw shines especially in rapid dialogue, but his style is always light, incisive, and perhaps too scrupulously sober. His nearest approach to fine writing occurs in Lydia Carew's glorification of our railway system from an aesthetic point of view, a passage which would probably tempt Mr Ruskin to place *Cashel Byron's Profession* beside the works of that noxious novelist W. M. Thackeray, at the very top of his blottesque Index Expurgatorius.

To what extent Archer was indulging in a little genteel logrolling on behalf of the protégé he had discovered in the Reading Room of the British Museum it is hard to say; in noticing the book at all, he could be accused of shedding the light of favourable publicity on a close friend, for the publication of the novel certainly inspired almost nobody outside the socialist coterie press to waste any time on it. In his day Archer had an enviable reputation for honesty and intellectual integrity, but Shaw seems to have believed that in this regard the world had made a very common error, which is to mistake the shadow for the substance:

> He has the reputation of being inflexible, impartial, rather cold but scrupulously just, and entirely incorruptible. I believe this impression is produced by his high cheek-bones, the ascetic outline of his chin and jaw, and his habit of wearing a collar which gives his head the appearance of being wedged by the neck into a jampot.[18]

And yet it was shrewd of Archer to have acknowledged the existence of *Cashel Byron's Profession*, which is at least as good as he says it is, and probably a great deal better. In his capacity as dramatic critic, resolutely refusing to be intimidated by Shaw's pretensions to genius, Archer repeatedly belaboured him for lacking all kinds of abilities and perceptions, including those of the born playwright. But this was later, when the protégé was already striding off into the utopian future, leaving friends like Archer to grapple with the uncomfortable problem confronting all friends of genius, which is how to admit to themselves that the person they know as a fallible, flesh-and-blood creature might also be a great man. The fact that Archer did not use the occasion of his review of *Cashel Byron's Profession* as a pretext for a disquisition on the art of novel-writing, is perhaps partly due to the fact that these were early Shavian days comparatively speaking, but surely also because his enjoyment was genuine.

Somebody else reviewed the book, someone who stands as high as any in the Shavian pantheon, and whose heroic stature dwarfs that of the clerical Archer. When Shaw had completed *Cashel Byron's Profession*, fourth of the novels of his nonage, he immediately set to work on his fifth, *An Unsocial Socialist*; and when the opportunity arose for his work to be serialised in the socialist press, naturally decided that Opus 5, being the most recent of his works, was also the best, and gave it out to the typesetters before allowing them to lay hands on the text of *Cashel Byron*. This established an inverse sequence of publication which was to confuse American reviewers of pirated editions, who 'unaware that the publisher was working backwards through the list, pointed out the marked advance in my style, the surer grip, the clearer form, the finer art, the maturer view of the world, and so forth.'[19] The first instalment of *An Unsocial Socialist*, the book in which the amateur pugilist Pakenham Beatty is sublimated as Chichester Erskine, appeared in *Today* in the issue of March 1884, and so diverted William Morris that he became curious to meet its author.

Morris's review of *Cashel Byron's Profession* appeared in the issue of *The Commonweal* on 17 July 1886:

A mere novel bearing on the face of it no controversial opinion, might not seem a suitable subject for review in these columns, but even apart from the author's well-known views and his power as a Socialist lecturer, a Socialist will find much in *Cashel Byron's Profession* to interest him as a Socialist. Everything that Mr Shaw writes must bear with it an indictment against our sham society, and it would be harder to find more incisive criticism of its follies than in this book. Perhaps, to a reader not a Socialist, and therefore not in the secret, it would be seen to be nothing more serious than a fantastic piece written on pessimistic lines, as all clever modern novels are, and with no further aim in it; but anyone must be forced to admit that it fulfils the first function of the novel by amusing the reader. As in all literary works of art, one is bound to accept its special atmosphere, which doubtless at first might rather confuse the ordinary reader, since the plot which one has to accept as possible consists of the development of the love at first sight of a very rich and refined young lady for a prize-fighter. The said heroine is not very much alive, is rather the embodiment of the author's view of life than a real personage; but the hero is most carefully studied and very successful, and every one of the minor characters is highly finished and natural. Indeed, Mr Shaw gives very good penn'orths in the manner of invention of incident, and is almost reckless in the care which he bestows on his scenes, as witness the sparring-match before the 'African King' in the Agricultural Hall, or the burst of confused excitement on studious solitude after Byron's great fight with Paradise. Mr Shaw sees his scenes clearly and accurately; indeed more after the manner of a painter than a dramatic writer. This is a quality which is much rarer than is generally supposed in these days of word-painting. It is probably a defect which naturally goes with it that the scenes are, so far as their artistic effect goes, isolated and lacking in the power that accumulation gives: the whole story rather leaves off than comes to an end, also. However, this is a defect which it shares with all novels of this generation that have any pretence to naturalism. As Mr Shaw is quite successful in establishing his claim to keen observation and vivid representation, one must not quarrel with him for not attaining to what is mostly beyond the aim of a modern novel, but which both Scott and Dickens now and then touched – the unity and completeness of a great drama. Whatever is attempted in *Cashel Byron* is done conscientiously and artistically.

Morris does well by Shaw, but in spite of the undoubted sincerity of his sentiments as expressed in the review, the modern reader begins to get the feeling that there has been a rallying-round in London socialist circles, that there is in the air a determination to see that their champion should get some kind of exposure before the world at large. It is a suspicion confirmed by the fact that another coterie periodical to review the book, with some acuity as it happens, was *Our Corner*, the magazine destined soon to take over the task of serialising Shaw's rejected fiction. In fact Shaw's Opus 2, *The Irrational Knot*, ran in *Our Corner* concurrently with the serialisation of *Cashel Byron* in *Today*. Shaw's comically uncompromising bellicosity towards anyone who dared to differ from him as to the relative merits of these fictional rejects, and his positively flamboyant refusal to deploy diplomatic wiles where literary impact might fail, is reflected in the shattering broadside with which he confounded John M. Robertson, editorial assistant to *Our Corner* and apparently a man who preferred *Love Among the Artists* to *The Irrational Knot*. In his letter of 19 January 1885, Shaw very quickly disabused Robertson of the idea that he was allowed to have any opinion in the matter at all:

> Mrs Besant writes to say that 'Mr Robertson fancies that *The Irrational Knot* is the least likely of your (my) novels to suit us'. Now I write to say that you have not read *The Irrational Knot*, that you ought to know better at your age than to dogmatise about novels that you haven't read, and that, by the Lord! you shan't have the other one that you want. What do the readers of *Our Corner* care about the life of a musician? they don't know Wagner's 'Tristan' from 'Pop Goes the Weazel'. *The Irrational Knot* is very long, and highly moral, and deeply interesting. A child can understand it, and a stern man can weep over it (if he likes). I am not going to be insulted before my time by being told at this stage of the proceedings that it won't suit. Run it through *Our Corner*, and when it is finished (in four years or so) perhaps you may get the other to follow it if you have behaved yourself in the meantime and refrain from telling Mrs Besant that my books are immoral and dull. I have no doubt that you have gone that length, though she is

too kind to say so. No sir: forbear these rash judgements until you have swallowed the MS, which you may expect any time in the course of the next fortnight. I must alter a few scenes – the alterations will remain to the good even if they fail to please you.[20]

Shaw signed the letter 'Champion Moralist'; he might have added the adjective 'triumphant', because Robertson went quietly, serialising *The Irrational Knot* in twenty-three monthly issues from April 1885, and earning his reward by being permitted to do the same with *Love Among the Artists* over fourteen issues from November 1887. Shaw may have not thought very highly of Robertson's perceptions as a literary critic – although the apparent wrath of the letter is shown to be bogus by the glint of levity which shines through every phrase – but it was Robertson who published, in the edition of *Our Corner* for 1 May 1886, the review of *Cashel Byron's Profession* which Shaw's official biographer Archibald Henderson described as 'the most sagacious and kindly':

No one can read the running comment in his story without seeing that to something of the Dickens faculty of humorous imagination he adds a much wider intellectual grasp than that of Dickens; that his satire is abreast of the times; and that he has looked at life from an adequate level of culture. His dialogue, too, is generally vivid and vigorous, and never feeble, though at times it curiously lapses into old-fashioned conventionality. And his style is that of a born writer, sound, elastic, various, unaffected . . .

Why does Robert Louis Stevenson, who is certainly as far away from life as Mr Shaw, and whose net action, as action, is quite as extravagant as that of *Cashel Byron's Profession* – why does he, in his best books, leave us pleased and applauding, while with Mr Shaw we are left objecting and wanting something else? It is not that the latter writer is less powerful or the less intellectually competent: we should rather infer from the two books, *Prince Otto* and *Cashel Byron's Profession* that his philosophy was the more comprehensive and the more solid of the two. It is this, it seems to me, that Mr Stevenson, if the lesser thinker, is, when at his best, the greater artist; that he achieves roundness, balance, and proportion in a successful art form, while Mr Shaw's many-sided satire is not artistically homogeneous; the satiric purpose being cramped by the fiction form, and the fictional effects being thwarted and deflected by the satiric purpose.

The extent to which reviewers resorted to Stevenson as a touchstone is perhaps surprising to an age which has long since forgotten how to take the author of *Weir of Hermiston* with much seriousness; but years later, when piratical American publishers brought out cheap editions of *Cashel Byron*, there Stevenson was, in James Huneker's article 'Bernard Shaw and Women' in *Harper's Bazaar* for June 1905:

> The Gods know that Bernard Shaw has many sins of omission to answer for when he reaches the remotest peaks of Parnassus; but for no one of his many gifts will he be so sternly taken to task as the wasted one of novelist. . . . There is more native talent for sturdy, clear-visioned, character-creating fiction in the one prize-fighting novel of Bernard Shaw than in the entire cobweb work of the stylistic Stevenson. . . . Shaw could rank higher as a novelist than as a dramatist – always selecting for judgement the supreme pages of his tales, pages wherein character, wit, humour, pathos, fantasy, and observation are mingled with an overwhelming effect.

Yet another American reviewer to invoke Stevenson in the context of Shaw is Christopher Morley who quotes Stevenson's by now famous remark about Shaw's 'insane chivalry and animated narration'. Remembering Stevenson's open question as to the chances of the Shavian style being 'thrown out like an untimely birth by the Daemon of the Epoch', Morley goes on:

> Well, the Daemon of the Epoch did have its effect on G.B.S. Whether for good or ill, it is too early to say. With his industry, as great as Trollope's, his seriousness, as intent as John Stuart Mill's, and his mad humour, as fierce as Meredith's, he might as well – and if publishers had had half an eye, certainly would – have gone on in a series of novels that would have been unlike anything in the course of British

fiction. No one can read *The Man of Destiny*, for instance, without saying, What a short story gone astray! No one can read *Cashel Byron's Profession*, no one but a publisher, at any rate, without seeing its extraordinary charm, humour, and subtle spoofing. I myself regard him as a great novelist gone wrong.

Two aspects of the case strike the modern reader with particular force. Surely no unpublished novel was ever so copiously reviewed; and, if those reviews are not altogether misleading, surely no unpublished novel was ever so badly treated by as well-intentioned a crew of publishers' readers as ever exposed their own imperceptions.

As to the stream of rejections which constitute Shaw's abortive career as a Victorian novelist, the evidence suggests that there arrived a juncture when even his rampant ego was at last stung by the ignominy and frustration of persistent failure. January 1885 marks one of the very rare moments in his Grub Street phase when the Shavian smokescreens disperse to reveal glimpses of a vulnerable hide. Shaw had spent the earlier part of the month amusing himself at the expense of the publishers Macmillan and Company, establishing over their readers an insolent intellectual superiority which must be most unusual in the history of literary rejections. The month began when Macmillans, in rejecting *An Unsocial Socialist*, added that they 'would be glad to look at anything else of a more substantial kind'. This drew a predictably comic lampoon of outraged literary virtue from Shaw, who wrote on 14 January:

Many thanks for reading *An Unsocial Socialist*. Your demand for 'something more substantial' takes my breath away. Your reader, I fear, thought the book not serious – perhaps because it was not dull. If so, he was an Englishman. I have met only one reviewer (J. M. Robertson) and one oral critic (William Archer) who really took the book in. They were both Scotchmen. You must admit that when one deals with two large questions in a novel, and throws in an epitome of modern German socialism as set forth by Marx as a makeweight, it is rather startling to be met with an implied accusation of triviality.[21]

On 22 January Macmillans replied so defensively as to apologise to Shaw for having had the impertinence to criticise him. In assuring him that *An Unsocial Socialist* had 'by no means been unappreciated', the firm hastened to assure Shaw that 'our reader is not responsible for the epithet "unsubstantial" which was perhaps not quite fortunate though we could not think of any other that would better express our meaning'. Shaw's prospective publishers, having by now been reduced to such intellectual disarray as to admit that their vocabulary was not commensurate with their professional obligations, now inspired in Shaw the closest approach to self-pitying pathos in which that resolutely unsentimental man ever indulged. After displaying admirable magnanimity by opening his reply 'I forgive your critic,' Shaw goes on to explain the difference between seriousness and solemnity, and then, in his closing lines, comes perilously close to making an appeal for sympathy:

> Surely out of thirty millions of copyright persons (so to speak) there must be a few thousand who would keep me in bread and cheese for the sake of my story-telling, if you would only let me get at them.[22]

But neither Macmillans, nor Bentley, nor Kegan Paul, nor Swan Sonnenschein, nor any other publisher ever did give young Shaw the chance 'to get at them', and in attempting to understand the nature of this astonishing professional folly of the publishing trade in refusing to have any part of one of the great prose masters of the last three hundred years, the question is bedevilled by the ambivalence of the prose master himself. As we have seen, Shaw was not above deriding his own books even in the act of attempting to sell them, and never tired in later years of poking merciless fun at them. Indeed, he appears to have worked out a tactical device for the next fifty years, which was that whenever confronted by the five skeletons hanging in the closet of his novel-writing nonage, always to make them dance. Fifty-seven years after his joust with Macmillans, he received a request from them for permission to publish the correspondence, and in the course of negotiations was given access to the original readers' reports on his novels. Shaw affected to be amazed by the generosity and insight of these reports:

I consider them highly creditable to the firm's readers: for they make it clear that what was wrong was not, as I thought, any failure to spot me as a literary discovery, but the strangeness at that time of my valuations. In fact they thought more of my jejune prentice work than I did myself; for I really hated those five novels, having drudged through them like any other industrious apprentice because there was nothing else I would or could do. That in spite of their disagreeableness they somehow induced readers rash enough to begin them to go on to the end and resent that experience seems to me now a proof that I was a born master of the pen. But the novel was not my proper medium. I wrote novels because everybody else did so then. . . .

I began, not very wisely, by calling on all the publishers in person to see what they were like; and they did not like me. I did not like myself enough to blame them. I was young [23], raw, Irish from Dublin, and Bohemian without being in the least convivial or self-indulgent, deeply diffident inside and consequently brazen outside, and . . . utterly devoid of reverence. . . . Altogether a discordant personality in the eyes of the elderly great publishers of those days, a now extinct species. As I had a considerable aesthetic culture, and the English governing classes, of whom I knew only what I had picked up from Thackeray and Trollope, had none, they were barbarians to me; and I was to them a complete outsider. I was in fact outside the political world until I had written the first three of my novels; and when I came in I was a Marxist, a phenomenon then inconceivable even to Mill, Morley, Dilke, Auberon Herbert, the Fortnightly Reviewers, the Positivists, the Darwinians, and the rest of the Agnostic Republicans who represented the extreme left of the most advanced pioneers in the eighties of the last century.[23]

That statement, balm for the corporate ego of Macmillans, is only one of several of a similar nature which Shaw issued periodically from the mountain-top.

As early as 1905, when he could hardly have dreamed of the

bright future still in store for his five bedraggled apprentice
works, he remarked:

> If I failed as a novelist to create a convincingly verisimilar
> atmosphere of aristocracy, it was not because I had any
> illusions or ignorances as to the common humanity of the
> peerage, and not because I gave literary style to its
> conversation, but because, as I had no money, I had to blind
> myself to its enormous importance, with the result that I
> missed the point of view, and with it the whole moral basis, of
> the class which rightly values money, and plenty of it, as the
> first condition of a bearable life.[24]

The accusation which Shaw is making against himself, that he
wrote of an aristocracy and a moneyed class of whose practical
morality he knew nothing, is one which he often invoked in his
assessments of other writers, particularly in an essay of great
distinction which was published as an introduction to *Great
Expectations* in 1947. In defending his great novelist-hero
Dickens from the wrist-slapping of gentlemen litterateurs, he
insists that 'Dickens knew all that really mattered about Sir
Leicester Dedlock and Trollope knew nothing that really
mattered about him. Trollope and Thackeray could see Chesney
Wold; but Dickens could see through it.' If for Chesney Wold we
substitute the Wiltstoken Castle whose walls are so triumphantly
breached by Cashel Byron's left jab, and fling on to Shaw's head,
as he repeatedly insists we do, all the imputations he makes
about Trollope and Thackeray, it would appear that what Shaw
is saying is that his novels deserved their failure because of their
social naïveté, a view he made clear yet again in a written
statement only a year before the publication of the *Great
Expectations* essay. In presenting the manuscript of four of his
novels to the Royal Library of Dublin, he remarks of *An Unsocial
Socialist*:

> The title of this novel finished me with the publishers. One of
> them refused even to read it. I had read the first volume of
> Karl Marx's *Capital* and made my hero a Marxian Socialist.
> This was beyond endurance. A clerk for my hero (my first) was
> not a recommendation, but at least he accepted the world as it

was and wore a white linen collar in its social eddies. I was perhaps to be encouraged. But my second, a working electrical engineer crashing through the castes and mastering them: that was distasteful and incorrect. I was going wrong. Then a British Beethoven, careless of his clothes, ungovernable, incomprehensible, poor, living in mean lodgings at an unfashionable address: this was absurd. The next, a prizefighter, wooing and marrying a priggishly refined lady of property, was a bit of romance without a child dying in it but with a fight or two. But a Socialist! A Red, an enemy of civilisation, a universal thief, atheist, adulterer, anarchist, and apostle of Satan he disbelieved in!! And presented as a rich young gentleman, eccentric but not socially unpresentable. ! ! ! Too bad.

And all the time I did not know that I was being ostracized on social and political grounds instead of, as I thought, declined on my literary merits, which, as is now clear, were never in question.[25]

Those sentiments may be taken as an expression of official Shavian policy whenever the subject of the five rejected novels was raised, a public attitude as carefully calculated as the contents of those printed postcards which he sent to people who wrote requesting either financial, intellectual or literary subsidy. But in private the sublime Shavian equanimity was animated by genial derision for those publishers' readers whose idiocy he was so ready to forgive in public. In fact, it could be said that for the next sixty years he resolutely refused to forgive any of them, gaily vilifying them instead, with a consistency which has actually bestowed upon at least one of them a kind of backhanded immortality. And in recalling the exalted frame of reference of those reviews, who can blame him? A taste in chivalry like Walter Scott's or Dumas's? Profound insight into the springs of human action? A much wider intellectual grasp than that of Dickens? A humour as fierce as Meredith's? Even if we deduct from the tributes the customary percentage of critical flapdoodle, it is an impressive reaction. So who were the blockheads who kept turning down this literary paragon? Who, for instance, the clerk who responded to the charming paradoxes of *Cashel Byron's Profession* with 'He has some promise of writing in him if he did not disgust us by his subject'? The identity of that particular noodle remains unknown, but the arch-villain of the piece, the reader who kept sending back Shaw's novels for year after platitudinous year was a famous public figure and, had Shaw only realised it, someone with whom he was already acquainted, and for whose morality and powers of literary discernment he had already developed a hearty contempt. And while he remained unaware who his persecutor was, his persecutor had quite forgotten he had ever met Shaw, and sincerely believed, as much as he could sincerely believe anything, that when he rejected *Cashel Byron's Profession*, his victim was a perfect stranger. It was an exquisite comedy of mistaken literary identity, a clash between the genteel parliamentary gradualism of the 1860s and the equally genteel Fabian revolutionary gradualism of the succeeding generation, with never a remote chance that either side would ever come to see the viewpoint of the other.

Like all ages self-consciously bent on reform against a background of rapid economic expansion, the Victorians have bequeathed to posterity a magnificent collection of stuffed owls, and it is doubtful if there exists any more perfect specimen of the genus than John Morley, who entered the interlocking worlds of literature and politics and for a while bestrode them like a pygmy. He began reading for Macmillans in the 1860s, concurrently editing the *Fortnightly Review* for fifteen years from 1868, and it was just before he left this post for the pastures of Westminster to transform his entire career into a comical contradiction, that Shaw first met him. For this free-thinking, forward-looking, liberty-loving Englishman had not been in the Commons five minutes before Gladstone made him Chief Secretary for Ireland, a success he eventually surpassed in 1905 when he was appointed Secretary for India. As neither the Irish nor the Indians at the time were altogether convinced that any coherent concept of freedom was compatible with the presence in their midst of a British secretary, it might be wondered how Morley contrived to square his advancement with his conscience. If he ever did so, he certainly kept the process a secret.

And yet the political contradictions in Morley's career are no less wonderful than its cultural cartwheels. As senior literary adviser to Macmillans, it was his duty to pass judgement on hundreds of novels, including Shaw's; but it was an open secret that so far as literature was concerned, he was one of those glum philistines who believe that if a thing has not happened, then it ought not to be written about – at least, not too much. His address 'On the Study of Literature', delivered at the Mansion House in 1887, included the extraordinary complaint that seven out of every ten books borrowed from public libraries were novels. He felt that this number was 'much too large' and that 'we should be better pleased if it sank to around forty per cent'. We consider that remark and conclude that he was a humbug. We then study his further observation that it is possible to stack a thousand octavo volumes in a space thirteen feet by ten by six inches and that 'everyone has that small amount of space at his disposal', contemplate its shocking tactlessness in the context of Morley's avowed social concern, and conclude that he is not a humbug after all, but a fool. The truth was that for all his inflated rhetoric, Morley had little inclination either for fiction or foreigners.

And yet it must have taken considerable courage to stand as he did against the Boer War, and to deliver against it his famous speech, that superlative example of windy Macaulayesque bombast masquerading as high art. It must have required something more than courage to resign, as he did, from the Cabinet in protest against the Great War. But what, one wonders, was so resolute and so strident a political moralist thinking of in committing himself to the administration of serfdoms like Ireland and India?

But if we are inclined to laugh at Morley today, our laughter is no more than an echo of the considerable amusement he evoked at the time, for he was one of those men whose outward manifestations of an imperishable rectitude inspire the scepticism of more worldly men. Nobody becomes known among his colleagues as 'Honest John' unless there is a hint of something distinctly shifty about him, but not even that label was explicit enough for Sir Henry Campbell Bannerman, who appointed him to the India Office and christened him 'Priscilla', although the order of sequence is not recorded. One historian looking back at the period has suggested that Morley was perhaps 'a little too obviously conscious of his own importance',[26] and even his close friend George Meredith once described his demeanour as that of 'an old maid telling off an errand boy'. However, it was not dishonesty which predisposed people against him, but what John Gross has admirably defined as 'the steady tick of ambition'. In a brief but exquisitely balanced sketch of Morley,[27] Gross suggests that Morley was 'the kind of Victorian liberal whom later generations take the greatest pleasure in unmasking', admits that it is not difficult to see him as a dupe, a doctrinaire and a humbug, but ultimately defends him, justifiably so, on the grounds that for all his dubieties, Morley really did believe in a fundamentally decent society. Doubtless Shaw would have replied that that fundamentally decent society, had Morley ever achieved it, would have frittered away much valuable energy goggling at worthless art.

G. M. Young once made a brave attempt to assess the condition of Morley's cultural soul, and suggested that for him, 'poetry meant Tennyson, fiction meant Dickens and George Eliot'.[28] We begin to see why things did not augur well for the aspiring author of *Cashel Byron's Profession*. Tennyson, Shaw decided, was 'an extraordinary musician with the brains of a third-rate village policeman',[29] and of George Eliot he wrote:

> When I was young George Eliot was thought to be the greatest writer of the day. I had to go to a Young Fabian meeting, held in the Hampstead Library, and as I came twenty minutes too early I took down a novel by George Eliot and shall never forget how disappointed I was. I could do that kind of writing, I thought. Until then I had never thought of writing for a living but what was I to do? I had discovered that I could never be a Michelangelo and I was without means, so I wrote a novel and it read like a bad translation. When, after trying five novels, I discovered that I would never become a George Meredith, I resigned myself to playwriting.[30]

With which declaration there enter the hind legs of the Macmillan pantomime horse, for it was Meredith who often deputised as publisher's reader for Morley; perhaps it was on one of these occasions that Morley wrote of his friend, 'He is Phoebus Apollo descending upon us from Olympus'. As Shaw put it when discussing the fate of Opus 1, *Immaturity*, 'George Meredith shared the guilt of its refusal with John Morley'. He then goes on to describe how some friends laid a jejune plot, and comments on Meredith in a style which reveals some idea of the sheer hopelessness of his early quest for acceptance:

> Once, when I had achieved the feat of speaking in the open air at Trafford Bridge, Manchester, for four hours at one stretch, a plot was laid by Henry Salt, Clement Shorter and others to take me down to Box Hill on the understanding that I should start talking the moment I entered the house and not let George Meredith get a word in edgeways. But it never came off; and I did not make the pilgrimage and the acquaintance until shortly before his death. I had thought of approaching him in 1898–9, when I lived on Hindhead, through Grant Allen; but I found G.A. had given up going to Box Hill . . . I valued Meredith as a poet and as a cosmopolitan *bel esprit* of a certain mid-Victorian type (represented by Dilke, Laurence Oliphant, Hyndman, etc.) but politically he was a Rip Van Winkle in the Socialist movement; and the literary life in the Surrey Hills was contrary to all my rules of conduct: even as gifted a man as Meredith could not live it as long as he did without becoming a walking anachronism. *Diana of the Crossways* is fifty years behind *Our Mutual Friend*: its social values were all out of date. That is why so many people who, like myself, have a very high opinion of his natural power, can read nothing of his except the poems and *Shagpat*.[31]

Shaw's summary dismissal of Meredith as a kind of *flâneur* disappearing into the swirling mists of literary antiquity is at least as brusque as it is justified, but it sounds like abject sycophancy when seen in the context of what Shaw had to say about the front legs of the pantomime horse which trampled all over his early manuscripts. The association with Morley begins on a note of unexpected geniality. In 1880, having succeeded Frederick Greenwood as editor of *The Pall Mall Gazette*, Morley actually wrote to Shaw saying that he had heard from a common friend (George Macmillan of Macmillan and Co.), 'that you might perhaps be able and willing occasionally to write for me on this paper. If you care to entertain the notion I shall be very happy to talk it over with you some day next week.' Macmillan's kindness in suggesting Shaw, and Morley's in acting on the suggestion, were stimulated by a certain guarded admiration on Macmillan's part for *Immaturity*, which the firm had just turned down with some hesitancy. On 22 May 1880 Shaw responded:

> I shall have pleasure in calling on you next week if you will be good enough to let me know the hour most convenient to you. You may name any time – morning or afternoon – without fear of embarrassing me. However, should I not hear from you, I shall call on Tuesday at two o'clock, but I have no reason for selecting this hour except that it may save you the trouble of writing a second time.[32]

Morley and Shaw then met, each later giving his version of what happened. Shaw manages, as usual, to justify Morley's rejection of him and at the same time make the man look ridiculous:

> When, as a beginner, I got an introduction to Morley, and he asked me what I thought I could do, I threw away the opportunity by saying that I thought I could write about art. In utter disgust he turned away, flinging over his shoulder a muttered 'Pooh! ANYBODY can write about art.' 'O CAN they? ? ?,' I retorted, with a contempt equal to his own; and I honestly thought I was showing great self-restraint in not adding 'you wretched Philistine second-hand Macaulay'. That concluded the interview; and Morley missed his chance of becoming my editor.[33]

Morley's version is more guarded, and does not mention Shaw by name at all, although it is hard to imagine who else he might be describing:

> I asked the young applicant for a post on *The Pall Mall Gazette* if he had any special qualifications. The applicant replied with one word: 'Invective.' 'Any particular form?' 'No,' casually replied the applicant, 'Just general invective.'[34]

Both Shaw and Morley are lying shamelessly, because it is

impossible to reconcile either testimony with the events which actually occurred. Morley invited Shaw to submit a review of a three-decker novel called *George Vanbrugh's Mistake*; it turned out to be Morley's mistake. On 2 June he wrote back to Shaw:

> I am not sure I can use your review, but I like the style of it. Could you not send me some short middle article upon some social or other topic?

In response Shaw sent Morley an essay and a review, with a covering note which implied that Morley had no intention of reading them and that Shaw did not blame him:

> In the very limited time in which my present occupation leaves at my disposal, I have only been able to produce the enclosed article on 'Exhausted Arts', which I am afraid you will find rather indigestible. I send also a paper on *The Merchant of Venice*, which of course I do not expect you to read through: but a glance into it will give you an idea of what (besides the usual 'shop') I can do as a dramatic critic. I should prefer writing on theatrical or musical events to manufacturing random articles, which is to me much the same thing as making bricks without straw.
>
> I expect in a short time to be offered a not very brilliant appointment which will leave me even less time for literary pursuits than I have at present. Should you advise me to accept it? I must have either one stool or the other to sit upon.
>
> I should be obliged by your returning me any papers of which you made no use. I will send you back the books you lent me, tomorrow. Wingfield's novel is a three volume pamphlet on penal servitude, and a review of it would be merely an article on that subject. The romantic part is too bad to waste powder on.

On the following day, 14 June, Morley returned Shaw's manuscripts, enclosing with them one of the funniest editorial gaffes of the nineteenth century:

> They are not quite suitable for this paper. . . . With regard to the question that you ask me, I cannot hesitate to say, that in my opinion you would do well to get out of journalism. It is a

most precarious, dependent, and unsatisfactory profession, excepting for a very few who happen to have the knack, or manage to persuade people that they have it . . . I wish I could have been of more service to you.

A day later Shaw replied:

I have received your letter, and also my last two MSS. . . . Thank you very much for your attempt to befriend me. I am sorry for having baffled it; but I fear I am incorrigible. Instead of cultivating that unfortunate knack, I laboriously rub all signs of it out. I wonder whether the public would really like it. Should you ever require anything particularly disagreeable written about anybody, pray remember

yours faithfully,
G. B. Shaw.[35]

With which ends all direct contact between the editor who happened to have the knack – or had managed to persuade the proprietors of *The Pall Mall Gazette* that he had it – and the author of *Cashel Byron's Profession*. But Shaw and Morley continued to sing their comic duet for some years yet, although neither performer realised who his partner was. Five years after the exchange of letters, Morley, reading for Macmillan, finds himself confronted by a prizefighting novel by an author whose name means nothing to him. Uninhibited, therefore, by any previous opinions he may have expressed, he now sings quite a new aria:

The novel is a *jeu d'esprit*, or satire, with a good stroke of socialist meaning in it. The story is designedly paradoxical, absurd and impossible as if it were one of Peacock's. But whoever he may be, the author knows how to write: he is pointed, rapid, forcible, sometimes witty, often powerful and occasionally eloquent. I suppose one must call his book a trifle, but it is a clever trifle. . . . The present book is Ruskinian doctrine; theories with a whimsical and deliberately extravagant story, served up with a pungent literary sauce. The result is a dish which, I fancy, only the few would relish, but the writer, if he is young, is a man to keep one's eye on.[36]

*Above*, G.B.S. newly transplanted
from Dublin to London
'Immature, and apparently an
arrant pig'
*Above right*, Pakenham Beatty
*Right*, John Morley by Spy

*Above*, Plates XLV and XLVIII from *The Art of Boxing* by Ned Donnelly. See page 82 *Right*, Frontispiece advertisement for Ned Donnelly's gymnasium, from *The Art of Boxing*

*Above left,* 'Gentleman' Jim Corbett in 1909
*Above right,* Georges Carpentier in 1920
*Below,* G.B.S. at the ringside in 1929

*Left*, Georges Carpentier *v* Jack Dempsey in 1921
*Below*, Battling Siki knocks out Georges Carpentier in 1922

If the report seems excessively carping, and perhaps even contradictory, it is still a catalogue of hysterical enthusiasms compared to what Morley had to say about some far more eminent men than Shaw was at the time – or Morley was either, for that matter. For it was he who had described Swinburne as 'the libidinous laureate of a pack of satyrs' and a passage from Rousseau as ' a vision of the horrid loves of heavy-eyed and scaly shapes that haunted the warm primeval ooze'. It appears, however, that Morley much preferred criticising others to being criticised himself. When in 1888 Shaw began writing merciless attacks on his politics in T. P. O'Connor's *The Star*,[37] it was not long before the fearless and incorruptible scourge of Swinburne and Rousseau was trying to have Shaw dismissed. One day in the Division Lobby of the House of Commons he showed O'Connor a particularly virulent Shavian paragraph in which he had, to use his own ambiguous phrase, 'been treated more faithfully than fairly'. The tactic succeeded; as Shaw later proudly boasted, 'the country was not ripe for my editorials by about five hundred years, acccording to the political computa- tion of the eighties'. O'Connor's assistant, Massingham, then moved Shaw across from the political pages to music criticism, so it could be said that after all it was Morley's influence which finally launched Shaw on a literary career. On the day he wrote to O'Connor offering to withdraw from the paper, he wrote also to Massingham, setting a tone to his references to Morley which he was to maintain for the rest of his life:

I have written to T.P. withdrawing from *The Star*. It is a pity that the experiment has been a failure; but I think you must see that T.P.'s conciliatory no-policy is hopelessly incom- patible with my aggressive policy. I can only relapse into reviewing novels for the P.M.G. and criticising pictures for Yates until I can get a paper of my own. T.P.'s attachment to John Morley is the final blow. It is impossible to attain even high mud mark in politics without taking that solemn literary obsolescence and shaking the starch out of him twice a week regularly.[38]

Two years later, in resigning for a second time from *The Star*, this time permanently, Shaw writes to T. P. O'Connor:

If you become an irreclaimable Whig, we shall exchange fearful blows as time goes on, but none below the belt. Besides, I shall knock the stuffing out of Honest John and convince you even before you find him out.[39]

In 1892 Shaw writes to the Birmingham Fabian E. D. Girdlestone:

There is not a man living who is not in favour of equality of opportunity, justice, and everything that is proper and sublime, consistently, of course, with an independent income for himself. J.M. is the worst of all political scoundrels, the conscientious, high-principled scoundrel. Robespierre was a mere trimmer in comparison.[40]

It would be instructive to know at exactly which point in his relentless proceedings against Morley, Shaw discovered the identity of his anonymous persecutor at Macmillan's. It seems certain that even without any literary or personal grudge, Shaw would have despised Morley, who represented precisely that brand of moth-eaten parliamentary radical agnosticism which Shaw held almost in more contempt than he did the landed gentry, which was at least capable of producing a Lydia Carew from time to time. But at which stage of the battle Shaw found himself able to save his shot by killing two dull dogs with the same dialectical stone, Morley the reader for Macmillan's, and Morley the Liberal statesman, is not certain. But he never forgave either Morley or Meredith. At the very end of his life, in conversation with the Boswell of his dotage, Stephen Winsten, Shaw remained contemptuous of those who had rejected him, telling Winsten that at the time of his marriage to Charlotte Payne-Townshend:

My possibility of future eminence was unlimited. I was already an unsuccessful novelist with not a single novel accepted and therefore an established genius frowned upon by the bourgeois publishers. What did readers like George Meredith and John Morley know about good work?[41]

And yet a few days later he was telling Winsten quite a different story. Winsten had been tactless enough to raise the ghost of Virginia Woolf, to which Shaw responded:

Anybody can write a novel. When a novelist cannot pad a story, she puts in a few hundred pages of psychology. Ricketts used to say that writing was very easy because everyone knew how to talk and write letters and so there is no technique to learn, but in painting you have to master a new technique, and every weakness is immediately exposed to the eye. The fact is the arts are exhausted. I thought when I arrived in London that it was the centre of literature and art but I got nothing for nothing and very little for a halfpenny. I was abused and vilified. I soon realised that a mighty harvest had left the soil sterile. From the habit gained in my commercial work, like Trollope I worked daily at my writing without waiting for inspiration.[41]

Yet perversely, Shaw's contempt for his novels seems to have been surpassed only by his contempt for the literary gentlemen who rejected them. A century later the student of such affairs cannot help feeling that Morley, who published his own biography of Gladstone and rejected *Cashel Byron's Profession*, might perhaps have served the causes both of Shavianism and Liberalism a great deal better by rejecting his biography of Gladstone and publishing *Cashel Byron's Profession*.[42]

If the Morleys and the Merediths of the Victorian literary establishment were so adamant in their rejection of Shaw the novelist, how did it come about that these unwanted items of literary baggage were eventually smuggled across the frontier of acceptance? If no publisher would touch them, how did the five books come to enjoy such a sensational and controversial career, attracting the attention of artists as distinguished as Stevenson and Morris? The answer seems to be that when impersonal literary appeal fails, a little nepotism will often work wonders. At the time he was composing his novels, Shaw may have been handicapped by the fact that he was part of a tiny intellectual minority, but at least that minority was an intensely articulate and vociferous one, determined that its voice should be heard. And quite understandably, the captains and the kings of its pathetic beleaguered garrisons discerned that voice in the curiously dispassionate overtones of Shaw's unorthodox fictions. Even as he was conducting his hopeless campaign against the great publishing houses, Shaw found himself advancing, apparently quite by accident, on a different literary front altogether, and always insisted later that the whole campaign had proceeded of its own volition.

In assessing the degree of truth in this scenario which Shaw so carefully designed for the edification of his biographers, it is as well to remember that the most important and influential of all the literary lions who thought something of *Cashel Byron's Profession* was its author. For all his avowals of repugnance, Shaw was at least kindly enough disposed towards his five early works, his 'brown paper parcels' as he derisively described them, to allow all of them entry into the pantheon of the Collected Edition. Indeed, Shaw appears to have been so genially acquiescent in the face of *Byron*'s eccentric and peculiarly

persistent publishing history that his public pretence of having
lost control of the monster may be taken as the Shavian
paraphrase of his private satisfaction that his once unwanted
sickly child should have proved such a boisterous and
glamorous survivor. Every time *Cashel Byron's Profession* surfaces
in one of its multifarious guises, Shaw does the right thing and
then hastily gives the wrong reason for doing it. When an
impoverished weekly political periodical serialises it, he
pretends that not only is the text mere journalistic padding,
but also that his acceptance of an author's fee from the pro-
prietress is an act of kindness on his part; when he takes the
considerable trouble of composing his own stage adaptation
(*The Admirable Bashville*) it is only to stop somebody in America
from producing their own pirated version; when, after a reput-
able American publishing house has paid him £10 for his
American 'rights', a rival house produces a pirated edition, as
it was legally entitled to do, he sends back the £10. As he said
in mitigation of all this:

> I was to find out later on that a book is like a child; it is easier
> to bring it into the world than to control it when it is launched
> there. As long as I kept sending my novels to the publishers,
> they were as safe from publicity as they would have been in the
> fire, where I had better, perhaps, have put them. But when I
> flung them aside as failures, they almost instantly began to
> show signs of life.[1]

Whether or not this predictably unpredictable Shavian levity
was retrospective it is difficult to know, but certainly as the years
passed and Shaw's rate of progress began to accelerate along the
route to his consecration as the Bishop of Everywhere, he
behaved as though no more uproarious farce had ever come to
his notice than this unexpected match of his rejected manuscripts, first into the columns of pulp journalism, then into the
tattered paper covers of late Victorian cheap fiction, and finally
into the legitimacy of the Collected Edition:

> The Socialist revival of the eighties, into which I had plunged,
> produced the usual crop of propagandist magazines, in the
> conduct of which payment of the printer was the main

problem, payment of the contributors being quite out of the question. The editor of such a magazine can never count on a full supply of live matter to make up his tale of pages. But if he can collect a stock of unreadable novels, the refuse of the publishing trade, and a stock of minor poems (the world is full of such trash), an instalment of serial novel and a few verses will always make up the magazine to any required size. And this was how I found a use at last for my brown paper parcels. It seemed a matter of no more consequence than stuffing so many broken window-panes with them; but it had momentous consequences; for in this way four of the five got printed and published in London, and thus incidentally became the common property of the citizens of the United States of America. These pioneers did not at first appreciate their new acquisition; and nothing particular happened except that the first novel (No. 5; for I ladled them out to the Socialist magazine editors in inverse order of composition) made me acquainted with William Morris, who, to my surprise, had been reading the monthly instalments with a certain relish. But that only proved how much easier it is to please a great man than a little one, especially when you share his politics. No. 5, called *An Unsocial Socialist*, was followed by No. 4, *Cashel Byron's Profession*, and Cashel would not lie quiet in his serial grave, but presently rose and walked as a book.[2]

The very fact that Shaw doled out his parcels in inverse order of composition suggests that he was rather more sensitive than he pretended to the ascending order of their relative merit, but he always insisted that the survival of Byron had less to do with its intrinsic literary appeal than with the fluke of a pugnaciously-inclined editor:

It happened in this way. The name of the magazine was *To-Day*, not the present paper of that name, but one of the many *To-Days* which are now Yesterdays. It had several editors, among them Mr Belfort Bax and the late James Leigh Joynes; but all the editors were in partnership with Mr Henry Hyde Champion who printed the magazine, and consequently went on forever, whilst the others came and went. It was a fantastic business, Joynes having thrown up an Eton mastership, and

Champion a commission in the army, at the call of Socialism. But Champion's pugnacity survived his abdicated adjutancy; he had an unregenerate taste for pugilism, and liked *Cashel Byron* so much that he stereotyped the pages of *To-Day* which it occupied, and in spite of my friendly remonstrances, hurled on to the market a misshapen shilling edition. My friend Mr William Archer reviewed it prominently; the *Saturday Review*, always susceptible in those days to the arts of self-defence, unexpectedly declared it the novel of the age; Mr W. E. Henley wanted to have it dramatised; Stevenson wrote a letter about it; the other papers hastily searched their waste-paper baskets for it and reviewed it, mostly rather disappointingly; and the public preserved its composure and did not seem to care.[3]

It is clear from this account that Shaw appreciated the importance of the quantity as well as the quality of the reviews which *Cashel Byron's Profession* inspired, and the circumstances surrounding at least one of those reviews illustrates the useful lesson that there are moments in a young writer's life when sexual magnetism will succeed where purely literary blandishments have failed. The periodical *Our Corner*, in which John M. Robertson had paid an unknown author the compliment of discussing his fiction in terms of Stevenson and Dickens, was edited by Annie Besant, who, by the time she published Robertson's review, had somewhat compromised her detachment in such matters by falling passionately in love with Shaw.

The details of Annie Besant's hopelessly one-sided romance with the author of *Cashel Byron's Profession* make instructive reading for any aspiring writer requiring guidance as to the best way of acquiring flattering reviews of his work. In the spring of 1885 the gladiatorial aspect of London utopian political life manifested itself in a performance by Shaw before the members of the Dialectical Society, who were to hear his address on the theme of Socialism. At this time Mrs Besant was renowned as one of the most irresistible demagogues in Europe, 'the most redoubtable champion,' said Shaw, 'of the old individualist free thought of which Bradlaugh was the exponent,' and a public orator so powerful that according to Shaw, 'if she asserted that "aye violet is not aye rose" and then thrillingly challenged the world in her contralto voice to contradict that profundity if they dared, all her listeners believed that they had been converted from thinking the opposite.'[4] When Shaw arrived for the debate, it was to find the congregation 'perturbed and excited' by her presence:

> I was warned on all hands that she had come to destroy me and that from the moment she rose to speak, my cause was lost.

Shaw claimed that he resigned himself to his fate, a comically implausible definition of his behaviour at any time in his life, but especially during his reign as the dialectical wizard of coterie politics. But on this occasion, not even Shaw himself was prepared for the effect of his oratory:

> When the discussion began, everyone waited for Annie Besant to lead the opposition. She did not rise; and at last the opposition was taken by another member. When he had finished, Annie Besant, to the astonishment of the meeting, got up and utterly demolished him. There was nothing left for me to do but to gasp and triumph under her shield. At the end she asked me to nominate her for election to the Fabian Society and invited me to dine with her.[5]

It appeared that in the course of his speech to the Dialectical Society, Shaw had inadvertently inspired Mrs Besant with a passionate adoration, a condition of existence to which, in the course of her life, that susceptible woman was to become very much accustomed. Until now she had been known to express distaste for Shaw's tendency to festoon the flowers of utopian progress with the bindweed of a facetiousness whose roots she was unable to locate; but now, seeing him in full flow, she was evidently converted to the theory that she was jousting with one of nature's princes. In fact, she was so utterly overwhelmed by what she took to be the earthly manifestation of intellectual grace and manly beauty that she began setting her cap at Shaw with a resolution at once comic and tragic. When Shaw accepted her invitation to dine at her house in Avenue Road, St John's

Wood, they played piano duets with a disparity of executant technique which somehow symbolised the irreconcilable differences between them:

> To please him with her playing in the duets she practised alone like a schoolgirl, and always played the right notes coldly and accurately at a moderate speed while he played wrong ones with a fire that she continually frustrated.[6]

Having graduated to Shavian Socialism via Bradlaugh's Atheism and Aveling's Evolution, Mrs Besant was already an experienced benefactress, and expressed her passion for Shaw in the most practical way, by making sure that *Cashel Byron's Profession* was reviewed at length, and then, when *To-Day* foundered, subsidising Shaw's hopeless financial predicament by serialising the rest of his fiction and appointing him to a regular post as contributor:

> She serialised his novels in her magazine *Our Corner*, appointed him art critic, and when she offended its secularist subscribers (Bradlaugh's old Guard) by embracing socialism and it ceased to pay its way, she paid for his contributions out of her private account until he found her out and removed himself from the pay list, padding the paper with his unpublished novels as he had before padded *To-Day*. They were constantly on the platform together; and he walked home with her, carrying the handbag that never quitted her, always complaining of its weight and defeating her indignant attempts to capture it from him until she at last guessed that his unmanly conduct was part of a puzzling side of him of which she had no comprehension:[7]

In his preface to *Cashel Byron's Profession*, Shaw most generously acknowledged Mrs Besant's part in his career as a novelist:

> *Our Corner* had the singular habit of paying for its contributions, and was, I am afraid, to some extent a device of Mrs Besant's for relieving necessitous young propagandists without wounding their pride by open almsgiving. She was an incorrigible benefactress, and probably revenged herself for

my freely expressed scorn for this weakness by drawing on her private account to pay me for my jejune novels.[8]

Realising that Annie was not a woman to be treated lightly, and knowing she had a husband to consider, he was not altogether surprised when she drew up a contract defining the conditions under which they were to live together; but he was positively stupefied by its terms, and reacted with 'Good God! This is worse than all the vows of all the Churches on earth. I had rather be legally married to you ten times over.' Hesketh Pearson, who reports this Shavian reaction, describes the end of the affair in the following pathetic terms:

> She would have nothing less than her contract, which she had expected him to sign with his heart's blood; and when he not only laughed at it but was evidently quite serious in refusing to be bound by it, she demanded her letters back. He collected what he could of them, and at a further and final interview gave them to her. She produced a casket in which she had kept all his letters, and, convulsed with suppressed tears, handed them to him. 'What! You won't even keep my letters!' he said. 'I don't want them.' The correspondence went into the fire. And that was the end of their private relations.[9]

But even Pearson, who is sometimes inclined to cast these Shavian romantic charades in a light perhaps too flippant for the tastes of those ladies unfortunate enough to be featured in them, adds that 'there can be no doubt that the parting for the lady was something worse than a mauvais quart d'heure. Her hair turned grey: she even thought of suicide.' In the last days of his life Shaw told Stephen Winsten, 'Annie had no taste. She bought an umbrella for me: it was so ugly that I wouldn't be seen at a funeral with it. I returned it to her and she threw it over a fence in Regent's Park. To tease her I did a drawing of the field with lots of little umbrellas coming through.'[10] Umbrellas were not all that Mrs Besant contributed to the Shavian cause. Besides publishing Robertson's review of *Cashel Byron's Profession*, she also serialised *The Irrational Knot* and *Love Among the Artists*.

In one of his several accounts of the saga of *Cashel Byron's*

*Profession*, Shaw added a few lines which suggest that even he, with his monstrous inability to experience normal human weakness, relished the discomfiture of frustrated and baffled publishers:

> When it crept into print through the back door of a Socialist magazine, it was praised by Stevenson and Henley where- upon Bentley, a leading publisher, hastily wrote to me to let him consider it again, and was furious when I had to tell him that he had lost his chance as it had just gone to a rival whom he regarded as an outsider.[11]

Henry Hyde Champion, Bentley's outsider, published an edition variously reported as five hundred and one thousand copies, all of which soon disappeared down the maw of late Victorian coterie journalism, and by 1887 Shaw was once again composing letters of only half-serious supplication to publishers in an attempt to interest them in a reprint of *Byron*. The publishing house of Walter Scott eventually took him up in 1889, and must very soon have realised that they had become embroiled with a very unusual type of impoverished author indeed. In a letter to the editor of the company in September 1890, after patiently explaining the economics of book publishing, Shaw closed with:

> Some time ago, you mentioned something about changing the cover of *Cashel Byron*, and introducing a design of some pugilistic kind. This is to give you formal notice that if you do anything of the sort without first submitting the cover to me, I will have your heart's blood.[12]

– a remark whose threatening overtones were reduced hardly at all by the fact that Shaw signed off 'Yours respectfully'.

A letter to T. Fisher Unwin in the following April finds Shaw referring sarcastically to *Byron* as 'that immortal work', and then goes on to report in distinctly peevish tones that up to 31 March, the novel had sold only 3193 copies, a statistic which to a later, more illiterate age, does not sound half so depressing a sales figure as Shaw evidently felt it to be. But then it appears that Shaw tended to adjust his own epistolary attitude towards *Byron* in accordance with the tastes of his correspondent. Writing to the bookseller-bibliophile-photographer Frederick Evans in 1895, by which time he had already crossed the rubicon of *Arms and the Man* and *You Never Can Tell*, Shaw disposes of his five brown paper parcels once and for all:

> I wrote five novels altogether: the first was the biggest, but the mice ate most of it; the next two appeared as serials in an extinct magazine and have never been dug up. They are all jejune and rotten: I shan't write any more of them.[13]

Jejune and rotten their creator may sincerely have believed them to be, but at least one of them had an oddly persistent habit of getting itself into new editions. In October 1901 Grant Richards published *Cashel Byron's Profession* complete with dramatised version purportedly written by Shaw to forestall the possibility of American piracy, and this eventually found its way, if only briefly, on to the English stage. Both Henley and James Runciman, uncle of the John F. Runciman who was music critic of the American *Saturday Review*, wanted to see *Cashel Byron's Profession* dramatised. Shaw dissuaded Runciman from taking any practical steps to this end by explaining to him that 'the means by which I had individualised the characters in the novel would prove ineffective on the stage, so that all that could be done was not to dramatise the novel but to take the persons out of it, and use them over again on the stage in an otherwise original play'.[14] The blandishments had their desired effect on Runciman but apparently none on Shaw, who in January 1901 began writing *The Admirable Bashville*, a three-act play in blank verse.

The first copyright reading took place in London two months later, the first amateur production was staged, again in London, in December 1902, and finally, on 7 and 8 June 1903 the Stage Society performed it at the Imperial Theatre. The cricketing Englishman-turned stage Englishman Sir C. Aubrey Smith,[15] playing the part of a policeman, hit upon the device, whose impudence can only be described as excessively Shavian, of appearing on stage disguised as the author. Almost at the very end of his life Shaw still remembered the comedy of the situation:

Aubrey Smith played in my *Admirable Bashville* and wanted to make up as myself. Nobody has ever succeeded in doing that, not even myself, and nobody could say what was wrong. But Granville-Barker came on the stage, saw what was wrong at once, and daubed some white here and some there on the beard and Aubrey was transformed. On the first night my mother came with me. When Aubrey Smith walked on the stage, there was loud laughter and again laughter which held up the play. My mother was quite bewildered. She turned to me and asked what the laughter was about. I told her that this actor was impersonating me. 'You?,' she said, 'but this man looks so elderly.'[16]

In his preface to the 1901 edition Shaw brings the reader up to date with that flourishing American career without which Byron could never have worked his strange magic. As long ago as 1883 *Cashel Byron's Profession* had been offered to Harper's, who, notwithstanding their announcement that it was no use to them, published it three years later in their *Handy Series*, sending Shaw the sum of £10 in lieu of the copyright payment which, because of the commercially convenient absentmindedness of American law, they were absolved from bothering about. In 1889 Shaw discovered that a pirated edition of brown paper parcel Opus 5, *An Unsocial Socialist*, was selling surprisingly well in America:

Columbia was beginning to look after her hitherto neglected acquisition. Apparently the result was encouraging; for presently the same publisher produced a new edition of *Cashel Byron's Profession* (Opus 4), in criticising which the more thoughtful reviewers, unaware that the publisher was working backwards through the list, pointed out the marked advance in my style, the surer grip, the clearer form, the finer art, the maturer view of the world, and so forth. As it was clearly unfair that my own American publishers should be debarred by delicacy towards me from exploiting the new field of derelict fiction, I begged them to make the most of their national inheritance; and with my full approval, Opus 3, called *Love Among the Artists* (a paraphrase of the forgotten line 'Love Among the Roses'), followed. No doubt it will pay its way; people who will read *An Unsocial Socialist* will read anything. But the new enthusiasm for *Cashel Byron's Profession* did not stop here. American ladies were seized with a desire to go on the stage and be Lydia Carew for two thrilling hours. American actors 'saw themselves' as Cashel. Mr James Corbett has actually appeared on the New York stage in the part. There can be no doubt now that my novels, so long left for dead in the forlorn-hope magazines of the eighties, have arisen and begun to propagate themselves vigorously throughout the new world at the rate of a dollar and a half per copy free of all royalty to the flattered author.[17]

The James Corbett to whom Shaw so offhandedly refers was none other than James J. Corbett, the stylist who took the World Heavyweight Championship away from an astonished John L. Sullivan and thus became the first boxer at that weight to acquire the championship in a contest where both contestants wore boxing gloves,[18] and whose fitness to play Shaw's hero is admirably hinted at by his professional soubriquet, 'Gentleman Jim'. As for the circumstances surrounding Corbett's imper-sonation, it is not clear whether it was his determination to play at being Byron which led to the protective device of a copyright reading of *The Admirable Bashville*, but if it was, then history (and Shaw) seem to have done Corbett an injustice, for subsequent evidence suggests that whether pirated or not, Corbett's stage impersonsations of Byron might have been paid for honourably enough. Around 1901 those unintentionally funny mercenaries, the Shubert brothers, produced Corbett in a stage version of *Cashel Byron's Profession*, but it was not for another five years, by which time he had retired from the prize ring, that Corbett managed to persuade anyone to take his histrionics with that due solemnity which is assumed to go with a grand opening in a prestigious Broadway theatre. Critical reaction was revealing.

By 1906 dramatic criticism in New York had reached that stage of apoplectic puritanism which, in England, had achieved its notorious climax fifteen years earlier with Clement Scott's review in the *Daily Telegraph* of the first English performance of Ibsen's *Ghosts*. Indeed, several of the American reviewers seem to have taken their tone if not their vocabulary from Scott. If in their columns there was no hysterical evocation of open drains, lazar-houses, and the rest of the municipal plumbing with which Scott appears to have been so morbidly preoccupied, at least the spirit of his style of abuse is very much apparent in their reactions to poor 'Gentleman Jim' Corbett. To what extent that thespian innocent was aware of prevailing fashions in New York in what might be called the 'higher criticism' remains unknown, but his knowledge need not have been very extensive for him to see from a glance at the theatre pages that his chances of approval were unlikely.

Then there were the precedents, which were more ominous still. In 1901 there had actually been not one but two Byrons vying for attention on the American stage, Corbett's rival being so severely battered by the local press that after a few days both the production and its star were carried from the ring and never heard of again. It is almost too painful to picture the reactions of Mr Harrison J. Wolfe, as he awoke on the morning of 5 January 1901, reached out a trembling hand across the counterpane, made contact with the *New York Dramatic Mirror*, and read this:

> Herald Square – *Cashel Byron*; play in four acts, by Harrison J. Wolfe; produced December 27.

> Mr Shaw's story might make a good play, but Mr Wolfe's arrangement was absolutely worthless dramatically. It was utterly without action, situation or merit of any sort, and it

was, moreover, of deadly dullness. Actors are few nowadays that can write plays. For some inscrutable reason the action and business that they will insist upon in the works of professional dramatists seem superfluous to them when they go into playwriting themselves.

Mr Wolfe played Byron no better than he wrote him. There was in his performance no tone, no color, no character nor shading. Equally uneventful was Jane Kennark's Lydia, though this must have been the fault of the play and not of Miss Kennark, who assuredly can act well when she has the chance. The most notable work was that of Billy Elmer, who, besides arranging a capital fight in the first act, acted the role of Mellish with much skill and real humour. Edward Emery gave a neat sketch of a sporting lord, Harry St Maur put in a good portrait of old Skene, Brinsley Shaw was an acceptable Weber, E. Brownell played a German socialist ably, and Margaret Dibdin Pitt gave another of her intelligent, forceful impersonations, with odds much against her. The other actors did what they could with their vague roles. The play was mounted fairly.

With which the unfortunate Harrison J. Wolfe, no doubt puzzled by the implication that everyone but the star had performed with consummate art, and failing to find much solace in the fact that two columns to the west of his own notice the same reviewer had slaughtered Sarah Bernhardt as a prose Hamlet, disappears from the Shavian record.

Five years later, Corbett, having long since been relieved of his title by the Cornish émigré Bob Fitzsimmons, and having subsequently been beaten twice by Fitzsimmons' conqueror James J. Jeffries, finally reached Broadway at no less a hallowed temple of the arts than Daly's Theatre. Since the critical flaying of Harrison J. Wolfe, marginal adjustments had taken place to New York taste. Where in Wolfe's day the locals had been offered *Trilby*, *Quo Vadis* and *The Gay Lord Quex*, melodrama was now being served by *The Squaw Man* and *More to be Pitied than Scorned*. Indications of a move towards an indigenous American musical theatre were to be found in the disappearance of *Florodora* and *San Toy* in favour of two George M. Cohan shows, *Little Johnny*

*Jones* and *Forty Five Minutes From Broadway*. Shaw's neighbour
J. M. Barrie, who in Wolfe's day had been represented on
Broadway by *The Professor's Love Story*, a work which later
mysteriously disappeared from reprinted editions of the
Collected Plays, was now enjoying a double success with *Alice-
Sit-By-The-Fire* and *Peter Pan*. And most significant of all, Robert
Loraine was appearing at the Hudson Theatre in *Man and
Superman*.

Newspaper reactions to this sluggish progressive tide varied
from one editorial headquarters to another, but nobody
connected with Corbett's début at Daly's would have been
surprised to learn that the most virulent reaction to *Cashel Byron*
was to come from the *New York Daily Tribune*, one of those pillars
of conservatism whose blunt dismissal of anything more
progressive than Dockstader's Minstrels had more than a touch
of comic truculence about it. The *Tribune* combined confidence
with ignorance to a spectacular degree, and clearly believed that
the best way of defending the old standards, whatever they
might be, was to carry the fight to the enemy, those disgusting
degenerates of the modern movement, and this it did with a
calculated insolence much funnier than any of the comedies its
reviewers went to see. The *Tribune* on the morning after the first
performance of *Cashel Byron's Profession* was a positive slaughter-
house of advanced thought in the theatre. The day's blood-
letting begins with a list of coming attractions:

Mr Ibsen's obnoxious play of *Ghosts* will be given, in the
Russian language, this afternoon, at the Criterion. This ought
to gladden all the sickly cranks in this region.

The Berkeley Lyceum Theatre is becoming a sort of
Chamber of Horrors. Last season several misguided persons
strove to impress the public, in that place, with the ghastly
humor of life in a lunatic asylum. Now, a foreign performer
named Miss Parsenow, who appears to have left Germany on
account of her great prosperity and fame there in Oscar
Wilde's nasty play of *Salome* and Mr Gorky's hideous drama of
*A Night's Lodging*, is disporting at this house, in a symbolic
fabric, by Mr Maeterlinck, called *The Death of Tintagiles*. Some
of the proceedings, in this gem of art, pass in a burial vault,

and the heroine rejoices in the name of 'Ygraine'. Mr Maeterlinck's play is fantastic and repulsive rubbish, and his mind is in a state of chronic obfuscation.

It is satisfactory to know that the authorities of Springfield, Mass. have prohibited the performance there, by Miss Olga Nethersole and her company, of the dirty, disreputable play of *Sappho*, and it is earnestly hoped that other cities will follow this good example. The pollution of the theatre is a blow at social order, and ought to be stopped.

There follows a long essay entitled 'The Tainted Drama' in which the plays of Ibsen are defined as 'the tainted trash of that erratic Norwegian pundit'. In this context it is not surprising that the *Tribune*, finding itself confronted by Byron's outrageous assumption that a man who earns his living by fighting people is no worse than one who earns his by writing about it, reacted by publishing not one but two attacks on Shaw on the same page. Under the heading 'A Feather-Brain Play at Daly's Theatre', the *Tribune*'s critic attempted to ignore the play and castigate it at the same time:

> Taking advantage of the evanescent notoriety of Mr G. B. Shaw, Mr Harris brings forth at Daly's Theatre a synopsis of his story of *Cashel Byron's Profession*, that of a pugilist; and presents an ex-prizefighter, Mr J. J. Corbett, in the principal part. A young woman, named Lydia Carew, encounters Cashel Byron at an English country house, mistakes him for a professor of athletic culture, and becomes interested in him, as he does in her; but when his actual vocation is made known to the lady, under somewhat ludicrous circumstances, she repels him. Later they are reconciled and betrothed. The piece is a skit. Miss Margaret Wycherly, an unconsequential actress of a sentimental order, appeared as Miss Carew. Mr Corbett received much applause from his friends.

But the writer of the notice, having stood back to admire the self-portrait which emerges from it, must have realised that to talk of mere 'evanescent notoriety' on the same page that disembowelled Ibsen, Maeterlinck and Gorky was to let Shaw off too lightly. There therefore appeared, immediately under the Byron review, a brief essay called 'The Shaw Fad':

It is difficult to think with patience or write with tolerance of the plays of Mr George Bernard Shaw, for, to a thoughtful mind, perceptive of their latent impurity and mischievous perversity, they are a source of mingled irritation and disgust. Mr Shaw is a clever Irishman, and, like most Irishmen, revolutionary in spirit and happy in a grievance against society. He possesses a spice of the nimble wit and reckless satirical sprightliness that have always been characteristic of the mind and speech of his race. He has had experience as a journalist. His style is glib and profuse, and his writings show some inventive skill, combined with some vigor of coarse, rancid animal vitality. Those writings, however, do not reveal a particle either of genius, refinement or grace. On the contrary, they show an unbalanced mind; a shallow nature, unsound, wavering, or wrong principles; prodigious vanity, and the mournful complacency of insensate conceit. Cursed with the desire to impress people as 'brilliant', this dramatist succeeds only in being impertinently smart. As a playwright he is an imitator, as to method (in a small way and at a great distance behind) of that original, brilliant author, William S. Gilbert. Mr Shaw's aim is to turn everything upside down and inside out; to exploit paradox; to shine in pert epigram. In this latter particular he is sometimes fortunate, just as, occasionally, a blind hog will root up a good acorn, because he cannot help it. But throughout his plays there is a pervasive spirit of insincerity, and in some of them (notably in *Candida*) there is a subtle taint of disease, a kind of miasma, that can scarcely be distinguished from downright immorality. Few persons so intrinsically disgusting as the sickly, sexless hysterical thing that he calls a poet in *Candida* have ever made their way to the stage; while the woman Candida herself, who listens to this snipe and allows his presence, is a gross libel upon decent, self-respecting womanhood. Another of his plays, now current, *Man and Superman* by name, is one long rigmarole of jaundiced satire, flamboyant paradox, and cheap cynicism. His *Captain Brassbound* is a vulgar, preposterous farce, fabricated of impossible story, impossible incidents, distorted, fantastic characters, and forced, haphazard situations, dependent on coincidence and accident for any effect they may chance to produce. A recent deliverance of this author, as to parents and children, sufficiently indicates the fibre of his intellect and the quality of his moral nature. Nobody lives with children, he said, except people who are obliged to do so, and it would be well that places of refuge should be provided, so that children might be 'rescued from the demoralizing influence of home'. In brief, Mr Shaw's purpose is to attract attention, and this purpose he has, in a measure, accomplished, by paradox of speech and by a topsy-turvy morality that seems to mean something to 'qualified old maids and disappointed widows', to dissatisfied, discontented women in general. Two of his plays, *Arms and the Man* and *The Devil's Disciple*, contain amusing dialogue, in the vein of such pieces as *Trying It On*, *Cool as a Cucumber* and *Used Up*, which he has imitated. When the path has been blazed it is not difficult to follow the trail. Tennyson, remarking on imitators of his poetic style, wrote that

> Most can raise the flower now,
> For all have got the seed.

So much for the perceptions of the *Tribune*, which had contrived to lavish considerable space on the Shavian theme without giving any of its readers the faintest idea of what they were likely to see were they to venture into Daly's. There was a sense in which one of the *Tribune*'s rivals, *The World*, did even worse, for although it was much more kindly disposed towards Shaw, and was positively effusive in its praises of Corbett, so incensed was it by what it took to be the ineptitude of the play that alone of the New York newspapers it invoked the Harrison J. Wolfe disaster as a point of reference. *The World* was one of those journals whose approach to the arts was anecdotal rather than textual. Having reached the conclusion that there were more people living in the city who enjoyed a good laugh than those who appreciated a good performance, its editors usually found some amusing or ribald anecdote with which to open their account of some sternly aesthetic experience. On the same day that *Cashel Byron* was noted, a review appeared of Caruso at the Metropolitan Opera House in *Tosca*; the sub-heading informed readers that in kissing the prima donna, Caruso had been 'too fervid and disarranged her hat'. Another musical item on the same page revealed that on the previous night a young Russian pianist called Arthur Rubinstein, finding the elevation of his piano stool unsatisfactory, had performed Saint-Saëns while sitting on the Brahms Second Symphony and one of the lesser works of Schumann. It was natural that a newspaper with so relentless an eye for the news-worthy should celebrate an event as eccentric as a Shaw play featuring a professional boxer:

James J. Corbett lent the presence that once inspired awe and terror in the prize-ring to a dramatisation of Bernard Shaw's novel, *Cashel Byron's Profession*, at Daly's Theatre last night. Heretofore he had only been toying with the stage; now he is in for a finish fight with that thing which, by courtesy, is called dramatic art.

And why not? The theatrical firmament is densely studded with less able citizens than he. Gay divorce court débutantes hustle pell mell to the alluring glare of the footlights. Dashing dames who have slipped off the edge of society fall joyously into the stage's outstretched arms. Ne'er-do-wells of the aimless rich answer the call of its beckoning fingers. Tom, Dick and Harry all aspire to be actors when they have proved conclusively that they can do nothing else.

Mr Corbett is different. He actually accomplished something in the field of his first endeavor. And now that he has outgrown his usefulness at the old game, why shouldn't he try his hand along with the rest at the new?

His was not the least scintillating opening on Broadway this season by long odds; Daly's Theatre was packed to the rear partitions. The applause, partly made to order, was long and loud. The bench, the bar – both kinds – and all the other learned professions were there to do homage. Literature was represented by Miss Jeanette Gilder.

Mr Corbett 'acted up' to the occasion. He was a bit shy at the start, but his diffidence soon wore off. He did more than exhibit himself. If the rest of the actors – excluding Miss Margaret Wycherly – had acted half as well as he, the play would have been twice the success that it was. Of course there was more or less rigidity in the Corbett poses. The Corbett elocution had a habit of running its words together. But Corbett deportment was, for the most part, easy. There are plenty of alleged actors who cannot navigate around the stage as handily as he. The leading role must have appealed to Mr Corbett's ex-professional tastes. For Cashel Byron was a prizefighter too. He was invented before Bernard Shaw discovered that it was profitable to pull human character out of all semblance of human form.

But the play in which he was set was a dreadful waste of words, considering the material with which Stanislaus Stange had to work. Like all other dramatised stories, it was one long-winded, actionless stretch of narrative put in the mouths of a collection of puppets. The talkative footman and maid should have been squelched. The scarecrow of a lover should have been given his quietus while the piece was 'on the road'. Hardly any of the characters gave a suggestion of real flesh and blood. A much better version of the novel was given at the Herald Square Theatre half a dozen years ago – and that one was bad enough, at that. Miss Wycherly struggled hard to put life into Lydia Carew, the heroine. It was anything but an agreeable or a consistent character and that this charming young actress succeeded as well as she did is a feather in her cap.

That notice, which suggests that Corbett might have made a better showing if only he could have found a better dramatist, gives posterity some idea of the immense respect with which Corbett was regarded, not only by the boxing fraternity but also by America generally. People wanted the conqueror of the braggart Sullivan to succeed in whatever enterprise he mounted, no doubt reading into his graceful movements and his pretensions to gentility a hopeful portent for the future of American respectability. The bar-room braggadocio of a fat Irishman may have been all very well in the old century, when prizefighting itself was shuffling uneasily on the rim of illegality, but now that the nation was growing up and settling down, surely it was better for the general welfare that its heroes should bear themselves with a little more modesty, even if they were still mere tradesmen hired to injure each other? Corbett, 'the first fighting man I ever saw in full evening dress',[1] was a distinct social advance on Sullivan, with his 'I can lick any man in the world'. By the time of Corbett's assault on the bastion of Daly's Theatre, Sullivan was an obsolescent type, a fact so irresistibly apparent that everyone accepted it except Sullivan himself, in whom egomania and blockheadedness appeared to have fused to form an unbreachable defence against the inroads of reality. Not even his conclusive defeat at Corbett's hands had done anything to reduce the bump of his self-esteem, and he continued to exist on the same assumption which had inspired his youth, which was that he could lick any man in the world.

And yet there was an ambivalence in attitudes towards Sullivan, an ambivalence which Corbett knew all about, and which must have helped him considerably in his attempts to convey on the stage of Daly's Theatre the irony of a thinking boxer outfighting a fearsome pug. As the twentieth century proceeded, there were still a great many educated and articulate gentlemen whose boyhood had been too deeply suffused with the reflected light of Sullivan's glory not to remain susceptible to him forever after. Ironically these idolators included Corbett himself:

> He used to be my idol when I was a young fellow, and when I was coming up the scale I hoped all the time I would one day reach his position in the fight game. My fond dreams were realised when the match was made for me to meet him. His reputation in the ring was big enough to frighten anybody, but I reckoned that as John L. was around thirty-four years of age and I was barely twenty-six, I would stand a good chance. I knew, too, that John had abused his physique considerably; I knew I hadn't.[2]

Corbett's deferential euphemism, 'John had abused his physique considerably, was, of course, a polite reference to the fact that in the years since his victory over Paddy Ryan, Sullivan had contrived to drink himself into a stupor of self-regard hardly compatible with the successful defence of his title against a scientific opponent.

Perhaps for those who worshipped him Sullivan represented a garbled idea of America's lost innocence, when men were men and were expected to build a nation with their bare hands. The concept was idiotic, but at least it was sustained for a while by Sullivan's apparent invincibility. The cities of America were crammed with tipsy fools among the ward politicians and the professional free-loaders who went around saying, 'Let me shake the hand that shook the hand of John L. Sullivan,' almost as though by some bizarre process of osmosis, vicarious hair might sprout on America's corporate chest. What is much more curious is that neither Sullivan nor his congregation of worshippers were chastened in the slightest by the débâcle of the Corbett fight, a fact which seems to suggest that Sullivan, with his red neck and his bulging forearms, was revered not so much as an athlete as an athletic ideal, and that it was an irrepressible schoolboy respect for brute strength rather than fighting prowess which attracted the loyalties of a sporting fraternity inclined to ignore its Cashel Byrons in favour of musclebound boors whose intellectual grasp would hardly have qualified them to post Byron's letters. It was a contradiction which Shaw, by writing his novel, had become the first man to postulate, which Corbett, by bringing down Sullivan, had become the first performer to act out, and which was at last to be consummated once and for all by a champion of the next generation. No American was ever heard to make the request that he be allowed to shake the hand that shook the hand of Gentleman Jim, and in later years it was Sullivan, not Corbett, who continued to behave as though life were a fight to a finish and he the only man in the world who knew the rules.

When the customary lip-service has been paid the noble art, all the world loves a slugger at heart, and Corbett, recognising the parallels between his own predicament and Cashel Byron's, must have grabbed at Shaw's prescient novel hardly able to believe his good fortune. As for the *New York Sun*, on the morning of 9 January 1906, its eagerness to bundle the world's first respectable prizefighter into the pantheon of fine art was almost indecent. Under the heading 'Corbett and the Shaw boom' there appeared the sub-title, 'Art blended with realism at Daly's produces first-rate fun – the ex-champion pugilist a sincere, intelligent and amusing actor'. The notice proceeds in the following gushing terms:

The portraits of Molière and Shakespeare, which confront each other across the proscenium arch at Daly's Theatre must have passed many a dubious glance over recent offerings in this powerhouse of the drama, but the chances are that last night they exchanged winks of amused approval. It is many years since James J. Corbett essayed the obscurer stage in a dramatisation of Bernard Shaw's serio-comedy of the prizefighter and amused the volatile Irishman by taking himself seriously as an actor, while delighting him with royalties honestly paid, but it remained for the tidal wave of the Shaw boom to bring him in triumph to the heart of Broadway. New Haven was of the opinion last week that with *Cashel Byron's Profession* Mr Shaw had redeemed himself in its pure eyes for *Mrs Warren's Profession*. However that may be, the performance last night provided plenty of first-rate fun.

The devotee of the Drama with a capital D no doubt had occasion to sniff, for realism mingled with make-believe in a manner that might well have dispelled the atmosphere of legitimate art. Most of the fun of the performance turned upon the fact that the protagonist was, in fact, a redoubtable fighting man. But the wonder was that Mr Corbett obtruded his personality so little – or, to put the case more fairly, that he succeeded so well in creating the illusion of impersonation.

To say that he is a consistent and finished actor would perhaps be stretching the truth. But this much is certain, he conducted himself with the same scrupulous intelligence and skill that gained him his prominence in the prize-ring. No prizefighter was ever more nearly created in the image of Shaw's sincere and downright hero; and to his native advantages he added a really surprising degree of histrionic spontaneity and address.

He was boyishly charming always, and suggested the roughness of the professional pug without in the least overdoing it. To the passages of lovemaking he brought a simplicity and an ardour quite adequate to the play – the seriousness of which so constantly verges on phantasy. Even the quick remorse and the childish despair of the outsider in love with the heiress he denoted with emotional conviction. To the women in the audience he proved as captivating as to the heroine of the play. Next to that of a bull pup, his is the most beautiful grin in the world. He is fortunate too, in the lines of the part.

Shaw has not always excelled in that impartial observation of life and character which is the essence of the art of the writer of comedy. Too often his people were embodiments of his own abstract and erratic theories. But here for once he worked with his eyes rather than from his brain. How the champion of the vegetable kingdom and the foe of diversions alcoholic ever came into such close contact with the world of the four-ounce mitt is one of the wonders; but the fact that he has done so is unmistakable. And the result is a part that richly rewards intelligent effort on the part of the actor.

The dramatization, which is the work of Stanislaus Stange, is superficially mechanical, the main features of the story being assembled in three scenes in a manner sufficiently arbitrary, and not always with the smoothness and inevitability essential to dramatic art. But the play has the virtue of relying on the book to an extent surprising. Many of the dialogues were the work of the scissors unaided and had true Shaw verve and flavor, proving again how keen is the amazing satirist's instinct for dramatic effect.

The length and the depth of that review must have gratified Corbett, but by no means all the newspapers took either him or Shaw half as seriously. Clearly the *New York Herald*'s policy so far as the fine arts were concerned was to be as lively as possible without actually saying much about the arts themselves, so it is no surprise that in approaching Corbett's portrayal of Cashel Byron, the paper decided to present the event not as a play at all, but as a boxing contest. Under the heading, 'Corbett knocks out Bernard Shaw', followed by 'Wins Readily in a Lively Three Round Go at Daly's, Get's the Decision Easily, receives a hearty greeting at the theatrical ringside on début as new Broadway star', it appended a full cast list and then went on:

Jim Corbett, former fistic champion of the world, had a dramatic go at Bernard Shaw last night and knocked Shaw out in three rounds. The mill was pulled off at Daly's Theatre. There was a very large attendance at the ringside, including all the managers in New York who were looking for knockouts. The decision went to the former champion, with much cheering and no dissenting shouts. Mr Stanislaus Stange was the accomplished and efficient referee. He made only one false judgment, and that was when, after the second round, he came on the stage with Mr Corbett and in a playful way put up his fists to the champion. It was bad judgment, but the champion mercifully overlooked it.

Mr Shaw laid down the rules for the contestants in a pleasant comedy called *Cashel Byron's Profession*. Mr Stange revised it to suit Broadway, Mr Corbett and real art, as it is known under the white lights. The result was highly satisfactory to all. Mr Corbett knocked 'em all out with his ingenuousness, his boyish smile, his physique and his real ability to play himself. He played with restraint, too, and only knocked down one of the characters. The actor only got what was coming to him.

First Round – 'Jim' let Mr Shaw, assisted by Mr Stange, prove that a highly educated heiress can fall in love with a prizefighter.

Second Round – Corbett fought fast and furious. He scored at every point, and, metaphorically, landed body blows on his rival Lucian, played by Lionel Adams, and made no little impression on the charming heiress (Miss Margaret Wycherly). He had them all going for that matter.

Third Round – Corbett floored every one who opposed him. It was a walkover to the final curtain when the heiress threw herself in his arms, and the audience went out. And they said that Mr Corbett was not by any means bad – not great as an actor, but not bad all things considered.

The assistants were competent and knew their business. Mr John Dixon, made up as John L. Sullivan, knew the game better than any. The play in its unique presentation is a success.

The *Herald*'s way of treating high drama may have been unusual, but compared to the policy of a daily newspaper called the *New York Press*, its policy seems positively conservative. This paper, which advertised itself as the publication 'with the largest

Republican circulation by many thousands', decided to ignore conventional methods of presentation altogether, and to carry instead a rambling essay comparing *Cashel Byron's Profession* with another production which happened to have opened on the same night. There was not the remotest connection between the two plays; they might have been written in different centuries on different planets, but the *New York Press* contrived somehow to believe that a single statement could cover them both.

A certain Reverend Thomas Dixon Jr had written one of those works which cleverly contrive to reconcile the Sermon on the Mount with the ethics of lynch law. This play, *The Clansman*,³ had been received with mindless ecstasy in the playhouses of the old Confederacy, but as it travelled north, so did its popularity steadily wither away, until by the time it reached Broadway on the same night as *Cashel Byron*, some of the applause had changed to mild derisive laughter, perhaps because New Yorkers had recently been surfeited with a flood of plays with similarly evangelical tendencies. Resolved on weighing the relative merits of two schools of dramatic thought which had no connection apart from the accident of their collision on Broadway, the *New York Press* decided that:

> If anything, the palm of glory must be given to Corbett. He has not been the sensational success of his fellow professional, the Rev. Mr Dixon, but on his merits as an entertainer he seems the more deserving. *The Clansman* has all the earmarks of a popular success. There are strong melodramatic situations in the play, but reducing the productions to the elements of popular entertainment the chief honor must be given to the conqueror of John L. Sullivan. Our stage has been brought to an amusing predicament. On the one hand we have a former heavyweight champion pugilist claiming attention through the medium of a dramatist, who, by the verdict of every woman's club in the city, has been pronounced superior to all of his contemporaries, and on the other hand we have three clergymen forsaking their pulpits to show how the theatre should be conducted, both in an artistic and a financial way. There is much in common between the

Rev. Dixon and Mr Shaw. . . . Shaw is the greater revolutionary of the two, for he pretends to a desire to reform the whole world, while Dixon merely assumes to direct these United States in their attitude towards the negro. The Irishman has taken on himself the vastly greater contract, but it appears that he has the larger chance of reaching the particular end he has in view.

The suspicion begins to form that the Republican *New York Press* is using the modest Corbett as a stick to beat a pretentious rabblerouser who 'had done more to ruffle the good nature of play-goers than any other stage writer of the day'. The suspicion grows as the essay proceeds:

Better far the honest frolic of Corbett and Shaw than the mockery of Dixon. It would be the safer plan to scoff at Corbett, but despite chance of general derision, it may be said that there are actors who flatter themselves that their names should be written in golden letters who could not give a more meritorious performance. Although George Bernard Shaw by this time may be wearing a halo, Corbett is better than the play drawn from the Irishman's novel. Shaw sniffed when told that Stanislaus Stange was to dramatise *Cashel Byron's Profession* and declined to accept royalties, believing there would only be a widow's mite of royalties to accept. But in the light of recent developments Shaw might well have been more condescending in his dignity, for, hard as Mr Stange worked, he was unable to extract more than a conventionally tame comedy from the book, and it must gall the soul of George Bernard to be associated in the slightest degree with a single convention of this conventional old world.

Corbett is a surprise. He acts his role in excellent fashion. He displays no false pride or conceited notions. He appears to be possessed of the wise idea that a little burlesque is expected of him, and he carries himself with refreshing liveliness through the play. He is not affected, and this is a modest trait that cannot be despised. Corbett is the best antidote known up to the present for the Shaw rattling and preaching. The prizefighter takes all the sting out of Shaw's cynicism, and robs his most captious comment of its sharpness. There is a keen relish in the rollicking vigor of Corbett, and instead of being an object of ridicule he has become a welcome addition to the ranks of stellar players. A meeting between Shaw and Corbett now will be in order, and the world should hang in interest on the outcome of the inevitable debate on vegetarianism vs pugilism.

The determination of the New York critics to praise the actor at the expense of the dramatist certainly produced no critical curiosity more bizarre than the *New York Press*'s suggestion that Shaw would have allowed the size of the royalties to influence his acceptance of them, or that Shavian polemics are more diverting when the sharpness is taken out of them.

It would have amused Shaw, had he been aware of the reaction to his fable by the New York press, that whether critics took the production at Daly's as an excuse to jeer at the presumption of an upstart prizefighter, or as an opportunity to fling a few brickbats at a mad Irishman, not one of them seemed to notice what the story was about, or to take the point which Shaw had so patiently made in the novel, which is plainly that one kind of professionalism is much the same as another, and that it is ridiculous for a society to countenance the act of making money by extracting a man's teeth with a pair of pliers, as young Valentine does in *You Never Can Tell*, while spurning the act of removing those same teeth with a scientifically placed right uppercut in the style of Cashel Byron. People who work for a living, says Shaw, are much of a muchness ethically speaking, and the would-be arbiter of moral standards who swallows, say, the kept woman of the heir apparent to the throne of England must not complain when suddenly confronted by Vivie Warren. No hint of this theme is ever mentioned by the New York critics.

Perhaps the oversight is understandable, for Shaw's moral instruction was being received only after it had been filtered through two forms not ideally suited to the delivery of the lecture, a novel and its literal translation on to the stage. Had the critics only been presented with the issues in a less cluttered setting, then perhaps they would have seen the fable Shaw meant them to see, instead of the one they imagined they saw. It is quite true that by the time Corbett's production opened on

Broadway, Shaw had long since forsaken the novel form as an effective means of disseminating Shavian propaganda; had he only discovered his own destiny ten years earlier than he did, it is probable that the text of *Cashel Byron's Profession* would have been couched in dramatic form, and its proposition, instead of rambling through nearly a hundred thousand words, would have been reduced to amusing absurdity over three acts.

How might Shaw have constricted his material to fit an evening at the theatre? A likely solution might have been to design the action to fit a single location, one lavish enough to allow Byron to perform a few pugilistic set pieces, and yet elevated enough for Shaw to be able to make his point, which is that in a frankly acquisitive society, all banknotes have the same colour. Let us assume that Shaw had chosen for his background a large fashionable hotel in a great city, and let us assume also that his prizefighter arrives at this hotel with enough money to pay for his accommodation, only to discover that the management refuses to accept that money because of the way he has acquired it. Let us assume also that in order to make sure that nobody misses the point, Shaw lets us see that even as Byron is turned away, financiers and market speculators of the most dubious ethical persuasions are being welcomed with open arms. Of course there would have been the usual complaints; that Shaw had rigged his facts for the convenience of the debate; that real-life hotel managers are too mercenary ever to turn business away; that real-life financiers never reveal their sins so blatantly in public places; above all that the allegory of the grand hotel as a microcosm of capitalism is an embarrassing platitude. The Shavians would have replied that allegories are not supposed to be realistic, or that capitalism is itself so blatant a cliché that only a platitude could possibly do it justice, and so on. The argument would have raged for a while and then subsided, quite suddenly, as the next Shaw play arrived in town. Had anyone suggested this kind of treatment to Stanislaus Stange, he would almost certainly have dismissed it as a silly impracticality, and explained that no hard-headed New York sophisticate who frequented luxury hotels would accept such a premise for a moment.

Stange and company would have been wrong, for not only

had our hypothetical Shavian scenario already been enacted in real life, but, by one of those comically appropriate coincidences which novelists and dramatists are always wise to avoid, it had actually been acted out concurrently with the opening of *Cashel Byron's Profession*. On the eve of Corbett's grand opening there had arrived in the city a pugilist of some renown called Mr John Hagen, who had for many years been conducting his business affairs under the trade name of Philadelphia Jack O'Brien. This Mr Hagen-O'Brien was known throughout the sporting world as a fighter of great technical skill and physical courage, whose proud distinctions included a No-Decision contest with Jack Johnson, and, only three weeks before Corbett's opening night, a twelve-round knockout victory in San Francisco over the same Bob Fitzsimmons who had once relieved Corbett of his world championship. O'Brien was a much respected man, who had always been seen to conduct himself with that comic punctilio which men in his profession will sometimes adopt once they have grasped the central paradox of Shaw's novel. New York's hotel managers, however, had most decidedly not grasped it, and reacted to Mr O'Brien's overtures accordingly. The most astonishing fact of all in connection with poor Mr O'Brien's social ostracism is that of all the New York papers, only one, the *New York American*, recognised its topicality, and that even the *New York American* failed so utterly to perceive the relevance of *Cashel Byron's Profession* to the events enacted along Fifth Avenue on 8 January 1906, that on the very same page where one critic was braying loudly at the proprietors of Daly's Theatre for allowing a mere pugilist on the stage, it ran an editorial defending O'Brien's cause, and defended it with a flair very nearly Shavian in its sprightliness:

> The sad case of Mr Jack O'Brien, né Hagen, in cold-blooded New York last Sunday recalls those inhumanities of man to man that make countless thousands mourn. Mr O'Brien had just returned from the large and hospitable West, where he had given an exhibition of his skill in that profession which George Bernard Shaw has applauded through the mouth of his hero, Cashel Byron. As a result of the skill he manifested

there he has become the most eminent professor of the squared circle in the United States, and yet when, with his valet, and his private secretary, his business manager and the rest of the personal staff necessary to the comfort and dignity of a successful heavyweight, he drove from hotel to hotel on Fifth Avenue, he was politely, but firmly, asked to seek some other spot, or, in the language of his associates in his own profession, 'to skidoo'.

As the poet has it:

> Ah, it was pitiful;
> In a whole city full,
> Rooms there were none.

It does not seem altogether in accordance with the highest principles of justice that the Fifth Avenue landlords looked with disfavour upon their would-be guest. He follows a profession which compels him, if he would succeed, to live cleanly, avoid the wine when it is red, and hold himself well in hand. When he practises his art, he does so only in communities where it is permitted by law, and cannot, like some eminent gentlemen who frequent these very hotels, coin money by violating the laws of a neighbouring State, and escape responsibility by avoiding legal summons, or by defying the law authorities. Strangely enough, in one of the hotels which 'passed up' Mr O'Brien, the house authorities, on the same day, rescued a millionaire trust magnate who had entrenched himself in his bathroom to escape the service of legal papers. At another hotel, according to the reminiscent Mr Lawson, eight connecting rooms were cheerfully put at the disposal of two frenzied financiers who wished to escape the observation of a friend whom they had meant to betray. Characteristically enough, the meeting ended by each one of the confrères trying with alternate success to swindle the other as well as their friend.

Mr O'Brien has to play his game fairly, under well-established regulations, with his hands up and in full view of the people interested in the outcome. He may not strike below the belt, nor hit his adversary when he is down. Of how many of the promoters, frenzied financiers, bucket-shop keepers and *chevaliers d'industrie* who haunt the corridors of Fifth Avenue hotels can as much be said? And yet they are made welcome while Professor O'Brien could scarce find in all Fifth Avenue a place to lay that block which Professor Fitzsimmons vainly tried to knock off.

Far be it from us to defend Mr O'Brien's profession. The task has been left to a higher authority, a literary gentleman, who of late years has taken to defending more than one curious profession. We quote from Mr George Bernard Shaw these illuminating words spoken by his hero, Mr Byron, to a lady who had expressed disapproval of pugilism:

Who did I see here last Friday, the most honoured of your guests? Why, that Frenchman with the gold spectacles. What do you think I was told when I asked what his little game was? Baking dogs in ovens to see how long a dog would live red hot! I'd like to catch him doing it to a dog of mine. Ay; and sticking a rat full of nails to see how much pain a rat could stand. Why, it's just sickening. Do you think I would have shaken hands with that chap? If he hadn't been a guest of yours I'd have given him a notion of how much pain a Frenchman can stand without any nails in him. And he's to be received and made much of, while I'm kicked out! Look at your relation, the general. What is he but a fighting man, I should like to know? Isn't it his pride and boast that as long as he is paid so much a day he'll ask no questions whether a war is fair or unfair, but just walk out and put thousands of men in the best way to kill and be killed? – keeping well behind them all the time, mind you. Last year he was up to his chin in the blood of a lot of poor blacks that were no more of a match for his armed men than a featherweight would be for me. Bad as I am, I wouldn't attack a featherweight, or stand by and see another heavy man do it. Plenty of your friends go pigeon shooting to Hurlingham. There's a humane and manly way of spending a Saturday afternoon! Do you think foxes like to be hunted, or that the people who hunt them have such fine feelings that they can afford to call prizefighters names? Look at the men that get killed or lamed every year at steeplechasing, foxhunting, cricket and football! Dozens of them!'

We would urge Mr O'Brien, who is clearly ill-used, to study the literature of the profession the practice of which he has so well mastered. So shall he be able to argumentatively uppercut inhospitable landlords who would expel a pugilist never charged with crooked work, and admit insurance, copper, oil, gas and traction magnates.[4]

With which truly remarkable example of life imitating art, the curtain falls on the spectacle of James J. Corbett as Cashel Byron.

If Shaw ever exulted in his astonishing triumph in tempting a flesh-and-blood boxing champion to masquerade as Byron on stage, he gave no indication of it, being too preoccupied with the pleasurable task of rubbing in the dust the noses of the old-time London publishers:

> Blame not me, then, reader, if these exercises of a raw apprentice break loose again and insist on their right to live. The world never did know chalk from cheese in matters of art; and after all, since it is only the young and the old who have time to read, the rest being too busy living, my exercises may be fitter for the market than my masterpieces.[1]

Although it must have been a belated vindication of unusual sweetness that a real-life pugilist was playing at being Byron, an altogether more brilliant, if far more belated, victory of a truly fantastical nature, was yet to come. Shaw was, of course, always a consummate master of the art of puffing his own work on the pretence of belittling it, and his ostensible deflation of *Cashel Byron's Profession* is choice enough to whet the appetite of even the most incurious reader:

> *Cashel Byron's Profession* is, at bottom, a mere boy's romance. It has a sort of cleverness which has always been a cheap quality in me; and it is interesting, amusing, and at one point – unique in my works – actually exciting. The excitement is produced by the brutal expedient of describing a fight. It is not, as usual in novels, a case in which the hero fights a villain in defence of the heroine, or in the satisfaction of a righteous indignation. The two men are paid to fight for the amusement of the spectators. They set to for the sake of the money, and strive to beat each other out of pure ferocity. The success of this incident is a conclusive proof of the superfluity of the

conventional hypocrisies of fiction. I guarantee to every purchaser of *Cashel Byron* a first class fight for his money. At the same time he will not be depraved by any attempt to persuade him that his relish for blood and violence is the sympathy of a generous soul in its eternal struggle with vice. I claim that from the first uppercut with which Cashel Byron stops his opponent's lead-off and draws his cork (I here use the accredited terminology of pugilism) to the cross-buttock with which he finally disables him, there is not a single incident which can be enjoyed on any other ground than that upon which the admittedly brutalised frequenter of prize-fights enjoys his favourite sport. Out of the savagery of my imagination I wrote the scene; and out of the savagery of your tastes you delight in it. My other novels contain nothing of the kind. And none of them have succeeded as well as *Cashel Byron's Profession* . . . which is like any other novel in respect of its hero punching people's heads. Its novelty consists in the fact that an attempt is made to treat the art of punching seriously, and to detach it from the general elevation of moral character with which the ordinary novelist persists in associating it.[2]

Who could resist so seductive a come-on? Indeed, the Shavian blandishments are so alluring as to be more attractive than the novel they purport to belittle. But for all his devious justifications for Byron's existence, Shaw appears to have retained a streak of shamefacedness for having indulged a schoolboy fancy. According to Hesketh Pearson, Shaw felt the book to be 'a streak of original sin', and added:

The glove fight and the conventional lived-happy-ever-afterwards ending, to which I had never previously condescended, exposed me for the first time to the humiliation of extravagantly favourable reviewing and of numbering my readers in some thousands. But long before this my self-respect took alarm at the contemplation of the things I had made. I resolved to give up mere character sketching . . . and at once to produce a novel which should be a gigantic grapple with the whole social problem.[3]

The gigantic grapple, which was to take the form of *An Unsocial Socialist*, falls outside the scope of any discussion of Shaw's connections with the prize-ring. What is very surprising indeed is that *Cashel Byron's Profession* should so consistently have fallen outside the scope of any discussion of Shaw as an emergent creative artist. The book has generally been by-passed by even the most conscientious Shavian critics and biographers, with the result that certain subtleties and witticisms in the balancing of characteristics have been overlooked. To be sure, the plot of *Cashel Byron's Profession* appears to be conventional enough. However, there is much more to Byron than at first meets the reader's eye, and in a brief but extremely acute attempt to till this neglected Shavian ground, at least one critic has taken the trouble to push aside the conventional heroics of the plot and see what lies beyond. Margery Morgan, after giving an airing to the familiar theory that in his early novel-writing days Shaw felt the influence of his great hero Dickens, goes on to suggest links with another writer not often invoked in the Shavian debate, Jane Austen, and cites as possible proof the voice of the ironist which asserts itself in the very first chapter of Shaw's novel:

> This Miss Carew was a remarkable person. She had inherited the Castle and park from her aunt, who had considered her niece's larger fortune in railways and mines incomplete without land. So many other legacies had Lydia received from kinsfolk who hated poor relations, that she was now, in her twenty-fifth year, the independent possessor of an annual income equal to the year's earnings of five hundred workmen. . . . In addition to the advantage of being a single woman with unusually large means, she enjoyed a reputation for vast learning and exquisite culture.

Miss Morgan has a suspicion that Shaw's attempt to disarm the reader with protestations that his novel is a device for 'stripping prizefighting of false glamour' is thoroughly bogus, and that what really constitutes the tension of the plot is not the conflict between the rationale of Byron's ring technique and the crudities of poor Paradise, but the contradictions inherent in a hero whose 'moral being seems rudimentary', and a heroine whose 'insufficiency of passion is deliberately exposed as a defect'. Byron utters shattering truths with the innocence of a naïf, but it takes Lydia, 'or the reader, to recognise the wider applicability of the truths Cashel speaks, and she is only able to do so because ignorance of how he makes his living allows her to remain open-minded.'

'I am a professor of science' said Cashel in a low voice, looking down at his left fist, which he was balancing in the air before him, and stealthily hitting his bent knee as if it was another person's face.

'Physical or moral science?' persisted Lydia.

'Physical science,' said Cashel. 'But there's more moral science in it than people think.'[4]

Byron's curious implication that there is a morality in punching people is finally justified in an hilarious set-piece at a London party where the boxer delivers what is virtually a lecture to the assembled company on the civilising effect of technique. After pointing out that in order to rescue a lady by vanquishing the rough who is assaulting her, 'you want to know how to hit him, when to hit him, and where to hit him; and then you want the nerve to go in and do it', Byron seizes on the nearby portrait of St George vanquishing the dragon:

The lady in the gallery is half-crazy with anxiety for St George; and well she may be. *There's* a posture for a man to fight in! His weight isn't resting on his legs: one touch of a child's finger would upset him. Look at his neck craned out in front of him, and his face as flat as a full moon towards his man, as if he was inviting him to shut up both his eyes with one blow. You can all see that he's as weak and nervous as a cat, and that he doesn't know how to fight. And why does he give you that idea? Just because he's all strain and stretch; because he isn't at his ease; because he carries the weight of his body as foolishly as one of the ladies here would carry a hod of bricks; because he isn't safe, steady, and light on his pins, as he would be if he could forget himself for a minute and leave his body to find its proper balance of its own accord.

This superlative exposition of the great athlete's golden rule, which is the unselfconscious application of a consciously acquired technique, or to put it another, more Shavian way, that habit can with mental application become an acquired characteristic, naturally draws the fire of the other guests, one of whom challenges Byron's theory. The boxer responds:

'Suppose you wanted to hit me the most punishing blow you possibly could. What would you do? Why, according to your own notion, you'd make a great effort. "The more effort, the more force", you'd say to yourself. "I'll smash him even if I burst myself in doing it." And what would happen then? You'd only cut me and make me angry, beside exhausting all your strength at one gasp. Whereas, if you took it easy – like this – ' Here he made a light step forward, and placed his open palm gently against the breast of Lucian, who, as if the piston-rod of a steam-engine had touched him, instantly reeled back and dropped into the chair.

'There!' exclaimed Cashel, beaming with self-satisfaction as he stepped aside and pointed at Lucian. 'It's like pocketing a billiard ball!'

Byron has come to understand that this executive power of his is as much a responsibility as it is a blessing. As he tries to explain to Lydia 'I know what a man is going to do before he rightly knows himself. The power this gave me, civilised me.' In one sense this is the most uncannily prescient sentence in the entire novel. Just as, ten years after Shaw wrote the book, his drawing-room exposition of what happens to a wild, purely physical puncher in a fight with a reasoning artist was to be followed down to the last detail in the Sullivan–Corbett débâcle, so his suggestion that some pugilists possess the gift of anticipating the physical intentions of others was to sound its echo far into the remote future, as we shall see.

Clearly *Cashel Byron's Profession* needs to be bracketed with *Mrs Warren's Profession* and *Major Barbara* (at one time very nearly entitled *Andrew Undershaft's Profession*) as part of the same argument against differentiation on spurious moral grounds between one way of earning money and another. Miss Morgan has even seen closer analogies with Undershaft in the scene where the African king, 'in whose primitive eyes the greatness of Cashel appears indisputable, had been taken to visit Woolwich Arsenal, "the destructive resources of which were expected silently to warn him against taking the Christian religion too seriously".' The joke at the expense of Christianity has the vintage Shavian quality, but the best joke of all is contained in the book's conclusion, which is perhaps not quite as happy-ever-afterwards as Shaw insisted it was. As Miss Morgan concludes:

> Part of the joke is that Lydia justifies their marriage on the theory that Cashel's warm spontaneity will repair her own want of impulse and his physicality will correct her own overbred, scholarly nature, when in fact the union is not a mésalliance because his intelligence is as good as hers; it is an alliance of truth and wisdom, but still nature employs its irony at the expense of human logic.[5]

The irony to which Miss Morgan refers turns up in the final chapter of the novel when Shaw, dealing a whimsical but deadly blow against the very theories of Eugenics in whose cause he will so tirelessly campaign, writes that:

> For as they grew up, and the hereditary scheme began to develop results, the boys disappointed her by turning out almost pure Carew, without the slightest athletic aptitude; whilst the girls were impetuously Byronic: indeed, one of them to Cashel's utter dismay, cast back so completely to his mother that when she announced, at thirteen, her intention of going on the stage, he bowed to her decision as to the voice of Destiny.

When he came to attach a *Note on Modern Prizefighting* to the end of the novel in 1901, Shaw tied Byron irrevocably to Mrs Warren and Andrew Undershaft by insisting that:

> As long as society is so organised that the destitute athlete and the destitute beauty are forced to choose between underpaid drudgery as industrial producers, and comparative self-respect, plenty, and popularity as prizefighters and mercenary brides, licit or illicit, it is idle to affect virtuous indignation at

their expense. The word prostitute should either not be used at all, or else applied impartially to all persons who do things for money that they would not do if they had any other assured means of livelihood.[6]

The consequences of Shaw's argument may be seen nearly a century later in dozens of professional sports whose practitioners never even stop to consider the outlandish idea that what they are doing might be considered by some people to be not quite decent. But if Shaw anticipated this development, the characters of *Cashel Byron's Profession* did not. Towards the end of the story, Skene's wife, trying to persuade a dubious Lydia to accept Byron's proposal of marriage, remarks 'Only think what a man he is. Champion of the world and a gentleman as well. The two things have never happened before and never will again.''

As it happened, Mrs Skene was quite wrong.

# PART TWO

# *FIGHTING*

'I consider my association with George Bernard Shaw
as one of the outstanding blessings of my life.'
Gene Tunney

# 1 / FROM DONNELLY TO DEMPSEY

In 1919 the World Heavyweight Championship had been held for four years by a man called Jess Willard. The seventh fighter to hold the title, Willard, an ungainly giant, was also the least gifted. Unlike the six champions before him, he had little natural talent, and had become a professional only in his thirtieth year, an age when most prizefighters are beginning to think about retirement. Even the lustre of his official position was tarnished by the suspicion, never since quite eradicated, that there was something fishy about his acquirement of it. The notorious championship fight with Jack Johnson – the climax of a seedy 'White Hope' campaign which was really no more than a protracted newspaper race war – had ended with Johnson sprawled on his back indolently shading his eyes from the Havana sun with one elbow. It was obvious to the connoisseurs that Willard was no more than a caretaker champion to be relieved of his duties the moment a challenger appeared in the great tradition of Corbett and Fitzsimmons. By 1919 Willard did not have much longer to wait. It was now his misfortune to be confronted by a rival from Colorado who had begun fighting as Kid Blackie and had later reverted to his baptismal name of Jack Dempsey.

Dempsey was wholly unorthodox but a born fighter. Donnelly/Skene would have been scandalised by his style but delighted by its effect. His technique was to advance on opponents in an ugly, crablike crouch, bobbing and weaving to make himself an ever-moving target, throwing short, swinging punches of great power with both hands. Poor Willard was no more than a sacrificial offering. After only two rounds he was so severely battered that for years afterwards, people half-believed the canard that Dempsey's handlers had sprinkled cement dust on the bandages taping their man's fists. Once hardened by sweat, the effect of the cement dust would be roughly the same as being armed with a couple of rocks. The charge, though ridiculous, gives some idea of Dempsey's terrific punching power, and of the terror which the mere thought of the new champion inspired in so many of his rivals throughout the 1920s. However, had the Willard–Dempsey fight taken place a few years later, it is quite possible that Willard would have won on a disqualification. Several times Dempsey clubbed the defenceless champion when he was either falling to, or rising from, the ring floor. And each time Willard went down Dempsey stood over him, ready to unleash a murderous barrage the moment his opponent was even halfway to his feet. Such tactics were conventional enough in the professional rings of the period, but their manifest unfairness soon caused the rules to be amended. After the Willard–Dempsey fight, it became compulsory for a fighter to retire to a neutral corner while the referee was counting over his fallen opponent, thus giving the opponent a reasonable chance to gather his wits and prepare to defend himself. It is this change in the rules, and Dempsey's total failure in a crisis to adapt to it, which brings into context for the first time the Shavian Life Force and Life imitating Art, although Dempsey no doubt remained in blissful ignorance of both those peculiar concepts for the rest of his days.

Meanwhile the new rule was passed and Dempsey, characteristically, proceeded to ignore it utterly. He was the greatest sporting idol in American history and a law unto himself, a truth which was very soon demonstrated in a most vivid way. One night in 1923 Dempsey spent an extremely uncomfortable few minutes in the company of an Argentinian bottle-washer called Luis Angel Firpo. An immensely strong and brave heavyweight with no pretensions to skill, Firpo opened his challenge for Dempsey's crown by literally knocking the champion out of the ring, with the kind of right swing which might have killed a normal man. By an enormous stroke of good fortune, Dempsey landed in the laps of the gentlemen of the press, who most obligingly pushed Dempsey back through the ropes into the ring – this being the only recorded occasion in sporting history when the press has been of any practical use to an athlete. Miraculously Dempsey resumed the contest, and after two rounds of bloody confusion was declared the winner. Both fighters were up and down so often, and each of them mauled his opponent so indiscriminately as to duplicate the conditions of a bar-room brawl, that had the neutral corner rule been enforced, both would have been disqualified for blatant breaches of the code. Dempsey, it appeared, was above the law, at least for the moment.[1]

Throughout the seven years of Dempsey's reign, the boxing world was pleasantly preoccupied with the problem of whether the champion was actually invincible. Although he fought with ominous infrequency (Dempsey defended his championship only six times in those seven years; in the seven months between December 1940 and June 1941 Joe Louis successfully defended the same title seven times), he always won through a combination of fierce punching power, speed of reflex, bull-like strength and indomitable courage. It soon became clear that only a remarkable alliance of pace, guile and sheer bravery would ever bring him down.

In the meantime, while the World Heavyweight Championship was moving resolutely into its golden age of ballyhoo and giantism, what had happened to the middleweight contender of Pakenham Beatty's Victorian tutelage? To what pugilistic ends was the Fighting Irishman of Fitzroy Square devoting his energies? To none at all, it seems, at least for a great many years. The musty world of the old prize-ring had fallen far away behind him in at least two senses, for not only had Beatty's old companion become transmogrified by the engines of his own publicity into one of the world's most renowned intellectual celebrities, but the prize-ring as he had once known it had virtually disappeared. A succession of brilliant Shavian careers had followed on to form a cerebral processional whose virtuosity was unparalleled in the modern era. The music critic had made way for the theatre reviewer who had cleared the ground in preparation for the dramatist who had usurped the theatre for his own mystical ends, and throughout this period there is no scrap of evidence to suggest that Shaw maintained even a peripheral interest in the affairs of either professional or gentleman pugilists.

In any case, had he attended any of the famous contests which took place between, say, Mr Gladstone's third administration and the outbreak of the First World War, had he chanced upon the legerdemain of Pedlar Palmer or Jim Driscoll or Jimmy Wilde, he would have found little that was recognisable to a graduate of Donnelly's gymnasium in Panton Street. In this respect, at first glance Donnelly's manual is misleading, because its illustrations present a pugilistic face whose expression is more or less consistent with what a later age tends to think of when prizefighting is mentioned. In the cosily two-dimensional world of Donnelly's textual illustrations, false leads are feinted and real ones blocked, crosses are delivered like so many postcards, and punch is parried by counter-punch. But the reader who has stamina enough to fight his way through to the latter stages of the book where the ultimate refinements are imparted, suddenly realises that this is a very different world from what he has imagined; Donnelly is after all, no more than a pugilistic Turveydrop whose punctilio has been rendered hopelessly quaint by the passage of time.

Although Donnelly published the revised edition of his manual as late as 1897, and although fifteen years earlier he had undoubtedly instructed two young gentlemen like Beatty and Shaw in the noble art according to the formal canons of the then newly-formed Amateur Boxing Association, he was still ready to recognise the sad fact that some men, gentle or otherwise, came to him in order to learn how to do other people a serious injury, in which ambition Donnelly seems to have acquiesced with a truly professional docility:

PLATE XLV:
Stop for right cross buttock by immediately putting left hand over opponent's right shoulder, and pulling his head well back, thus taking all strength out of the body, and at the same time hitting with right hand on face.

As if to preserve the remnants of his own gentility in the face of such fearsome goings-on, Donnelly adds a parenthetical warning: 'It is a very nasty throw – man throwing you and falling on you at same time'. A few pages later he reveals the secret of something he describes, with a nice appreciation for euphemism, as the 'Back-Heel':

PLATE XLVIII:

. . . by putting left fore-arm well under opponent's chin, draw at same time left foot back and throw weight of body on him to cause him to fall on back of his head, which is a dangerous fall.

The fact that all this strikes the modern reader as bizarre is probably due to his misconception that once the Queensberry Rules were introduced, everyone immediately began observing them. The Marquis gave his official blessing to the code as early as 1867, when Shaw was still a Dublin schoolboy, but a generation later there were still pugilists who disregarded it. The trouble was that in prohibiting such tactics as kicking, gouging, butting and biting, the revised code was taking a great deal of the harmless fun and good sportsmanship out of a recreation whose followers included a great many for whom the vicarious joys of kicking, gouging, butting and biting were, in the manly fulfilment they afforded, second only to the act of witnessing the ritual dismemberment of a fox. Not until as late as 1892, by which time Shaw had passed on from Lillie Bridge to his tryst with posterity, was there a contest for the World Heavyweight Championship in which both contestants wore gloves, the champion, John L. Sullivan insisting on this arrangement and his challenger, James J. Corbett, taking nonchalant advantage of it.[2]

In 1897, the year when Donnelly brought out his revised primer and Shaw was involving himself in the world première of *The Man of Destiny* at Croydon, Corbett lost his title to a gnarled, balding Cornishman called Fitzsimmons, who had made the interesting discovery that if you hit a man in the stomach hard enough to stop him breathing, the chances are that he will not be feeling quite himself for a little while. Fitzsimmons' famed exposition of the solar plexus punch was a heartwarming reassertion of the old English genius for scientific pragmatism, but it seems to have drawn no flicker of interest from Shaw. But perhaps the lack of interest was understandable. After all, Fitzsimmons was English only in the technical sense, having emigrated as a young man to New Zealand and done his fighting in Australia and America. In any case, there could have

been very few people at that time who saw anything particularly sensational in a British-born fighter becoming World
Heavyweight Champion. Fitzsimmons was only the third in the
succession, after Sullivan and Corbett, and was already
beginning to make a habit of acquiring such titles. Back in 1891
he had won the World Middleweight championship and hung
on to it so tenaciously that six years later, faced with the
opportunity of a fight with Corbett, he had relinquished it
undefeated. Even after his eventual loss of the heavyweight
crown to James J. Jeffries, Fitzsimmons contrived to win yet
another world championship, this time of the Light-
Heavyweight division in 1903, by which time he was reputed to
be over forty years of age – although it is fair to add that nobody
seems to have been quite certain when Fitzsimmons was born,
not even Fitzsimmons. When he lost his heavyweight crown to
the giant Jeffries, the British, who had invented and codified
virtually all the world's sports and games in an astonishing burst
of inventive genius between 1860 and 1880, and were
accustomed to being champions at them all, must have assumed
they would not have long to wait before another local fighter
emulated Fitzsimmons. That was in 1899 and today they are still
waiting.

Jeffries later retired undefeated, and was succeeded by a
diminutive Canadian called Burns, who was willing to take on
all comers provided he was allowed to choose who they were.
Eventually he was cornered in Australia and duly defeated by
Jack Johnson, that consummate artist destined to bow out of the
succession lying under the Havana sun, shading his eyes with his
elbow at the one moment in his career when one might have
supposed him to be indifferent to prevailing weather
conditions. The unlikely apotheosis of Jess Willard in Havana
took place in 1915, by which time the lions of the old London
prize-ring were historically as obscure as the proverbial
philosophies of Martin Tupper, or the two half-centuries scored
by Henry Hyndman for the Sussex county side. Nobody
remembered Donnelly and his quaint little book of instructions,
and the administrators of the English amateur championships,
had they set out to find Lillie Bridge, might well have got lost on
the way.

By the turn of the century Pakenham Beatty, the amateur who had first introduced Shaw to the pleasures of boxing, had most sadly declined into a cipher whose fortunes, had they not been supervised by old friends, and one in particular, would have degenerated into unmitigated disaster. Beatty's is perhaps the saddest fate of all those involved in the curious story of *Cashel Byron's Profession*, embodying a perfect example of the type of obscure literary dabbler who hovers quixotically on the periphery of great events for a while and then vanishes imperceptibly like the Cheshire Cat. Beatty was as far above that kind of damnation as he was below Shaw's eminence, but only through the happy accident that he went in for boxing and that his sparring partner happened to become a great man. For all the grandiloquence of his ambitions, he has left only the very faintest of imprints on the memoirs of the period, and were he to stand purely on his own achievements, nobody would remember his name. And yet Pakenham Beatty did acquire a kind of immortality after all which enables us to catch a glimpse of him, even if only through the distorting prism of Shavian satire.

In the fifth and last of Shaw's novels, *An Unsocial Socialist*, in Chapter Eleven, the author's doppelgänger Sidney Trefusis is introduced to a dashing young bicyclist to whom everybody addresses as Chester. Trefusis asks 'Have I the pleasure of speaking to Mr Chichester Erskine, author of a tragedy entitled *The Patriot Martyrs*, dedicated with such enthusiastic devotion to the Spirit of Liberty and half a dozen famous upholders of that principle, and denouncing in forcible language the tyranny of the late Tsar of Russia, Bomba of Naples, and Napoleon the Third?' Erskine blushes at this because he feels that 'this description might make his drama seem ridiculous to those present who had not read it'. A few pages later the figure of Erskine emerges more substantially:

> He was a young man of gentle birth, and had inherited fifteen hundred a year from his mother, the bulk of the family property being his elder brother's. Having no profession, and being fond of books and pictures, he had devoted himself to fine art, a pursuit which offered him on the cheapest terms a high opinion of the beauty and capacity of his own nature. He had published a tragedy entitled *The Patriot Martyrs*, and an edition of it had been speedily disposed of in presentations to the friends of the poet, and to the reviews and newspapers. Sir Charles had asked an eminent tragedian of his acquaintance to place the work on the stage and to enact one of the patriot martyrs. But the tragedian had objected that the other patriot martyrs had parts of equal importance to that proposed for him. Erskine had indignantly refused to cut these parts down or out, and so the project had fallen through.

One wonders if that paragraph ever fell under the eye of Henry Irving, and, if it did, what that 'disemboweller of Shakespeare' thought of it. Further signs of the embryo drama critic are revealed in the following paragraph:

> Since then Erskine had been bent on writing another drama, without regard to the exigencies of the stage, but he had not yet begun it, in consequence of his inspiration coming upon him at inconvenient hours, chiefly late at night, when he had been drinking, and had leisure for sonnets only. The morning air and bicycle riding were fatal to the vein in which his poetry struck him as being worth writing. In spite of the bicycle, however, the drama, which was to be entitled *Hypatia*, was now in a fair way to be written, for the poet had met and fallen in love with Gertrude Lindsay, whose almost Grecian features, and some knowledge of the differential calculus which she had acquired at Alton, helped him to believe that she was a fit model for his heroine.

From such fragments and from the surviving letters which Shaw sent him, we can begin to piece together the career of an archetypal bohemian-dilettante of the period.

Beatty was born in 1855, a year before Shaw, of Irish parents in Maranhao, Brazil, and, like his sparring partner, spent part of his boyhood at Dalkey. But the two men did not meet before they were both coping with self-imposed exile in the London of the 1870s. At an early stage in their friendship Shaw dubbed Beatty 'Paquito', a name which was later to serve as an alias for the eponymous hero of *Captain Brassbound's Conversion*. The first surviving letter from Shaw to Beatty is dated 1 November 1878, and concerns Shaw's receipt of his friend's new book of poems, *To My Lady and Other Poems*, whose appearance in print gave Beatty several years publishing seniority over Shaw. Three months after the publication, on 22 February 1879, Beatty married Edith Benigna Isabel Hutton Dowling, known as Ida. She had studied the piano under Gounod and read and spoke French fluently; Shaw, who was notorious as the master of the maladroit art of being the bachelor friend of newly-weds, visited them almost every Sunday for the first six years of the marriage, donning boxing gloves and sparring with the husband, and practising his French with the wife, who affectionately dubbed him 'old grandmother Shaw'. This was the period when the two young men were attending Donnelly's boxing classes, and *Cashel Byron's Profession* progressed from conception to completion. Only in 1885, when the Beattys moved out to the village of Mill Hill on the northern fringes of London, did Shaw's visits fall away and finally peter out.

In 1881 the Beattys' first son was born and most unfairly saddled with the burden of his father's idealism, being christened Pakenham William Albert Hengist Mazzini; Shaw only made matters worse by facetiously adding the nickname 'Bismarck'. Many years later, in *Heartbreak House*, Hesione Hushabye explains the curious christian name of Mazzini Dunn by saying 'Mazzini was a celebrity of some kind who knew Ellie's grandparents. They were both poets, like the Brownings; and when her father came into the world Mazzini said "Another soldier born for freedom!" So they christened him Mazzini; and he has been fighting for freedom in his quiet way ever since. That's why he is so poor.' In 1884 Beatty published his verse-tragedy *Marcia*, which Shaw, masquerading as L. O. Streeter in the periodical *To-Day*, pilloried so unmercifully that his father, alone now in Dublin, and no doubt relieved to be so, wrote 'I am afraid Mr Streeter deserves the title of "Ruffian" from Mr Beatty.'[1] It was this poetic effusion of Beatty's which later appeared in the thin disguise of *The Patriot Martyrs* in *An Unsocial Socialist*. There was something else which prompted Shaw's father to write to him in that same year, Paquito's apparent infatuation for Shaw's sister Lucy: 'I hope that fellow is not still annoying Lucy. It must be very distressing for her.'[2] And presumably also for Ida, to whom Shaw wrote on 22 September 1885 explaining that he had no idea where her husband might be. Beatty and Shaw, accompanied by Henry Hyde Champion and the Russian nihilist Stepniak, had dined at the Criterion and walked on to the Socialist League Hall in Farringdon Road, with Paquito and Stepniak bringing up the rear, lagging further and further behind, although Shaw says, 'we could hear them most of the time above the din of the traffic, shouting one another down about Victor Hugo or the like'. By the time the party reached Holborn the two laggards had cut adrift completely: 'when we looked about for the poet and the Nihilist, they were invisible, nor were their voices heard in the land'. It is not till the last paragraph of the letter that some hint is conveyed of the magnitude of the task which poor Ida had undertaken in becoming Mrs Beatty. Earlier that evening Paquito had enjoyed a bout of sparring with another of his partners, the poetry reciter C. H. Johns. Shaw ends his letter:

> What on earth made Paquito ill? Was it the glee dinner, or did he quarrel with Stepniak? Or was it the combat with Johns, and the bowl-foaming at the American Bar subsequently? Suggest to him to do a month with me. The compulsory abstinence would renovate his exhausted frame, and would greatly amuse,
>
> > yours, dear Mrs Beatty, most lowspiritedly,
> > heroically,
> > George Bernard Shaw.[3]

The letter paints an affecting picture, of two bohemian stragglers, the nihilist who believed in nothing, and his impetuous friend the poet who believed in everything, except, it seems, behaving like a responsible husband. Matters had hardly improved two months later, when Shaw wrote once more to Mrs Beatty: 'If you are still on speaking terms with Paquito, please tell him that I found his cheque waiting for me on my return from Leicester, and that I hope to see Champion soon, and make enquiries about the poem'.[4] In March 1886 the Shavian web became infinitely more tangled when Lucy went to stay with Jenny Patterson, the widow who in the previous July had performed the superhuman feat of relieving Shaw of his virginity. Discovering Lucy's whereabouts, Beatty promptly paid a visit to Mrs Patterson's home in Brompton Square, only to be met by an alliance of deadly indifference. Ida then visited Brompton Square herself, drawing from Shaw this comment on 10 March:

> Your visit to Brompton Square has produced an impression utterly fatal to the poet. I have just received a letter from Mrs Patterson in which she says '*Mrs* Beatty we shall always be charmed to see. She is simply delightful.' Now what do those four lines under 'Mrs' mean? Evidently a strong distinction between Mr and Mrs. It is plain that the rascal represented himself as being the victim of cruel parents, who forced him in his early youth into a detested union with a harsh, ill-favoured, parsimonious, puritanical woman of fifty, with no poetic heart to beat in unison with his own. Who would not be kind to a poet in such a predicament, however suspicious his eye might be? But now the murder is out. Don Juan is unmasked. The young, charming, neglected wife is *en évidence*. The suggestions of the wicked eye are verified; blue spectacles even will be in vain should he have the hardihood to visit her now, which she strongly objects to his doing. Brompton Square, in fact, is up in arms against him. Such is my interpretation of 'Mrs'.[5]

Beatty evidently did have the hardihood to call again at Brompton Square, on the very day that Shaw was sending his letter to Ida, and this time Jenny Patterson wrote to Shaw, saying that neither she nor Lucy desired to know Mr Beatty, whom she described as 'a Hass', and that if he called again they would not be at home to him. 'Will you do a kindly action and save him a useless journey?'.[6] Shaw, perhaps recollecting the circumstances of his own deflowering by Jenny a few months earlier, was not impressed by her affectation of defenceless femininity cowering before the deadly onslaught of a practised philanderer, and wrote back with some lack of charity:

> As to Beatty, do as you please. Only remember that –
> There are more considerate ways of getting rid of a man than shutting the door in his face.
> If a man's acquaintance has been accepted by a woman, and he has not behaved improperly, he has a right to be dealt with in the most considerate way.
> You and Lucy have about as much reason to be frightened as a pair of vigorous and experienced cats have to recoil before an exceptionally nervous mouse.
> And (general aphorism) people always act cruelly and stupidly under the influence of unreasonable fear.[6]

Evidently Shaw was unperturbed by the news that at the home of his mistress, his sister was the object of a seduction by his best friend. His letters to Ida at this time betray not the faintest tremor of lost nerve as she asks his advice on how to bring up Paquito's children. In September 1886, answering a request for children's book lists, he responds facetiously by claiming that 'When I was two months old or so, my favourite books were *The Arabian Nights*, *The Pilgrim's Progress*, Homer's *Iliad* (translated by Lord Derby), *Gulliver's Travels*, *The Skeleton Horseman* (in penny numbers), Shakespere (sic), and La Rochefoucauld's *Maxims*; especially the latter.'[7] By February 1887, Paquito had evidently woken up to the fact that his own sisters-in-law were female and therefore possible objects of his boundless affection. Shaw's letter to Ida on 8 February 1887 also discusses in ambiguous terms the non-existent romance between her and himself. Presumably Ida's sister Florence was unmarried at the time, although this would have made no difference at all either way so far as Paquito was concerned:

> Don't talk to me of romances: I was sent into the world expressly to dance on them with thick boots – to shatter, stab and murder them. I defy you to be romantic about me (I

understand your fable of my decease to be an advance in that direction) and if you attempt it, I will go straight to Paquito; tell him that you are being drawn into the whirlpool of fascination which has engulfed all the brunettes I know; express my opinion that it serves him right for having made an unmitigated ass of himself about Florence; and give him his choice between instantly knocking that insincere poetic affectation of blighted affection on the head, and seeing me arrive, clad in an irresistible new Jaeger samite, and vanquish his Florence, his Ida and everyone else at one dazzling flash. All these foolish fancies only want daylight and fresh air to scatter them. Once or twice, or three times at most, I may have allowed myself a moment's weakness out of sheer good nature, but only to spring upright again with added resilience.[8]

Having given Ida close instructions as to her purchase of a piano, her selection of schools for her children, and her choice of books to give them, Shaw turned to give the benefit of his commonsense to Paquito. The date is 27 May 1887, and Shaw was clearly alarmed at his friend's reckless generosity:

Go slow, my friend, or you will be milked like a cow. If you sanction such a division of labour as the Social Democratic Federation getting themselves into trouble by dint of bad judgment and you getting them out by dint of good money, you will soon be a beggar. And then, by the Lord, sir, you will taste the wane of your popularity.[9]

No advice, however, seemed to affect Beatty in his profligate pursuit of his own temperament, and by 27 April 1890, when Shaw wrote to Archer about him, he was clearly becoming a burden for everyone who knew him:

I was prevented from coming to tea by the plight of my drunkard, who, still in a state of horror, was surrounded by his whispering relatives, who were assembled as if for a funeral. I dispersed them with roars of laughter and inquiries after pink snakes, an exhibition of bad taste which at least converted the poor devil's wandering apprehensive look into a settled grin. I then took him out for a walk, and endeavoured to relieve his mind of the strong illusion that nothing will ever tempt him to taste liquor more. Tomorrow he goes to a retreat at Rickmansworth, to be reformed.[10]

Three years later Beatty was apparently still interested enough in Lucy's whereabouts to ask Shaw for her address, the situation having become even more convoluted by now owing to Lucy's marriage to an actor six years before. Shaw responded with a brisk lack of sympathy;

Haven't the least idea of Lucy's address. I think she is in Birmingham with one of her husband's sisters. Write to her here and ask her: she gets her letters sent on from time to time.[11]

By 1898 Beatty's career had become so exemplary a homiletic on the evils of drink that Shaw used it as a cudgel with which to batter both sides in the Temperance war. A group of local reformers at Hindhead, having reached what might laughingly be called the age of maturity without divining that people generally attend public houses in order to consume alcoholic beverages, and that anything else they might do on the premises could fairly be defined as peripheral, were attempting to open an inn which would 'discourage inebriety'. Lady Murray had written to Mrs Shaw on the matter, and Shaw took the opportunity to answer for himself:

The Drink Question is the question of supplying the people with drink in the best way. The ordinary workman requires a certain quantity of beer to keep him amiable and happy. If he does not get it, he sulks, mopes, beats his wife and children, envies his neighbour, and gets into a state which it is impossible for him to say a civil word to anyone about him. It is a bad thing to be the wife of a drunkard; but it is ten times worse to be the wife of a man who wants drink and cannot get it. A friend of mine drank himself mad twice. In my innocence I wanted him to become a teetotaller. Finally I discovered that the chief obstacle was his unfortunate wife. The house was so miserable, and her children so wretched, when he was abstaining, that the evil of his periodically drinking too much was less than the continuous evil of his not drinking at all. If you don't understand this – if you imagine that everybody is strong enough to endure life without an anaesthetic, you don't understand the Drink Question a bit.[12]

In time Lady Murray's opposition was either withdrawn or swept aside. The locals were presented with an establishment called *The Fox and Pelican* which offered them hot meals, social evenings, periodical smokers, a reading room, dominoes and draughts. And presumably beer, some of it perhaps being consumed by Beatty, who by the end of the century had apparently run through his legacy with enough efficiency for Shaw to write to young Mazzini on 15 December 1899 that 'both your mother and your father look enormously better and happier than ever they did when they were comparatively affluent.'[13]

But in spite of his raffish persistence, Beatty still commanded the confidence of his friend, especially in that nebulous area where prizefighting and literature merged. In April 1901 Shaw wrote thanking Beatty for his advice about the verse in *The Admirable Bashville*, stage version of *Cashel Byron's Profession*. In all other matters, however, Shaw more and more assumed the role of a kind of father confessor cum family solicitor, paying for the education of the Beatty children, and finally, in November 1904, making a mighty effort to extricate Beatty once and for all from the pit of his own making:

Look here, I am not altogether satisfied that you are not wasting energy in struggling along always some months behind your rents. And overwhelmed as I am by rehearsals, and by the frightful arrears of work and business which rehearsals leave after them, I haven't time to go and see you or even to write promptly when I hear from you. It seems to me that unless you were living quite madly beyond your income in the old days, the economies of the last few years ought by this time to have produced some degree of recuperation. Unluckily economies sometimes cost too much when you have to raise money at ruinous rates, or stave off creditors by practically throwing your children to the wolves.

As to work, that is all my eye . . . As to attempting serious literary work, you WON'T do that. It is one of the mysteries of life that you, being perfectly capable of writing amusingly, humorously, wittily, scholarlily, and like a gentleman in a private letter, are invincibly persuaded that real professional writing is a dull, artificial, precedent-limited, imitative, lamp-smelly ceremony, and that there is something indecent in a man putting his real thoughts and feelings and whims on paper for the mob to read. It is too late to hope that you will ever get out of that paralysing belief now; and since it is clear that nature offers you as work, literature or nothing, and since some fatal *mauvaise honte* forbids you to choose literature, I think it would be far wiser for you to give up all nonsense about working, and frankly consider how you can live like a gentleman.

Now there is only one way to do this; and that is to borrow money enough to enable you to recapture your property, or at least to wait until the remnant of it gets level with your wants. It is useless to be delicate about the matter: a man who has committed the crime of lending as you have done has no right to be squeamish about the comparatively venial offence of borrowing. One disadvantage of lending is that it makes borrowing difficult, because no man likes to lend money to a man who cannot keep it, and will, as likely as not, be bled of it by the first spunge he meets. In short, you must cease lending and begin borrowing.

In mid-flow Shaw is interrupted by a letter from Beatty which gives a few details about the nature of his recent business transactions, details which take Shaw's breath away even as he is offering his friend a form of financial salvation:

Your letter has just come; and I really cannot express my feelings. You have borrowed £50 at 62½% per annum, and given your furniture as security. Are you mad? Or are all your advisers and friends sharks? I enclose a cheque for £100. Go immediately and pay off the two instalments and the principal, at once, *before another day's interest accrues*. (Need I rub in the fact that your blasted delicacy about getting that £50 from me has ended in my having to pay the 62½% interest to Shylock when I could have borrowed it myself at less than 4%. This is what you call business and friendship. Get out!)

and, if possible, husband the change so as to get on to the first of January in a solvent condition. Keep this dark; for if you let it be known that you have a penny in hand somebody will borrow it – Tavy [his daughter] or another. Better put a fiver in your pocket and give the rest to your wife.[14]

With each succeeding letter, spanning a period of twenty-six years, a portrait of Pakenham Beatty gradually emerges, until with that last business letter, we find ourselves confronted with a familiar type of the period, the would-be romantic troubadour, the charming poetaster whose creative vein peters out while his eye for a pretty face and a trim ankle remain as keen as ever, the idealist who moves through the maze of lilliputian revolutionary societies and debating clubs, buttressed by an independent income which he disperses with profligate generosity. Money always had a way of trickling through Beatty's fingers, either into the pockets of equally bohemian but less well-appointed associates, or to the treasurers of struggling emergent political cabals. He was one of those immensely engaging men with the very best intentions and the very worst effects, one of those faintly ridiculous philanderers who mistake their own failure to respect the marriage vows for a heroic rejection of a corrupt and worthless society, and one of those hedonists who conduct their youthful affairs on the assumption of their own immortality, and whose tragic ineffectualness is revealed only gradually as the years slip by disclosing the eternal adolescent. Among the illustrations to Shaw's Collected Letters, there we find him, staring with a stolid, glassy bewilderment at a point to the left of the camera, his drooping moustache unable to conceal the boyish lines of his features, the stiff wing-collar of his shirt and the velvet collar of his single-breasted, fly-fronted overcoat lending him an elegance which must have slowly faded as the years – and the legacy – slipped away.

Shaw appears to have loved Beatty almost more than he loved anybody, taking care never to forget the debt he owed him for having sponsored his entry into the boxing world of the early 1880s. He betrayed that affection in two very Shavian ways; through financial generosity, and by preserving in literary form the spirit of the bachelor high jinks of the old days, when the two of them had knocked each other about by kind permission of Ned Donnelly and the Marquis of Queensberry, and above all that most famous day of all, astonishingly ignored by every one of Shaw's biographers, when two young Irish intellectual sparks went along to Lillie Bridge to try their luck in competition. This quirk of preserving the old relationship manifested itself in the true style of a compulsive writer. In corresponding with Beatty, whenever possible Shaw drew on the metaphor of the prize-ring. There is no question that for the rest of his life following the episode in the gymnasium in Panton Street, Shaw found the prizefighting profession as an allegory of Capitalism too convenient to overlook, or that when he came to compose the longest book of his career, *The Intelligent Woman's Guide*, almost half a century after his introduction to Donnelly, the ghost of the young Beatty was still peering over his shoulder:

> It may seem scandalous that a prizefighter, for hitting another prizefighter so hard at Wembley that he fell down and could not rise within ten seconds, received the same sum that was paid to the Archbishop of Canterbury for acting as Primate of the Church of England for nine months; but none of those who cry out against the scandal can express any better in money the difference between the two. Not one of the persons who think that the prizefighter should get less than the Archbishop can say how much less. What the prizefighter got for his six or seven minutes boxing would pay a judge's salary for two years; and we are all agreed that nothing could be more ridiculous, and that any system of distributing wealth which leads to such absurdities must be wrong. But to suppose that it could be changed by any possible calculation that an ounce of archbishop or three ounces of judge is worth a pound of prizefighter would be sillier still.

That passage was composed in 1928, and within a year of his death, Shaw was still using the terminology of Ned Donnelly to express his view of the world, this time to Stephen Winsten:

> I know too much about boxing to take for granted that capitalism is going to be counted out. What seems a deadly blow often makes no impression.[15]

Shaw had acquired this habit of discussing world affairs in terms of the prize-ring forty years earlier when corresponding with the Beattys. In a letter to Ida he closes with:

Tell Paquito that the Socialist League have been challenged by C. Bradlaugh to pick a man to fight him at catch weight – three rounds of thirty minutes, fifteen minutes, and again fifteen minutes apiece – St Jas's Hall or anywhere in the home circuit. Customers being backward for the John L. Sullivan of the platform, the League has appealed to the Fabian champion, who admits his liability to defend the belt. The set-to promises to be a rare one.

Need I explain that the Fabian champion is

> yours marmoreally,
> G. Bernard Shaw.[16]

In 1893 Shaw wrote to Beatty concerning the reactions of the poet Richard Le Gallienne to an adverse Shavian review of some poems:

Why all this fury against a poor little sensitive plant like Richard? Why, his fighting weight is not two and a half ounces.[17]

And in 1895, by which time it could have been assumed with a reasonable degree of safety that both Shaw and Beatty had hung up their gloves, there is this description of a famous incident in which two of the best brains of the century, those belonging to Shaw and Bertrand Russell, were very nearly ruined for ever in a bicycling mishap:

I have had a most awful bicycle smash – the quintessence of ten railway collisions – brother of Earl Russell of conjugal rights fame dashed into at full speed flying down a hill – £3.10.0 damages to machine – got up within the prescribed ten seconds, but had subsequently to admit knockout – Russell bereft of his knickerbockers but otherwise unhurt.[18]

But as the years went by and Beatty's effectualness shrank in inverse proportion to the growing fame of the 'pantomime ostrich',[19] Paquito steadily faded away into the past. Shaw, ever practical, seemed more concerned about the children than with Ida and Paquito. As for the noble art, by the time Jess Willard was half-carried from the ring at Toledo, Ohio after his ritual defeat at the hands of Dempsey, Shaw seemed to have dismissed such adolescent trifles from his mind. A terrible war had swept away Victorian England even as the young Fabian had predicted. Donnelly was dead, his gymnasium long since closed down and some of his most promising gentlemen students sleeping in Flanders or Gallipoli. Hubert Bland, one-time sparring partner, was dead and his widow remarried, while Mazzini, the baby boy with the burdensome name, was now a thirty-eight-year-old engineer; the conventions of the old prize-ring were buried so deep in history that modern boxing could hardly be considered more than its distant descendant. There was no more talk in utopian dovecotes of Henry George, or Hyndman or Bradlaugh. The world had done with such affairs, and anything Shaw might have to say about them surely belonged to a remote past.

And then, suddenly in 1919, there appeared at the ringside of an international contest in London, an apparition from that remote past, an apparition with a long white beard. It was Shaw, putting in an appearance both of his own accord and in a professional capacity. The editor of a weekly periodical, *The Nation*, had somehow prevailed upon him, or perhaps Shaw had prevailed upon the editor of *The Nation*, to compose an eye-witness account of the main contest of the evening. To those sporting journalists in the congregation who were too young to know much about Shaw's pugilistic past, the arrangement must have seemed little more than a stunt, although perhaps their ringside grins were just a shade inhibited by the fact that back in the old century, in the time of Gladstone and the ageing Pre-Raphaelites, Shaw had written a novel about prizefighting. In the issue dated 13 December 1919, *The Nation* published a report headed 'The Great Fight, by the author of *Cashel Byron's Profession*'.

The essay in *The Nation* is one of the most perceptive ever written about a boxing match, and its tone very quickly reveals the depth of Shaw's affection for his own fighting youth. Like all old men, even Shavian ones, he viewed the present down the long perspective of his own past, time and again including references to men and places which not one in a thousand of his readers could have appreciated. No doubt Shaw was stimulated in this exercise by a curious coincidence which must truly have delighted him. The referee for this big fight of the London season of 1919 was a figure from out of the Panton Street past, which constituted a fluke so melodramatic that Shaw actually invoked a famous melodrama from his theatre reviewing days to describe it. He also referred to a quartet of gentlemen who, the context makes clear, were once great figures in the world of boxing but whose names no longer meant anything. To take the measure of these real-life Shavian heroes, we have to fall back once more on Donnelly's primer, where, in the list of Queensberry Cupwinners we find that four gentlemen named Chinnery, Douglas, Michel and Frost-Smith won thirteen competitions between them, that all but one of their triumphs were in the heavyweight and middleweight divisions, the two classes in which Shaw had once entered the amateur championships, and that all thirteen victories took place in the years between 1867 and 1881, the period which encompasses Shaw's own casual boxing career. To a young Dubliner, footloose in London with neither an occupation nor an effective parry for the Backheel, they must indeed have seemed great men.

What was it that drew Shaw back to his old pugilistic haunts so many years after he had forsworn their savage diversions? To his literary contemporaries Shaw's performance at Holborn must have looked very much like one more irresponsible exhibition of Shavian levity. Almost none of them seems to have been aware of his youthful sporting abilities. As for that cheerfully philistine sub-section of the community, the boxing fraternity, the descent into their preserves of the Great Sage must have appeared a quaint joke which would perhaps do a disreputable trade no very great harm. In retrospect it is evident that Shaw was drawn back into the boxing world by his anticipation of an astounding event. He had come back to his old haunts in the belief that his irrepressible character Cashel Byron was to take his own apotheosis a stage further, out of that limbo between fact and fiction, represented by Jim Corbett's unlikely dramatic impersonation, into the realms of reality itself. For when Shaw turned up at Holborn to report on a contest for the European Heavyweight Championship, it was in the conviction that Cashel Byron had at last been rendered flesh and blood. The irony was that although Cashel Byron had indeed been rendered whole, and was at that time stalking the prize-rings of the world, he had no intention of turning up at Holborn to contest the European Heavyweight Championship. Although it was to be a few years yet before he realised it, Shaw had discovered the wrong model.

The boxer in whom, for the moment, all Shaw's Byronic dreams erroneously resided was a French ex-coalminer called Georges Carpentier (soon to be known among the poetasters of the American popular press as Gorgeous Georges the Orchid Man). Carpentier was one of those extremely rare athletes whose physique and carriage imply a nobility which their style confirms; even in the existing primitive moving pictures of some of Carpentier's contests, there can be perceived, behind the arthritic convulsions of the early cinematograph, the debonair good looks and the insolent, co-ordinated grace of the true artist, evocative of Shaw's dream-fighter. Indeed, there was something positively cerebral about Carpentier's deadly choreography inside the ring. Whatever the fortunate editor of *The Nation* thought he was buying, what he received was Shaw's first reconnaissance report to himself on the extent to which, in the threadbare days in Fitzroy Square, he had imagined the perfect pugilist and thereby anticipated nature by forty years.

The report begins with a few authentic Shavian flourishes, moving briskly from a treatise on the immorality of functional architecture to a satirical study of the audience. A note of genuine pathos is then struck which is quite uncharacteristic in the context of Shaw's habitual levity when confronted by the ghosts of his own apprenticeship. Into the ring there clambered a lion from Panton Street days, Jack Angle, once a renowned gladiator but now a referee. It is at this point, when the old gentleman from Shaw's past ducks under the ropes, that Shaw involuntarily scans the assembly for signs of Chinnery and company, only to be saddened by the realisation that, like Bland and Donnelly and the rest of them, they belonged to a remote past. At that moment, while Shaw is lost in a dim recollection of hero-worship, the challenger Beckett enters, having been grouped by reporters to play Orson to his opponent's Valentine as, conversely, Cashel Byron had once been placed by William Archer and others as Valentine against Orson.[1] Carpentier too is awarded his cultural identity, that of Charles XII. What then follows is a bravura exhibition by the writer of his perceptions regarding style, physique, gambling on the outcome of prize-fights, and punching power, on all of which subjects Shaw displays his customary omniscience.

How much of this omniscience is retrospective? After all, the fight reporter is in the same fortunate position as his cousin the drama critic; no matter how comprehensive his ignorance of the business at hand, he has at least the inestimable benefit of knowing what happened in the end. When Shaw insists his experience tells him that it is Carpentier and not Beckett who has all the physical advantages, that Beckett is not the indomitable British bulldog he appears but a sacrificial lamb, and that it is his orchidaceous rival who will conduct the slaughter, we begin to wonder if Shaw would have reached the same conclusion with half the certitude five minutes earlier, before events revealed the outcome of the contest. And yet, towards the end of his report, when Shaw, having been satisfied by the preliminary evidence, considers the ensuing 'Byron-Paradise' confrontation, he offers a prediction of truly startling prescience, one which only the very shrewdest observer of the noble art could ever have reached. In effect he predicts with perfect accuracy not only the result of a future encounter between Carpentier and Dempsey, but also the way in which that result will come about. The essay then closes with a gesture showing how clearly Shaw has retained the texts of his old 'Grub Street' jokes. One day in 1890 he arrived outside Her Majesty's Theatre:

> The other day, seeing from a placard that a Christmas pantomime was going on inside, I realised I had not seen one for fourteen years. So I went in. I do not think I shall go again for another fourteen years.[2]

And now, having witnessed a very different kind of pantomime, he paraphrases the same joke, reminding us in the process that thirty-five years is a considerable length of time even in a philosopher's life:

> If you were not at the Great Fight, and are at all curious about it, imagine four thousand people packed by night into a roofed enclosure with a gallery round it. I had better not call it a building, because that word has architectural associations; and this enclosure has none. It is fearfully ugly, and calls itself a Stadium, probably to provide modern poets with a rhyme for radium. The four thousand people are all smoking as hard as they can; and the atmosphere, which will be described in the morrow's papers as electric, is in fact murky, stifling and fumesome. In the midst is a scaffold, or place of execution, twenty-four feet square, fenced by ropes, and glared down upon so intolerably by arc lights that some of the spectators wear improvised brown paper hat brims to shield their eyes. On the scaffold is a mild man, apparently a churchwarden, but really a referee, patiently watching two hard-working Britons earning a precarious livelihood by boxing for the amusement of the four thousand. They are tired, and have not the smallest animosity to give a bitter sweet to their exertions; but they are most earnest and industrious; and one feels, in spite of the sportive alacrity which they keep up like a ballet dancer's smile, and their attempts to give a little extra value when the arc lights are increased to cinematograph the last round or two, that they are thinking of their little ones at home. One of them

presently gets a tooth, real or artificial, loosened. His second extracts it with his fingers; his opponent apologetically shakes hands; and they return to the common toil, the nightly toil. It seems indelicate to stare at them; and I proceed to study the audience.

Like all sporting audiences it consists mostly of persons who manifestly cannot afford the price of admission. My seat has cost more than ten times what I have paid to hear Parsifal at Bayreuth or Beethoven's Ninth Symphony at a very special performance at the Grand Opera in Paris. Certainly there are people here who can spare ten guineas or twenty-five easily enough; honourables and right honourables, explorers, sporting stockbrokers, eminent professional men, plutocrats of all sorts, men with an artistic interest in the display like Robert Loraine, Granville Barker, Maurice Baring, Arnold Bennett and myself. But the prevalent impression is the usual one of a majority of men who have sacrificed a month's wages to be present, and hope to retrieve it by bets on the result. Here and there is a lady. Not any particular sort of lady or no lady; just an ordinary lady. The one who happens to be sitting by me is one next whom I might find myself in the stalls of any theatre, or in church. The girl at the end of the next row would be perfectly in place in any West End drawing room. My lady neighbour watches the weary breadwinners on the scaffold, and tries to feel excited when they seek rest by leaning their heads affectionately on one another's shoulders, and giving one another perfunctory thumps on the ribs and on the nape of the neck to persuade the audience that they are 'mixing it', and dealing out terrible 'kidney punches' (this is modern in-fighting, which seems to me simply despicable). But I fancy she is trying to stifle a suspicion that she had better have stayed at home and spent the price of her ticket on a new hat. As for me, nothing would have induced me to stay in the place four minutes had I not been waiting for the not very far off undivine event towards which the sporting section of creation had moved.

Everything comes to an end at last, even the minor items in a boxing programme. The boxers retired, presumably to their ain firesides; and the scaffold was occupied by men unknown to me; for I belong to an older generation. One of these philanthropists earned my gratitude by adjuring the audience, if it loved the champions, to refrain from smoking; after which the atmosphere cleared until it was no thicker than an average fog. Suddenly a figure from the past – from my past – was announced and appeared. It was Jack Angle, no longer a trim, clean-shaven young amateur athlete, but a *père noble* in white moustaches, exactly like Colonel Damas in *The Lady of Lyons*. I found myself saying involuntarily 'Thank Heaven! here at last is somebody who knows something about boxing'. I looked round for his contemporaries, Chinnery, Douglas, Michel, Frost-Smith, and the rest; but if they are alive and were present I could not identify them. He instructed us politely but authoritatively how to behave ourselves.

Then the cheering began, rather localized, because from most of the seats little could be seen except the platform. Even the Prince of Wales had had some difficulty in procuring silence for his brief speech when he entered; and several people believed for some time that it had been made by Carpentier. As it happened I was near the gangway by which the champions came in, and therefore saw at once that the cheering was for Mr Joseph Beckett, who was approaching in an unpretentious dressing gown. Mr Beckett, though the descriptive reporters insisted on making him play Orson to his opponent's Valentine, is by no means ill-looking. His features are not Grecian; but he can be described exactly as a very sensible looking man; and I may say at once that he behaved all through, and has behaved since, more sensibly than most men could in a very trying situation. I liked Mr Beckett very well, and did not change my opinion later on, as some of his backers did. He mounted the scaffold, and went to his corner. A burst of louder cheering made me look round again to the gangway; and this time I was startled by a most amazing apparition: nothing less than Charles XII, 'the madman of the North', striding along the gangway in a Japanese silk dressing gown as gallantly as if he had not been killed almost exactly two hundred-and-one years before. I have seldom received so vivid an impression; and I knew at once that this could hardly be Charles, he must be either Carpentier or the devil. Genius could not be more unmistakable. Being in that line myself I was under no illusion as to genius being invincible. I knew that Mr Beckett might turn out to be Peter the Great, and that Charles might be going to his Poltava; but genius is genius all the same, in victory or defeat. The effect of the audience on the two men was very noticeable. Beckett, too sensible to be nervous, put up with the crowd of people staring at him as a discomfort that was all in the day's work. Carpentier rose at the crowd, and would have had it forty thousand instead of four if he could. He was at home with it; he dominated it; he picked out his friends and kissed hands to them in his debonair way quite naturally, without swank or mock modesty, as one born to move assemblies.

The descriptive reporters began to scribble their tale of a frail French stripling and a massive British colossus. Utter nonsense. The physical omens were all against the Briton. Beckett, who was trained, if anything, a little too fine, has a compact figure, a boxlike chest, stout, stumpy arms useful only for punching, and a thickish neck too short to take his head far out of harm's way. Carpentier, long and lithe, has a terrible pair of arms, very long, with the forearms heavy just where the weight should be. He has a long chest, a long reach, a long flexible neck, and, last but not least, a long head. Nobody who knew the ABC of boxing could doubt for a moment that unless Beckett could wear him down and outstay him, and stand a good deal during the process, he could not win at the physical odds against him except by a lucky knockout.

When the men stood up, another curious asset of Carpentier's raised the extraordinary question whether he had not been taught to box by a lady. Some years ago Miss Diana Watts, a lady athlete who believed that she had discovered the secret of ancient Greek gymnastics, reproduced with her own person the pose and action of the Discobolus and the archer in the Heracles pediment in the British Museum, both of which had been up to that time considered physically impossible. Her book on the subject, with its interesting photographs, is still extant. Her method was to move and balance the body on the ball of the foot without using the heel, and to combine this with a certain technique of the diaphragm. Now the moment 'Time' was called, and Carpentier on his feet in the ring, it was apparent that he had this technique. He was like a man on springs; and the springs were not in his heels but the balls of his feet. His diaphragm *tenue* was perfect. Whether his lady instructor was Miss Diana Watts or Dame Nature, she has turned out a complete Greek athlete. This really very remarkable and gymnastically important phenomenon has been overlooked, partly because it has not been understood, but partly also because in the change in Carpentier's face when he sets to work is so startling that the spectators can see nothing else. The unmistakable Greek line digs a trench across his forehead at once; his colour changes to a stony grey; he looks ten thousand years old; his eyes see through stone walls; and his expression of intensely concentrated will frighten everyone in the hall except his opponent, who is far too busy to attend to such curiosities.

There was no fight. There was only a superb exhibition spar, with Beckett as what used to be called a chopping block. For a few moments he wisely stuck close to his man; but Mr Angle gave the order (I did not hear it, but was told of it) to break away; and Beckett then let the Frenchman get clear and faced him for outfighting. From that moment he was lost. Carpentier simply did the classic thing: the long shot with the left: the lead-off and get-away. The measurement of distance – and such a distance! – was exact to an inch, the speed dazzling, the impact like the kick of a thoroughbred horse. Beckett, except for one amazed lionlike shake of his head, took it like a stone wall; but he was helpless: he had not time to move a finger before Carpentier was back out of his reach. He was utterly outspeeded. Three times Carpentier did this, each hit more brilliant if possible than the last. Beckett was for a moment dazed by the astonishing success of the attack: and in that moment Carpentier sent in a splendidly clean and finished right to the jaw. It is not often that perfect luck attends perfect style in this world; but Carpentier seemed able to command even luck. The blow found that mysterious spot that is in all our jaws, and that is so seldom found by the fist. There was no mistaking the droop with which Beckett went prone to the boards. In an old-fashioned fight he would have been carried by his seconds to his corner and brought up to the scratch in half a minute quite well able to go on. Under modern rules he had to lie unhelped; and at the end of ten seconds Carpentier was declared the winner.

Carpentier had made the spar so intensely interesting that the seventy-four seconds it had occupied seemed like ten; and I could hardly believe that four had elapsed between the moment when Beckett dropped to the boards and the jubilant spring into the air with which Carpentier announced that the decision had been given in his favour. He was as unaffected in his delight as he had been in his nervousness before 'Time' was called, when he had asked his bottle holder for a mouthful of water and confessed to a dry mouth. The usual orgy followed. Pugilists are a sentimental, feminine species, much given to kissing and crying. Carpentier was hoisted up to be chaired, dragged down to be kissed, hung out by the heels from the scaffold to be fondled by a lady, and in every possible way given reason to envy Beckett. Beckett's seconds, by the way, so far forgot themselves as to leave their man lying uncared for on the floor after he was counted out until Carpentier, indignant at their neglect, rushed across the ring and carried Beckett to his corner. I suggest to the masters of ceremonies at these contests, whoever they may be, that this had better not occur again. It is true that the decision was so sudden and sensational that a little distraction was excusable; but if Carpentier, who had the best reason to be carried away by his feelings, could remember, those whose duty it was could very well have done so if they had been properly instructed in their duties.

Now for the seamy side of the affair, the betting side. As I pushed my way through the crowd in Holborn, I could see by the way my news was received that every poor dupe of the sporting papers had put his shillings or pence or even his quid or two on Beckett. Never had a betting ramp been more thoroughly organized. When the war was over nobody knew whether military service had spoiled Carpentier for boxing purposes or left him as good as ever. If he were as good, or better, then clearly oceans of money could be made at a risk no greater than any gambler will take, by persuading the public that his sun has set and that the Carpentier who knocked out Wells in seventy-three seconds was a back number. Accordingly, the situation was taken in hand in the usual fashion. A British pugilist of something less than commanding eminence was sent to France and pitted against Carpentier, who gave a poor display and obtained the decision with difficulty. Here was proof positive of his decadence. Then the press got to work. Beckett, progressing rapidly from victory to victory, was extolled as invulnerable and invincible. Carpentier's reputation was discounted until hardly a shred of it remained. His two youthful defeats were retold. The public were reminded that he had obtained a decision against Gunboat Smith only on an unintentional foul by that gentleman; and ring reporters solemnly declared their conviction that but for this accident Carpentier could not have lasted another round. I was informed on the strength of private information from 'the French colony' (whatever that may be) that Carpentier had sold the fight, and that it was arranged that Beckett should win. Then came a clump of boxing articles, each giving a dozen reasons to show that nothing but a miracle could prevent Beckett from wiping the floor with the obsolete and exhausted Frenchman. I do not know how high the odds were piled at last; but on the morning of the fight every ringstruck sportsman who knew nothing about boxing (and not one in a hundred of the people who read about boxing, or for that matter, who write about it, knows anything worth knowing) had his bet on Beckett. Most of these poor devils do not know even now how completely they were humbugged. They blame Beckett.

Beckett is not to blame. What happened to him happened to Sayers sixty-six years ago when he was beaten for the first and only time by Nat Langham. Langham taught Donnelly, who taught Mr Angle's and my generation the long shot with the left and get-away of which Carpentier gave such a brilliant demonstration; and it beat even the invincible Sayers.

Langham could not knock him out, because the knock-out, though effective for ten seconds, does not last for thirty; and Langham had to keep hitting Sayers' eyes until they were closed, and poor Tom, blinded, had to weep over his solitary defeat. But Sayers' most famous achievements came later; and there is no reason in the world why Beckett should not be as successful as ever in spite of his having shared Sayers' fate. When he described his defeat as a million-to-one chance, he exaggerated the odds against a knock-out; but the knock-out is always a matter of luck; and Beckett has probably taken dozens of clouts on the jaw as heavy, if not so artistic, as Carpentier's, without turning a hair.

As to the brutality of the affair, Beckett was chatting to his friends over the ropes without a mark on his face, and with £3,000 in his pocket, before they had stopped kissing Carpentier. There are many industrial pursuits more painful and much more dangerous than boxing. The knock-out is probably the most effective anaesthetic known to science; that is why it is so conclusive. Many women would let Carpentier knock them about for twenty rounds for a pension of £150 a year. The valid objection is the old Puritan objection: it is not the pain to the pugilist, but the pleasure to the spectator that matters. To the genuine connoisseur it is simply distressing to see a boxer hurt beyond the harmless point up to which every reasonably hardy sportsman is prepared to smart for the sake of the game. Mr Angle's expression of concern as he contemplated Beckett on the boards was a study, though he knew that Beckett was fast asleep. But unquestionably many of the spectators believe that they are witnessing acts of cruelty, and pay for admission for their sake, not understanding boxing in the least. Also, the contests, like all contests, act as a propaganda of pugnacity and competition. Sometimes the demoralizing effect is visible and immediate. I have seen men assault their neighbours after witnessing a rough and tumble fight for some time. But the effect of a highly skilled display such as Carpentier gave overawes the spectators. It often reduces them to absolute silence. It fascinates the connoisseurs, and frightens the novices and the riff-raff. The question of the suppression of prizefighting is, therefore, not a simple one. The commercial exploitation of prizefighting is bad like the commercial exploitation of everything else; for in pugilism as in other things 'honour sinks where commerce long prevails'; and though such atrocities as the poisoning of Heenan and the rest of the blackguardism which compelled the authorities to make short work of the old prize-ring in the eighteen-sixties are now hardly possible, yet Mr Cochran and other entrepreneurs of the ring must bear in mind that they can secure toleration only by being on their very best behaviour. The belief that pugnacity and the competitive spirit are the secrets of England's greatness may give way at any moment to the equally plausible theory that they are the causes of her decline.

The world now waits breathless for the meeting between Carpentier and Mr Dempsey. The general sentiment on the night of the fourth was undoubtedly 'May I be there to see'. I know nothing of Mr Dempsey's quality as a boxer; but if he can play at lightning long-shots with an instinctive command of the duck and counter, and on occasion side-step a boxer who, as the cinematograph proves, has a dangerous habit of leading from off his toes without stepping in, with the certainty of falling heavily on his nose if his adversary takes in the situation and gets out of the way in time, Charles XII may find his Poltava yet.

Such are the impressions of one who has not for thirty-five years past dreamt of attending a boxing exhibition. If I be asked why I have abstained for so long, I reply that any intelligent person who frequents such exhibitions will soon be convinced that the English are congenitally incapable of the art of boxing. When you have seen a hundred contests between two hundred Britons, and have concluded that every single one of the two hundred must be the very worst boxer in the world, and his admirers the most abject gulls that ever tipped their way, like Mr Toots, into pugilistic society, you are driven to the conclusion that you would be happier at home, or even in a theatre or concert room. The truth is, of course, that boxing such as Carpentier's demands qualities which their possessors will not waste on so trivial and unamiable a pursuit in such rude company. It was worth Carpentier's while to escape from the slavery of the coal pit and win £5,000 in seventy-four seconds with his fists. It would not have been worth his while if he had been Charles XII. Thus the prizefighters are either geniuses like Carpentier, too few and far between to keep up one's interest in exhibitions, or else poor fellows whose boxing is simply not worth looking at except by gulls who know no better. And so I doubt whether I shall go again for another thirty-five years except when Carpentier is one of the performers.

What is most striking of all about this essay is not the shrewdness of its technical insight, nor its percipience regarding the likely outcome of the future encounter between Carpentier and Dempsey, but the special plea which its author is intent on making on behalf of prizefighting. Shaw of all people must have known that his minimising of the physical damage sustained by fighters was deliberately misleading, and that outside every arena of the period could be found shambling old men with flattened ears and coarsened features who could have testified against his argument merely by standing before him. He must have realised that his comparison between boxing disfigurement and industrial injuries was bogus, and that what sorely troubles the Puritan conscience is that of all human recreations, boxing is the last surviving sport in which it is the *intention* of the contestants to injure each other. Even in describing the nature of such damage Shaw is being shamelessly disingenuous. He carefully selects his vocabulary to impart to a brutal business the cosy sanction of domestic quietude. In his years with Beatty and Donnelly, Shaw had surely discovered that sometimes in the course of a contest a fighter will sustain a blow on the head so damaging that he will suffer an interlude of amnesia in which he will fight on by instinct, often acquitting himself quite well (as Peter Kane once did against Benny Lynch), and yet be so unaware of what had happened to him that his later attendance at a cinema showing of the fight comes to him with the force of a revelation. Shaw described Beckett's comatose condition on the ring floor as 'being asleep', when he knew perfectly well that if a man falls asleep many times as

Beckett did that evening against Carpentier, he stands a reasonable chance of ending his days unable to tie his shoelaces or sign his name. Shaw knew all this, better than almost anyone else on the premises, and yet he chose to apply the cosmetics of Shavian dialectic to the battered face of prizefighting. It is this very dubiety of his moral stance which indicates the depth of his affection for the the sport.

Obviously the return to London of the great, the romantic, the all-conquering Carpentier was one of those social occasions when the glamour transcends the event itself, and which as Shaw's list of distinguished spectators suggests, draw to them those who normally would never have been seen in such company. It so happened that one of those other literary notables present at Holborn that night was, like Shaw, there in his professional as well as his private capacity. Arnold Bennett had come along to perform for *The Statesman* the same deed which Shaw was performing for *The Nation*, and although he was a thoroughgoing professional in the prime of literary condition, with an impressive list of victories behind him, Bennett was clearly out of his class. He appears to have been aware of this and to have erected the usual Bennett defence in such situations, a kind of condescending amusement at the quaint but really rather endearing things which the philistines will sometimes get up to. But all the condescension in the world cannot hide for a moment the one deadly difference between his report and Shaw's, which is that while Shaw knew nearly everything about what was going on, Bennett knew nothing, and, knowing he knew nothing, was obliged to treat the whole affair as a bit of larky intellectual slumming.[3]

What distinguishes Shaw's reactions from those of other professional writers who dabbled in the sporting life is, of course, that while Bennett and company usually indulged in the pardonable error of using a prizefight as an excuse to display their democratic tendencies and their erudition in other fields, Shaw was preoccupied by the recollection of a philosophic concept contained in a novel he had written as a young man. Doubtless·he was utterly intrigued by the possibility that the character he had once put together from the component parts of the playboy Beatty and the professional Burke, was now a real person whose only deviation from the Shavian scenario was to have learned his boxing in Paris instead of in Australia. By 1921 Carpentier was a hero of France and undisputed master of the European circuit, and he was now about to throw down the gauntlet, on behalf of Europe, at the feet of Dempsey himself. One English schoolboy later recollected the element of trans-ferred patriotism which caused him to support Carpentier's cause:

> It was a fight between a European and an American, and because Europe was nearer to us than America, and because the European had, in fact, massacred our own Champion, we British boys felt that the prestige of our own country was at stake, even though the standard-bearer was a French-man. . . . Because we could not bear the idea of someone so godlike-looking as Carpentier being battered by someone who clearly came from Bashan, we sought reasons to justify our faith in Carpentier's victory.[4]

This very curious appropriation of a Frenchman's persona by the sportsmen of another country had begun several years before, when the British, gazing with dismay at Carpentier's one-round dismemberment of one of Beckett's predecessors, a gentleman with an iron will and a glass jaw called Bombardier Billy Wells, sensed that Carpentier was likely to continue making local boxers look excessively foolish for several years to come. When Shaw adopted a foreigner as his *beau idéal* it was hardly unexpected, because by the time he recognised Byronic overtones in Carpentier's style, the Frenchman had already become an honorary member of the British Empire.

And so Carpentier 'sailed away on his quest, and Europeans who could not sail with him in body sent their spirits across the Atlantic'.[5] But the truth was that Carpentier should never have been matched with Dempsey at all. He was really no more than a pumped-up light-heavyweight of around twelve and a half stones, obliged to take on heavier, stronger men because of the lack of worthy opposition in his own class. But it was one thing to give weight against performers of purely parochial ability like Joe Beckett and Billy Wells, and quite another to do the same against Dempsey; and although Carpentier possessed consummate skill in boxing, it was to be useless to him on the one night in his life when he needed it most. Some people were puzzled that Carpentier should have begun the fight with Dempsey as he did, tearing into the bigger man, carrying the contest to one of the deadliest punchers in the history of the sport. But the fight was held in New Jersey, where, under the State laws of the time, points decisions in prizefights were illegal. This meant that unless Carpentier actually knocked Dempsey out, his challenge must fail. In the second round Carpentier caught Dempsey flush on the point of the jaw with one of the hardest right hands he had ever thrown in his life, but Dempsey, who later denied any recollection of having received the punch, paused momentarily in his operations, blinked and then resumed. The outcome was inevitable, and Carpentier was counted out in the fourth round, his great bravery mocked by Dempsey's sheer physical strength.

After this most decisive defeat of his hero, Shaw's faith in Carpentier as the incarnation of Cashel Byron could have been shattered beyond repair. On the contrary, having studied the event most carefully, Shaw decided that the contest only confirmed his original belief that Carpentier (alias Byron) was the better man. On 3 September 1921, just thirty-two days after the fight, Shaw attended the Leicester Square Cinema in London to watch a film of the event, later returning home to compose a report which was published in *The Observer* on 11 September:

On September 3, 1921, I saw the Carpentier–Dempsey fight for the heavyweight championship of the world in London at the Leicester Square Cinema, where you can go and see it tomorrow (or even today) for yourself. I had a much better view of it than nine-tenths of the people who saw it in the flesh from Mr Tex Rickards' benches in New Jersey. I could have seen it three or four times over without leaving my seat. Perhaps I should have done so had it not been padded out with a great deal of matter (including some very dull boxing and some bogus training) of the sort that bears seeing once and once only. I am tempted to moralise on the enormous propaganda of pugilism that is being effected by this film, which repeats the fight again and again before millions of people all over the globe, and goes on for a year after the newspapers have been compelled to reject every allusion to it as intolerably stale. But I refrain, and return to the subject matter only because of its technical interest for boxers, and the right of a boxing film to its criticism equally with ordinary sob stuff.

And first, I must warn those who have seen Monsieur Carpentier only at New Jersey or in this film that they have no idea of what he is like and what he can do when he is at the top of his form and master of himself and of the situation. The film shows only what he can do when he is sandbagged. This is no excuse for his defeat. It was Mr Dempsey's business to sandbag him, and it was his own business to prevent Mr Dempsey from sandbagging him. Instead of doing so, he offered Dempsey (who will allow me to drop the ceremonious Mister) every facility for the operation, and got it very literally in the neck. That he nevertheless put up a tremendous fight is true: Dempsey again and again escaped defeat by a millimetre; but in boxing a miss is as good as a mile; and though Carpentier only once failed to get his blows home, he had not the luck to land them on the fatal spot which makes it possible for one blow to decide a boxing contest. He rose indomitably to a desperate situation, and fought fiercely and formidably to the last second with heroic pugnacity when all save honour was lost; but though able to box he was not able to think. His form was gone; he could not time his terrible left to stop his always aggressive adversary; and his right, though it could still stagger Dempsey by its mere impact, was not the perfectly artistic straight right, like a fencer's thrust, that laid out Beckett. His side-stepping was so perfect that Dempsey never once succeeded in getting him against the ropes with his retreat cut off; and after every such evasion he dashed at his man with a one-two that seemed to smash in before Dempsey could lift an elbow; but swift and fierce as it was, it was not the considered and finished delivery of Carpentier the artist; it was like the one-two of any other boxer who feels like a rat in a corner. Except in the first round, when he was so plainly beaten that I do not quite know why Dempsey did not finish him. He was a possible winner up to the last moment, even assuming that his right was disabled by the sensational blow which might have, but did not, put Dempsey to sleep in the third round; for he still had a knock-out blow in him, and Dempsey, like Beckett, could not stop it or dodge it. But even if he had landed on the right spot and won the fight, it would still have been true that the spectators would have been left without any notion of what Carpentier's style is at its best.

On the other hand, the film does Dempsey the justice that the printed reports of the fight (at least those that I have seen) denied him. The belief that he is a mere ruffian who is so tough that he will take everything that any boxer can give him, and batter him to bits afterwards, winning his fights as a gorilla might, has hardly half a grain of truth in it. He fights with an intense seriousness and a will to victory not less formidable than the same qualities in Carpentier. For fighting purposes he is not on a lower level than Carpentier: the two adversaries were worthy of one another in that respect, though I doubt whether they knew it: indeed, I think that each undervalued the other; and I can well believe that Dempsey, as a *Times* correspondent reported, was amazed, when he saw the film, by the fighting quality of the man whom he had been too busy beating to criticise. Another surprise is that his knock-out punch is not as decisive as Carpentier's. It did not come in the first round when it seemed to be called for. When Carpentier first dropped in the last round he rested in the most self-possessed professional manner until nine was counted, and then sprang to his feet in good order; and though the *coup de grâce*, which came presently, jolted him out of all power to co-ordinate his movements, he was quite conscious, and made a desperate struggle, half-raising himself and turning over with all his limbs reaching wildly to get a purchase somewhere before the fatal ten was called. Beckett had no such nightmare when he was knocked out by Carpentier; he did not hear the count, and woke up an astonished man, having no idea that the fight was over.

I must repeat here what I said before the fight, that the plea that Dempsey had an unfair advantage as the bigger man is all nonsense. Carpentier was quite big enough and strong enough to make the match a fair one. Some of the greatest boxers have been middleweights; and the giants have seldom justified the faith inspired by their inches. Both men displayed extraordinary physical power; and the result had nothing whatever to do with the weights and measurements. The film exhibition of their muscles shows Dempsey as muscle-bound and Carpentier as perfectly lithe. The odds were on Carpentier all the time for those who, like myself, had never seen Dempsey at work. And if the two were to meet again, and Carpentier were to take the lesson of his defeat to heart, and change his tactics accordingly, the betting would be on him again; for he is Dempsey's master at outfighting and footwork.

And now for Dempsey's positive technical qualities. He is the best in-fighter in the American style I have ever seen. If Carpentier had been well advised he would have entered the ring with these words branded on his brain: 'When you hit Dempsey, and he is still alive, get away, and get away quickly'. And by getting away I do not mean the side-stepping and slipping by which Carpentier saved himself so cleverly every time Dempsey tried to rush him. I mean what he did with Beckett when Mr Angle was referee: that is, step straight in with his lead and spring straight back out of half-arm reach when he landed, the referee being in his proper place out of the ring, and bent on having a display of boxing as distinguished from pollywogging. This is the old English style; and none of its ancient practitioners ever heard or dreamt of hitting or being hit on the back of the neck. In modern American practice, however, the occiput seems to be the favourite mark. It is *de rigueur*, when you have led off, or countered a lead-off, to crouch, clinch, and begin pounding your man on the atlas process, or banging him over the kidneys, trying meanwhile to hold his arms locked under yours until the referee, who is in the ring all the time, takes part in the combat and violently tears the clinchers asunder. (Incidentally I may say that if ever I act as referee in an American glove fight I shall demand at least an equal share of the gate money and cinema rights with the rival champions, and I shall have to work just as hard and get no glory by it.) At this game Dempsey is consummately skilful, cool, systematic, indefatigable, and ruinously damaging. Carpentier, his superior at out-fighting, cannot touch him at it. I suppose Carpentier, vain of his weak point, fancied himself at it, and went into the fight confident that he could beat Dempsey as easily at it as at long shots. At all events, in the very first exchange, instead of getting away, he deliberately followed up to close quarters, crouched, and clinched. In ten seconds he had lost the fight. Dempsey had him hammered silly before he knew where he was. Dempsey's fists never stopped for a moment, though they never moved wildly. Jab and jolt, bang and pound; they were all over Carpentier, especially on the occiput. That was the sandbag. It left Carpentier in such a state that he was forced to clinch again and again lest Dempsey should treat him as he himself had treated Beckett, and knock him out with a pot-shot whilst he was dazed. And every time he clinched the hammering began again as insistently, as skilfully, as destructively as ever. If Carpentier had not had a demon of endurance and determination in him he could not have got through the round. As it was, he went to his corner a desperate man, without having given a single demonstration of the classical pugilism that has made him the idol of artists as well as of bruisers.

The issue was now pretty narrow. Dempsey was bound to win at in-fighting; and as Carpentier persisted in the American routine of going into a clinch at every exchange, he played Dempsey's game for him. But there were still his terrible long shots, which were too quick for Dempsey (who, however, is by no means slow); and any one of them, if it jarred the funny-bone which Dempsey must have in his jaw like other mortals, would win him the fight. He did land a veritable thunderbolt in the third round. I cannot say, as Carpentier has said, that I saw Dempsey's knees give, nor, as Corbett has said, that I saw his eyes roll up; but I saw enough of its effect to know that Dempsey had a piece of luck like that of the batsman who skies into the hands of mid-on, and sees it slip through his fingers. But instead of disabling Dempsey it appears that it disabled Carpentier by laming his hand; and at this, the only moment at which it seemed the right policy for him to follow up, he could not do so effectively. He got in many other long shots; and Dempsey stopped most of them with his countenance as far as I could see; but the end was always the same: a clinch, and Dempsey master of his opponent, weakening him with body blows, and stunning him with thumps on the spinal cord. Dempsey never lost his form, and never gave the French champion a moment's rest. Carpentier avoided all his leads by slipping him, but Dempsey always knew where to find him and follow him up; and though, as he came on, Carpentier, with an unquenchable fighting spirit, would dash at him and let him have both fists in his face, he never hesitated nor hurried, and was presently hammering away body to body as systematically as if he were working on a ship's plates instead of on a living antagonist, and a very dangerous one, too.

In short, Dempsey did just the last thing that was expected of him: he not only won the fight, but impressed us by his *moral*. In his different way, and for the purposes of his profession, he is as remarkable a genius as Carpentier. He has been very much belittled, both by the absurd underrating of his opponent which went on before the fight, and by the failure of the Press critics of pugilism to appreciate his skill, his generalship, and his resolution in carrying out his own methods. I feel sure that he must have received in the days before the fight enough bad advice to secure his defeat ten times over. I am equally sure from what I saw on the screen that he went his own way to the end. There was something in the way he picked up Carpentier the moment the count was finished that made one feel that he had foreknown his victory almost as certainly as the cinema spectators foreknow it now. His face before the fight begins is well worth studying.

And yet the odds were against him. If he ever meets a boxer of Carpentier's powers who will stick to the English classical school of boxing, and refuse to 'mix it' in the American manner, he may be hard put to it to keep his championship. Meanwhile he has taught the best boxer in Europe a terrible lesson; and it will be interesting to see whether it will be taken to heart by Carpentier or his successors. Meanwhile the verdict of British boxing on Carpentier must be 'Serve him right for doing in America as the Americans do instead of sticking to the classical method of Euopean civilisation, of which he is the superlative exponent!'

For my part it would greatly revive my interest in boxing if the order 'seconds out of the ring' were to include the referee, and if crouching and occipital piledriving went the way of up-and-down fighting, and all the other practices that once made the ringside no place for a gentleman, not to mention a lady. Ladies are becoming as common at glove fights and the films thereof as at polo matches. At the Leicester Square Cinema, several ladies saw the fight when I did; and they were ordinary ladies, not Leicester-square ladies. Possibly this criticism may help them to understand what they are seeing, and encourage them to protest against American in-fighting as dull, ugly, and indefensible as a protaganist spectacle. It produces decisions, because it produces disablement; and decisions are necessary to betting. But betting has always been the bane of honest boxing; and now that the star pugilists draw the same fees whether they win, lose, or draw, they would be well advised to make their films as spectacular as possible by cultivating exhibition boxing; and leaving the minor practitioners to make more money by selling fights than by winning them.

The reader can sense Shaw straining with every cadence to preserve his own faith in the scholar-pugilist's ability to beat the man from Bashan. There are moments in studying his report when the reader begins to wonder if there has not been some mistake and that it is Carpentier who has defeated Dempsey. And so he learns that Carpentier has been overcome not because he is the inferior specimen but because he has adopted the wrong tactics, a postulation leading to the extraordinary quixotry of Shaw's claim at the end of the fourth paragraph to the effect that in any return match Carpentier ought to be the favourite to win. And perhaps Shaw was right. After all, would one defeat under adverse circumstances have changed the essence of Cashel Byron's temperament? Would an accidental punch or a momentary tactical solecism have affected the cerebral issues at stake? Perhaps not, and Shaw might just conceivably have been right in his assumption that Carpentier would have learned sufficient lessons from the first Dempsey contest to have emerged triumphant in a second.

But Carpentier was destined never to fight for Dempsey's title again, although few people could have suspected it at the time. Routed by the champion though he had undoubtedly been, he remained at the pinnacle of his bizarre profession and could look forward, with Shaw, to the reasonable expectation of many victories to come. Having recovered from the débâcle in Jersey City, Carpentier now surveyed his own prospects and found that his stature at home, so far from being diminished by his unfortunate American escapade, was actually enhanced by the insidious glamour which attaches itself to lost causes and gallant defeats. He was still, after all, World Light-Heavyweight Champion, and surveying the mediocre field, could anticipate several seasons of enjoyable sport toying with the pretensions of his challengers, several of whom were now in training. And so, casting all thoughts of his last fight from his mind, Carpentier drifted somewhat casually into preparations for his next one, taking easeful delight in the more parochial affairs of his own weight division, and never suspecting that his career was now about to be broken in the most sensational way.

On 16 September 1897, while Shaw was deep into his brilliant campaign to seduce Ellen Terry by kind permission of the Postmaster-General, the birth took place of a citizen of France called Louis Fall. This Monsieur Fall was no ordinary Frenchman, for his birthplace was that most incongruous of all departments of metropolitan France, Senegal, out on the western tip of the African continent, and linked to home more through the self-interested idealism of paternalist zealots than by any geopolitical realities. Fall was born in the township of Saint Louis, on the Senegal River, where there were venerable fishing connections with Brest, Bordeaux and Marseilles, and a tradition of conservatism so strong that when in 1789 certain adjustments were being made to the national constitution, the locals had sent in a memorandum of protests to the revolutionary congress.

It is hardly surprising, therefore, that Fall was so sadly lacking in even the most rudimentary grasp of those knotty concepts, Liberty, Equality and Fraternity, and that his attachment to them went no further than a casual mastery, while still a small boy, of diving for coins flung into the local waters by passengers from passing ships. One day in 1909 young Fall's expertise at retrieving the coins attracted the attention of a lady travelling on board a ship moored at Saint Louis. She turned out to be a Dutch professional singer who so admired Fall's technique in the water as to decide there and then to adopt the boy and take him back with her to her villa in the south of France – a sudden admirable flash of patronage most kindly considered by posterity to have been purely philanthropic in its intent. To add to the bizarre quality of the story of this alliance, soon after her acquirement of Fall, the benefactress suddenly disappears from the records and is never mentioned again. Whether she absconded or died has never been discovered, but whatever her fate, she certainly left her twelve-year-old protégé to his own devices. He was, at least, a strong lad possessed of a certain natural athleticism, and soon drifted into the life of a casual semi-professional pugilist, working with the itinerant troupes who travelled across France, setting up rings in villages and towns, challenging all comers to last so many rounds for so much money.

Fall was hardly the type to take much interest in political developments back home, yet it seems he paid some attention to the great events of June 1914, when a black Senegalese called Blaise Diagne won a famous electoral battle at Saint Louis and became a delegate to the French Assembly; when European war broke out two months later it was because of the propagandising of Diagne that so many Senegalese rallied to the Allied ranks and tasted the refinements of western civilisation. By this time Fall, a reasonably skilful lightweight, had learned to read and write, and, stirred by Diagne's entreaties, enlisted in the French army, fought on the Western Front, was wounded several times, won the Croix de Guerre, and was later rewarded by being permitted to work in postwar Paris as a dishwasher and street sweeper during those interludes when he was unable to obtain a fight.

Mediocrity, however, is a more highly prized attribute in the councils of pugilism than the outside world sometimes realises, for a champion like Carpentier, brilliant though he might be, does not care to spend his entire professional career putting that brilliance to the test of engagements like the one with Dempsey. Scaling the Alps may be a heroic and spectacular enterprise, but there are times when the occasional browse through the foothills of one's art can be just as rewarding and it must be accounted a stroke of desperately bad luck for Carpentier that, in the autumn of 1922, the foothill in question turned out to be Louis Fall. After the Dempsey fight, Carpentier, still boxing on foreign soil, had quickly despatched a pair of apprentice-journeymen called Cook and Levinsky, and was now considering what extravaganza he might lay before his idolatrous Parisian supporters. When it came to selecting a human punchbag on which the great Carpentier might give an exhibition of his favourite shots, who more suitable than the obscure and, in pugilistic terms, eminently uninspired Louis Fall? Admittedly there might be difficulty assuaging Fall's fear that in exposing himself in the same ring as the terrible Georges he might be performing the last foolhardy act of his life, but surely once everyone understood that this was hardly to be a fight at all in the accepted sense of the word, there seemed no reason why events should not run as smoothly as theatrical events usually do. Senegal buzzed with the rumour of an 'arrangement', and Carpentier appeared not to be bothering to train at all. Pa Levy, acting as Fall's promoter, was thought to have explained to the challenger that in the unlikely event that he found himself in a position to hit M. Carpentier very hard, it might be more tactful not to grasp the opportunity.

Exactly what happened at the Buffalo Stadium on 24 September 1922 has never been quite clear, and never will be now. Witnesses have testified to the abject terror of Louis Fall as he sat in his corner awaiting the start of his execution; others have suggested that Carpentier had promised the newsreel companies that he would prolong the rites sufficiently for them to be able to put an attractive film together. The latter theory in particular is wonderfully cynical, but the newsreel pictures do exist, and they show an overweight Carpentier toying with the utterly ineffectual Fall for the first two rounds. In fact, so woebegone was Fall's performance that it made a mockery of his recently adopted professional soubriquet, 'Battling Siki'. The same English schoolboy who had earlier adopted Carpentier as a kind of proxy-Englishman wrote:

Siki's terror persisted through the first two rounds, in which Carpentier flicked light punches at his chin, and generally played with him. In the third round Carpentier began to feel that it was time to draw the farce to an end, and therefore knocked Siki down with his right hand. While Siki was on the floor shaking his head, he turned his face slightly, and saw Carpentier strike a disdainful pose for the benefit of the photographers. This sight suddenly maddened him. In an instant he was no longer the cowed and cowering punchbag, but a wild savage with all the fiercest instincts of his ancestors blazing from his eyes. He leapt at Carpentier, who, taken quite unawares, received a terrific swing on his chin. Carpentier, rather dazed, tried to dodge, but it was no use. Siki tore after him, slamming blows into his body. At the end of the round the untrained Carpentier was badly marked and breathless. The interval between the third and fourth rounds did nothing to quieten Siki. Indeed, the buzz of the crowd, which suddenly realised that uncontrollable forces had broken loose, and that through them the wildly improbable had become fantastically probable, seemed to stir him still more, just as the drums of a war dance will inflame an African tribesman. He could hardly be restrained in his corner, and when the bell went for the fourth round and he was again unleashed, he went at Carpentier with redoubled frenzy. He battered through Carpentier's science with a continuous flail of blows, and when the science was battered, Carpentier had nothing but courage to offer in its place. His flaccid muscles would not respond to the orders from his brain, and his lungs seemed incapable of holding his breath. He did try one trick, which was to charge Siki head-on; and the sound of their two skulls cracking against each other seemed to shake all Paris. But it was no good. Siki in his frenzy would not have noticed a slam from a sledge-hammer. The gay cavalier of the world's boxing, instead of having the night out in Paris which he had planned, was taken to hospital by ambulance, and never fought again.[1]

That version of the sequence of events at the Buffalo Stadium may be described as the hagiology of the affair; the actual developments were a little less romantic. Nevertheless, the outcome was by no means as clear-cut as most accounts suggest. The referee on this occasion was a M. Henri Bernstein, and one can understand his deep confusion. With bedlam breaking out all around him, with 60,000 hysterical experts screaming as loudly as possible in order to clarify the situation, it must have been difficult for Bernstein to put two thoughts together. One thought, however, was not beyond him. He suddenly perceived that in counting away the ten seconds over Carpentier's crumpled body, he, Bernstein, was presiding over the demolition of a national monument. Bernstein was an honourable

man, an exemplar of that moral rectitude for which the professional prize-ring has always been distinguished, and he
saw no escape from the inexorable workings of fate. It was at
this stage that the unfortunate functionary was suddenly
vouchsafed a vision which inspired him to an act of sublime
moral courage. It was revealed to him that the whole thing was a
dreadful mistake; it had never happened. Siki had not knocked
Carpentier down at all, but had tripped him. He had no choice
but to disqualify the challenger and award the decision to the
champion, who, to do him justice, was in no condition to take
much notice. The crowd, however, took a great deal of notice,
and set up such a storm of protest as to suggest that even in their
crazed condition, they had rather more sense of fair play than
Bernstein had. They had been dismayed to watch their beloved
Georges slaughtered, but it was after all something to have seen,
and they were not prepared to stand by and watch Siki be
deprived of his laurels. But the baying of disorganised mobs at
boxing matches has never been very much of an impediment to
a crooked verdict, and it seemed unlikely that anything much
would have been done to redress Bernstein's decision, had it not
been for the presence in the crowd of a good friend of Siki's.

This was the same Blaise Diagne whose call to battle eight
year before had inspired Siki to volunteer for the French army.
By the night of the Siki–Carpentier fight, Diagne had become a
figure of considerable influence in France, having risen to
ministerial eminence as Deputy for the Colonies under that
distinguished patriot Pierre Laval. Diagne, realising that Siki
had won fairly, and determined that his victory should not
be stolen from him, decided to intervene. The official adjudi-
cator had seen a trip, Diagne, a prominent member of the
government, had not, and the boxing establishment found itself
in a hopelessly untenable position, presiding over a deadlock
whose political and racial overtones were not to be dispersed by
anything in the Queensberry rules. On being apprised of M.
Diagne's outraged sense of honour, M. Bernstein, psychic as
ever, was the beneficiary of a second vision; he now saw that Siki
had not after all tripped the champion up, but had in fact
knocked him down fairly and squarely. He accordingly
performed his second act of sublime moral courage and

reversed his disqualification. Siki was the winner after all, and World Light-Heavyweight Champion. Carpentier was done for.[2]

There were those who felt that because a white Parisian had been battered by a black Senegalese, western culture was suddenly threatened. There were others who believed that Siki's triumph went too strongly against the pugilistic grain to be altogether genuine. All in all, the enigma of the events began to assume such bewildering proportions that the British press fell back on the tactic it came to love so dearly through the first half of the twentieth century. Unable to discover either the truth or anyone who knew the truth, it decided to ask Bernard Shaw. In the edition of *The Sunday Chronicle* dated 1 October 1922, there appeared the following report:

> A representative of *The Sunday Chronicle* asked Mr Bernard Shaw what he thought of Carpentier's defeat, and whether it was likely to have any serious political reaction. Mr Shaw's reply is given below, supplemented by his impressions after he had seen the cinema film of the fight.

> 'Don't be alarmed', said Mr Shaw, 'civilisation will survive the shock. The fall of the mark is more important than the fall of any pugilist, though the sporting public may not think so. Most of us can remember when the possibility of Jack Johnson beating Jeffries made many unworthy people tremble lest America should perish in a sanguinary racial conflict. Well, Johnson triumphed, but America pulled through the crisis, and Africa remained tranquil.

> Siki will not assume the title of Emperor of Senegal and march on Paris. He will, like the rest of the thirty million black subjects of the French Republic, feel more dependent on Paris than ever. The fact that there are fifteen million negroes under Monsieur Poincaré's hand who are as good as white men when it comes to fighting, whether with fist or rifle, may perhaps increase our enthusiasm for the League of Nations: that is all. As to the victory of Siki being a surprise, why should it have surprised anyone? Since Carpentier contemptuously announced that his wonderful display against Beckett was the mere ABC of boxing, and devoted himself to the XYZ of it, he has invited defeat. He got it, and

got it hard, from Dempsey. He deserved it from Cook; and the utmost that can be said of his victory over Lewis is that it was legitimately stolen.

Besides, he is growing too old for these games; he has been staking everything on bringing off an early knockout, and carelessly exaggerating what he can afford to let the other fellow do to him while he is playing for it. He now says, 'They (the Senegalese) are not made like us'. But they are, only more so. Somebody ought to have told Carpentier that it is waste of time to punch a negro's head. However, as I have seen neither the fight nor the film, I have no right to discuss what happened. Tom King beat Jem Mace, a much better boxer, by a lucky bang under the eye which knocked him all to pieces morally and physically; and there may have been some luck of this kind in Siki's case. But really when I read of champions being knocked out by thumps in the back at what are supposed to be boxing matches, I cannot take any interest in the business. Boxing is only pardonable when it is very well done.

There will always be people who will crowd round anything in the shape of a fight – dog fight, cock fight, woman fight, or what you like – if only it is savage enough; but they are not, to say the least, influential people; and I doubt whether general public opinion will stand much more of the sort of thing that the glove-fighters of today are giving us. I, for one, find it not only rather disgusting, but unbearably boresome.'

Next day, however, *The Sunday Chronicle* representative had the luck to catch Mr Shaw red-handed, emerging from a West End Cinema.

'Well, Mr Shaw? Now you have seen it, what do you think?'
'I think that Carpentier does not know how to fight a negro. and has a good deal to learn from him. Siki made nothing of Carpentier's long shots, which dazed Beckett and made even Dempsey look serious. Siki not only understands the art of getting away and being hit by a spent bullet only, but, like all negroes, he does what no white man dare do – meets a straight lead by dropping his head neatly and taking the shock on the ridge of his eyebrow, where it makes about as much

impression as a mushroom on a minotaur, and jars the assailant most discouragingly.

Almost any white pugilist of Siki's build would have been down and out half-a-dozen times from the punches that Carpentier got home, but they did not worry Siki for a moment. When he took a count of seven he was calmly resting himself on one knee, bolt upright from hip to shoulder, just amusing himself. His in-fighting did not seem to be much more effective than Carpentier's: that is, it was not effective at all: Dempsey, I should say, would kill him at that game. The decisive blows were all whole-arm ones.

Carpentier retrieved the reputation he lost with Cook; he is by no means finished yet; and if he would get away when he has brought off a lead or had the best of an exchange, instead of always butting doggedly into a clinch, we should see the present proportion of a pound of pollywogging to an ounce of boxing reversed. Once he butted Siki quite outrageously. But the blow he struck Siki after Siki had helped him up from the ropes was quite fair. He waited until Siki was in a posture of complete defence and watching, like himself, for an opening. The film does not show clearly the blow which disabled Carpentier some time before the finish. On the other hand, it shows a knock through the ropes by Carpentier of which we heard nothing. On the whole, it proves that Carpentier puts up a much better fight and has much more left in him than the reports suggested. What is wrong with him is that, like a true Frenchman, he does not know when he is beaten; and that means Waterloo for him. Siki has all the negro qualities as a pugilist; toughness about the head, trickiness, and speed on his feet (much cleverer and quicker here than Carpentier), and the characteristic negro combination of romantic pluck and good humour. Like Dempsey, he was at no disadvantage whatever with the Frenchman in the matter of *moral*; and if Carpentier can get on a return match with him he will have to take him much more seriously.'

'And the finish, Mr Shaw, was it fair?'

'Oh, perfectly fair. Siki's leg was between Carpentier's legs, and the film does not show where Siki's right landed. I suppose it was on Carpentier's back; but there was no question of a wrestling trip. It was a legitimate knock-out, and, as in the Dempsey fight, spinal, not maxillary. I wish, by the way, they would allow wrestling. It would make these eternal clinches much more interesting. Good afternoon.'

But when the topic of conversation was so controversial, not even Shaw could terminate it quite so abruptly. The events at the Buffalo Stadium proved to be only the first act of a hopelessly confused melodrama which obstinately refused to pass into history. M. Diagne, evidently determined to make the Siki–Carpentier fight a political issue, disclosed circumstantial proof of skulduggery between the two pugilistic camps. Ten weeks after Carpentier had been divested of his titles, the scandal was still considered newsworthy enough for *The Sunday Chronicle* to interview Shaw once again, on 10 December 1922, to the following eloquent effect:

A representative of *The Sunday Chronicle* asked Mr Bernard Shaw whether he believes the story told in the French Chamber by the Senegalese deputy that the Carpentier–Siki fight was an arranged affair in which Siki had agreed to lose for the usual consideration, and had changed his mind in the course of the combat.

'There is nothing whatever incredible in it,' said the Sage. 'Many a pugilist has made more money by losing than by winning. But you must not rush to the conclusion that Carpentier's honour is involved. His military record and general good character entitle him to complete belief in his good faith when he pledges his word, as he does, that the story is not true.'

'But you say it may be true.'

'Yes; but how is Carpentier to know whether it is true or not? When such things are done, it is not the champion who does them: it is his manager, who takes good care, if his principal is at all fastidious, not to let him know that things are being made safe for him'.

'But would any honourable manager do such a thing?'

'My young friend', said the Sage paternally, 'the position of a boxer's manager is a very responsible one. The only people

Jack Dempsey flooring Gene Tunney in 1927

Tunney is down and Jack
Dempsey is sent to his corner

The famous long count, Dempsey *v* Tunney in 1927

*Left*, Gene Tunney poses with G.B.S. in 1929 at Brioni, and join their wives, *above*, to watch a polo match

who are defrauded by what used to be called a cross or barney – I don't know what they call it now – are the people who bet on boxing matches. Now the manager has nothing to do with that; if people choose to gamble, that is not his affair. It is wrong to gamble; and the interests of the sinners who do it should not be taken into account. The only legitimate side of the business is the honest earning of the gate money. And as the Parisian public would have been much better pleased if the Frenchman had beaten the negro than it was by the negro beating the Frenchman, Siki's ringside repentance – assuming it to have taken place – led to the public actually getting less value for their money than it would have got from the manager's arrangement – assuming that he arranged it.'

'Are you paradoxing, Mr Shaw?'

'Paradoxing is a useful rhyme to boxing: I will make a note of it. But I am not paradoxing. In so far as the fact that many fights are arranged discourages betting, it is a highly moral fact. You must also look at it from the point of view of the manager's duty to his principal. Suppose you were Carpentier's manager, and he had one of his great fights ahead: say the one with Dempsey. Would you really allow him to risk that great opportunity in a trumpery fight with a boxer of less pretensions than Dempsey: say with Levinsky?'

'I should see that the fight was a fair one'.

'I am afraid you will not succeed as a boxing manager; so do not take to it. But nothing can be fairer than an arranged fight, if the loser is honestly paid. If I were Carpentier's manager under such circumstances I should go to Levinsky and say, "If you beat Georges you will have to fight Dempsey. But do not turn pale, my friend: I take a great interest in you; and I have made up my mind that if Georges knocks you out you shall not lose by it". That would be my plain duty as a man of business. But of course I should not tell Carpentier anything about it. He might knock me down. And his natural good opinion of himself would prevent his having the faintest suspicion that his opponent was not quite so fast asleep during the ten seconds as he seemed'.

'But this Siki business –'

'A parallel case. Carpentier had before him the return

match with Beckett and the return match with Dempsey. If I had been Carpentier's manager do you think I could have reconciled it with my conscience to take any risks in a comparatively insignificant affair with Siki? No. I should have gone to Siki. I should have said "Siki my boy, you know you have not a dog's chance against Carpentier. Still, accidents may happen even in the ring; and with the best intentions you might land one on the soft spot which Carpentier, like all mortal men, has in his jaw. And then what would become of the Beckett match and the Dempsey match and all the money they mean? You must be reasonable, Siki. You must do enough for honour, and enough to give our patrons something for their money; and then you must submit to the inevitable knockout. You see, you would be lynched if you knocked out Georges; so I am speaking in your own interest. And I will see to it that you are none the poorer for your defeat."'

'I see. That would make the affair quite safe'.

'Not quite safe. It would be what is called a cross; and there is such a thing as a double cross. Somebody else might get at Siki and make it worth his while to fight to win, and thus double-cross me. Or there would be the possibility that Siki, on discovering in the ring that Carpentier's terrible right, so fatal to the European eggshell, makes no impression on the Senegalese cocoa nut, might see the championship within his grasp and be unable to resist the temptation'.

'You think, then, that Siki double-crossed Descamps?'

'Certainly not', exclaimed Mr Shaw indignantly. 'I have not mentioned the name of Monsieur Descamps. I am not telling you what M. Descamps did: I am telling you what I should have felt it my duty to do if I had been Carpentier's manager. These things are not done in France. Have you not heard how horrified – how shocked – the members of the French Boxing Federation are at the very suggestion of such a thing? Why, they demand that the delegate who accuses Carpentier's friends of having squared Siki should have his parliamentary immunity taken from him so that they may prosecute him. They would think me a very, *very* wicked man if they heard what I have just said to you'.

'Well, I am a little taken aback myself, Mr Shaw. Do you consider this crossing and double-crossing morally justified?'

'They are usages that spring inevitably out of commercial prizefighting. They do not interfere with the amusement of the public. They afford a living wage to many pugilists who would have a very poor time if they had to live by their victories alone. The amount of money that changes hands is not affected. Sometimes – not always – Peter loses to Paul instead of Paul losing to Peter; that is all; and Peter would not lose if he did not bet'.

'Well, I call it a rotten swindle'.

'Young man: you do not know the world; and your language is unclassical. The cross and the double cross are freely practised in diplomacy, in finance, in party politics, and in commerce; and pray who are you that you should set yourself up against these great developments of modern civilisation? There are always naïfs like you who have to be humoured – people who are determined to go on the straight and not on the cross. Yet the only result is that the crosses have to be arranged for them behind their backs. I have no doubt that Carpentier is one of them. Pitt, you will remember – or you would if you had studied history instead of fancying pugilism – absolutely refused to bribe the House of Commons; but that did not prevent his Parliaments from being steeped in corruption. Carpentier exhibits X-ray photographs of the broken bones in his hands to prove that he fought for all he was worth; but he can prove nothing by that or by any other evidence. For all he knows every fight he ever fought may have been a cross, his defeats, of course, being double crosses. All that he can say for certain is that he never sold a fight; he cannot say that his manager never bought one. We know that his victories over Wells and Beckett were not crosses, nor his defeat by Dempsey a double cross, because nobody believes that Wells and Beckett and Dempsey sell their fights. Like Carpentier, they have attained a position in which it would not pay them to sell, even if such a transaction were within their personal characters. But not one of them could prove that his manager had not bought a fight:

they could only say that they did not know it, and would have indignantly refused to fight if they had known it. That is what ring finance is like; and do not forget it, young man, when next you feel tempted to go betting'.

'What I cannot understand about it is this. I see that the big fights are all right; but why do the big men take on the little fights? Why did Carpentier take on Levinsky and Siki instead of waiting for Dempsey?'

'Be reasonable: champions must live. They cannot live on one big fight in eighteen months when they have to provide for their whole lifetime before they are thirty. Think of the gate money!'

'Well, if I had only known – '

'Do not be cast down. You realise that though you thought you knew all that was to be known of the sport, you were in fact, a mug. So you were; but then professional pugilism is pre-eminently a mug's game for the public. Cheer up; you will enjoy it just as much now that your eyes are opened: perhaps more. Good morning.'

Siki's subsequent career is an interesting example of the ways in which, as the author of *Cashel Byron's Profession* once pointed out in a different context, the conversion of a savage to Christianity very often turns out to have been the conversion of Christianity to savagery. Any last lingering doubts as to the existence in Siki of an irresistible lunatic streak are dispelled by his behaviour following the Carpentier scandal. He soon began to indulge his taste for the expansive gesture by drinking large quantities of brandy, wearing a dinner suit in the morning, taking to the streets of Paris with a lion on a lead, and scoring a succession of technical knockouts over his favourite opponent, his wife. Ridiculous as the acquirement of his title had been, he now achieved the apparently impossible by contriving to lose it in circumstances more ludicrous still. For the new champion, perhaps not altogether conversant with the eccentric expression of patriotic excess in certain outposts of Western European culture, fell in with a comical plan to defend his title in Dublin on 17 March 1923, against a gentleman called Michael McTigue. The ominously celtic overtones of his opponent's name were surely lost on Siki, and one wonders also if he knew the special significance of the date of his appointment with McTigue. However this may be, McTigue, by relieving him of his championship, gave the locals something wonderful to drink about. Not that many of them could have needed much encouragement: 17 March is St Patrick's Day.

It seems just possible that the memory of this unfortunate confluence of Irish forces arraigned against him embittered Siki to the stage where it eventually cost him his life. At the end of 1923 he decided to try his luck in America. When he was beaten in a contest at Baltimore on 14 November 1925, it was his farewell appearance, for on 15 December of that year he achieved the most extravagant feat of his freakish career when he actually succeeded in being murdered in two different places at the same time. In September 1975, by which time the Senegalese authorities, independent at last, were desperately attempting to repair the image of the first ever African World Champion to something approaching sanity, *Le Soleil* of Dakar reminded its readers that their great hero had fallen before a rain of seven bullets near 3rd Avenue in New York. If this is so, then Siki's powers of recuperation must have been even more remarkable than Carpentier had found them to be, for the body is said to have been discovered in an insalubrious section of Chicago called, by people who didn't have to live there, Hell's Kitchen; the seven bullets had left only stab wounds. The assassin was never found; nobody cared very much who did it, or why. Blaise Diagne's son has testified that Siki was 'rubbed out' by gangsters who were piqued by his refusal to throw a fight. But one British journalist researching Siki's bizarre life and times has described how one of the locals, on a trip to Chicago, met a man who told him that 'Siki was killed because he insulted two Irishmen on St Patrick's day'.[3] Perhaps it was Siki's way of getting his own back on McTigue and company.

Once Siki was out of the way, there were those, especially in France, who harboured dreams of a second coming by Carpentier. But boxing titles, once lost, usually prove impossible to recover, and in pursuing the identity of the next true virtuoso to succeed to the World Light-Heavyweight Championship, it is not to Carpentier that we must look, but to one of the more obscure supporting players in the melodrama of the earlier Dempsey–Carpentier fight. Sensational as that event undoubtedly was, the real romance had taken place outside the ropes, because it was on that July night at Boyle's Thirty Acres in Jersey City that the ghost of Cashel Byron, its ground prepared by the new rule requiring a fighter whose opponent has been floored to retire to a neutral corner while the count proceeds, first began to walk, and life to imitate the art of a failed Victorian novelist.

# 5 / TESTIMONY TO TUNNEY

In 1921 America was still basking in the afterglow of wartime chauvinism. Its warriors were still heroes to be fêted, and the promoters of the Carpentier–Dempsey contest, combining patriotism with box-office awareness, decided to feature, in the main supporting bout to the championship, an unknown ex-Marine whose claim to fame was that he had won the Light-Heavyweight Championship of the American Expeditionary Forces. The ex-Marine's name was James Joseph Eugene Tunney, and because he is the least typical of all the professional fighters who ever ducked under the ropes, it is worth studying him a little more closely.

Born in New York City on 25 May 1898, a few weeks after Corbett had lost the Heavyweight Championship to Fitzsimmons at Carson City, Nevada, Tunney is unique, not because of his regard for boxing as a means to an end, but for his vision of what that end might be. Thousands of fighters have come out of New York, as Tunney did, hungry for the substantial purses a successful career can offer. But for Tunney the cash rewards were no more than the first arduous step on a road of dizzying social improvement. He seems to have seen himself from the first as some kind of aristocrat of the mind and spirit, an unwitting parody of the foundling heroes of nineteenth-century pulp fiction who compensated themselves for the obscurity of their own beginnings by dreaming that they were the rightful heirs to a seat in the House of Lords. From the very beginning of his career Tunney moved through the jungle of professional boxing with the fastidious detachment of a man in search of his rightful exalted inheritance, and the very fact that he was able to create this conception of himself shows how alien his sensibilities must have been from those of the men he despatched so efficiently inside the boxing ring. Compared to men like Dempsey and Willard his horizons were vast, and he remains the only pugilist of the twentieth century to whom the social pretensions of Cashel Byron would not have seemed utterly absurd. Many champions might see in Byron's victory over Paradise a reflection of their own professional skill. Tunney alone would have recognised Byron's country estate and the successful entry into political life as the most significant victory of all.

Even in his early ring days Tunney was shrewd and reasonably well-read. When a fellow-Marine repaid a debt by offering him one of two books, thrusting upon him *A Winter's Tale* and keeping *Julius Caesar* for himself, the boxer remarked, 'He knew what he was about, as anyone who knows Shakespeare will attest.'[1] This is hardly the voice of Madison Square Garden or the barrack-room. Later Tunney worked his way through the rest of the Shakespearean canon 'with ease', and long before his retirement from the ring was echoing the Shavian view that *The Way of All Flesh* is 'a neglected masterpiece enjoying a belated fame'.[2] It is hardly surprising that he approached the problem of his own boxing technique with the same scholarly detachment he brought to the theme of his self-improvement. And because the pursuit of self-knowledge is always the most arresting narrative of all, the story of how Tunney stalked and finally tracked down a hypothetical hero – himself – who would dethrone the great, the all-powerful, the apparently invincible Dempsey, has about it the tautness of a well-constructed piece of fiction.

The quest begins with a boat trip down the Rhine in the year 1919. Tunney, light-heavyweight champion of the A.E.F. was one of a group of touring athletes giving exhibitions for the troops. The corporal in charge of the troupe, an ex-newspaperman, had recently seen in action the latest heavyweight sensation, Jack Dempsey, and when Tunney asked him for his impression, the corporal replied, 'He's a big Jack Dillon.' Now Tunney, like all aspiring amateurs, was well-versed in the mythology of the sport he practised, and knew all about Dillon, a destructive middleweight with a reputation as a killer. After thinking for a moment he added, 'Jack Dillon was beaten by Mike Gibbons, wasn't he?' The corporal agreed

Gibbons was a fast-moving, ingenious defensive artist who never allowed Dillon to get within destructive range.

I said to the Corporal: 'Well, maybe Jack Dempsey can be beaten by clever boxing.'

His reply was reflective, thought out. 'Yes,' he said, 'when Dempsey is beaten, a fast boxer with a good defence will do it.'[3]

The conversation ends, but Tunney said that as they sailed down the Rhine, 'I thought maybe I might be a big Mike Gibbons for the big Jack Dillon. It was my first inkling that some day I might defeat Jack Dempsey for the Heavyweight Championship of the World.' He admitted readily enough that it was this kind of presumption which reduced him to a mockery in the eyes of so many of the hardened cynics inside the boxing world:

> The laugh of the Twenties was my confident insistence that I would defeat Jack Dempsey for the Heavyweight Championship of the World. To the boxing public, this optimistic belief was the funniest of jokes. To me, it was a reasonable statement of calculated probability, an opinion based on prize-ring gossip.[4]

What does Tunney mean by 'a reasonable statement of calculated probability'? He means that the outcome of any contest between two fighters might be resolved by purely intellectual processes, that by reasoning away his own short-comings, an underdog is perfectly capable of turning the tables. The absurdity of the theory in the context of a world where brute force, physical strength, endurance, the will to win, remain the dominant factors at the highest levels, explains why the boxing fraternity laughed so loudly and so consistently at Tunney, and why also it could never bring itself to warm to his personality. The wiseacres were not used to fighters who uttered metaphysical imponderables, and backed uneasily away from a man who, they knew instinctively, would enjoy nothing more than backing uneasily away from them. Compare Tunney's reasonable statements of calculated probablity with the innocent philistinism of Dempsey's 'I wanted to be a prizefighter, and win the Championship of the World. Even going to college mustn't interfere with that,'[5] and it becomes clear why the boxing public never forgave the triumph of the metaphysician over the philistine. In any case, during those years of Dempsey's undisputed sway, when Tunney was persisting with his theories, experienced judges knew perfectly well that the reasoning process has a peculiar habit of disappearing at the very moment when most needed. Where, for instance, was Corbett's expert fighting brain at that watershed in boxing history when Fitzsimmons sank his left jab into the champion's solar plexus? The precise answer has been provided by of all people P. G. Wodehouse, who has correctly observed that:

> Of all cures for melancholy introspection a violent blow in the solar plexus is the most immediate. If Mr Corbett had any abstract worries that day at Carson City, I fancy they ceased to occupy his mind from the moment when Mr Fitzsimmons administered that historic left jab.[6]

What the pundits could not possibly have known was that with Tunney, there had finally arrived the exception who proved the rule. Here was a remarkable, perhaps unique fighter, who could apparently divorce intellect from muscle to the extent of watching his own performance with a dispassion which took no account of physical pain at all. No more remarkable testimony to the poise of a reasoning brain exists throughout the entire literature of sport than the description by Tunney, the ironist, of his notorious first contest with a light-heavyweight rival called Harry Greb. Greb was a rough, uncompromising, one-eyed ex-middleweight with whom Tunney fought a series of brutal and bloody contests. Later whenever the belittlers, angry with Tunney for having so tactlessly destroyed their hero Dempsey and then compounded the crime by behaving so casually about it, were tempted to equate his fastidiousness with lack of courage, there were always the Greb fights to pull them up short. Nobody who could outface Greb as Tunney outfaced him could be lacking in those qualities of raw bravery which will usually endear a fighter with the mob more passionately than all the recondite skills of the noble art. Greb was the only

professional boxer who ever defeated Tunney, so it is natural
that Tunney should never have forgotten the details:

While training for the Greb match I had the worst possible
kind of luck. My left eyebrow was opened, and both hands
were sorely injured. I had a partial reappearance of the old
left-elbow trouble which prevented my using a left jab. . . . In
the first round of the fight I sustained a double fracture of the
nose which bled continually until the finish. Towards the end
of the first round my left eyebrow was laid open four inches. I
am convinced that the adrenalin solution that had been
injected so softened the tissues that the first blow or butt I
received cut the flesh right to the bone.

In the third round another cut over the right eye left me
looking through a red film. For the better part of twelve
rounds I saw this red phantom-like form dancing before me.
I had provided myself with a fifty percent mixture of brandy
and orange to take between rounds in the event I became
weak from loss of blood. I had never taken anything during a
fight up to that time. Nor did I ever again.

It is impossible to describe the bloodiness of the fight. My
seconds were unable to stop either the bleeding from the cut
over my left eye, which involved a severed artery, or the
bleeding consequent to the nose fractures. Doc Bagley, who
was my chief second, made futile attempts to congeal the
nose-bleeding by pouring adrenalin into his hand and having
me snuff it up my nose. This I did round after round.

At the end of the twelfth round, I believed it was a good
time to take a swallow of the brandy and orange juice. It had
hardly got to my stomach when the ring started whirling
round. The bell rang for the thirteenth round; the seconds
pushed me from my chair. I actually saw two red opponents.
How I ever survived the thirteenth, fourteenth and fifteenth
rounds is still a mystery to me. At any rate the only
consciousness I had was to keep trying. I knew if ever I
relaxed, I should either collapse or the referee would stop the
brutality.

After the gong sounded, ending the fifteenth round, I
shook hands with Greb and mumbled through my smashed

and swollen lips, 'Well, Harry, you were the better man tonight!' and I meant that literally.

Harry missed the subtlety of the remark, for he said, 'Won the championship,' and was dragged away from me by one of his seconds, who placed a kiss on his unmarked countenance.

I discovered through the early part of that fight that I could lick Harry Greb.[7]

The modest self-assertion of that concluding sentence gives some idea of the kind of trouble lying in wait for Dempsey. So far as Tunney was concerned, each opponent presented an abstract problem, a cryptogram of boxing style to be cracked by research and analysis. He would digest the nuances of that style, become familiar with its mannerisms, memorise the path through the labyrinth of its permutations. Then sift, select, synthesise; and finally settle on his counter-measures to comprise a grand strategy of containment, control, domination. For all the savagery of Harry Greb's approach to his chosen profession, and his none too fastidious regard for the rules of infighting, he was just one more conundrum to be resolved.

We can only marvel at Tunney's detachment, and wonder what the crowds watching the massacre would have made of it all, had they had access to the thoughts whirling round inside his much battered head. They would surely have dismissed him as a lunatic and jeered at his presumption. But Tunney was right, as usual, and the boxing profession utterly, hopelessly wrong. As the series of Greb–Tunney fights proceeded, so was the balance subtly adjusted, until in the final confrontation it was Greb and not Tunney who was put to the sword, Greb who was led away by his handlers, Greb who was patently no match for an opponent superior in every department of the boxing art. In the moment of his astonishing triumph over Greb, as he saw his theories so gloriously vindicated, Tunney must have acknowledged to himself only one slight misgiving. The mastery over Greb had taken several bouts to establish; no such luxuries would be accorded to anyone who fought Dempsey. One defeat would signal the end of all hopes, as it had for Willard, for Firpo, for Carpentier. In approaching the ultimate riddle of his

career Tunney knew he would have to get it right at the first
attempt or never.

Over the years his dossier on the great Dempsey steadily grew.
Dempsey was the dragon he would one day have to slay, and so
he became an analytical St George, studying every aspect of the
monster's reflexes and working out his own careful counters
with an ingenuity which would have met with the full approval
of Donnelly in his Panton Street crammer. In Jersey City on
the night of the Dempsey–Carpentier fight, his own bout
successfully concluded, Tunney crouched under the ropes, a
nonentity snubbed by the mob, convinced that one day it would
be he, and not Carpentier, who would be confronted with the
riddle of Dempsey's style. What he saw that night confirmed his
view that the champion would be beaten only by speed and an
immaculate defence. A big Mike Gibbons. But there was still
something missing from the equation, something ineffably
Shavian, something closely linked to the theory of the Life
Force. Tunney, being the kind of creature he was, had yet to find
a way of rationalising his own irrational belief in his superiority
over Dempsey.

Perversely he found the answer in the very aspect of
Dempsey's style which terrified everyone else, his killer instinct.
Nobody who saw Tunney in a ring would ever describe him as a
savage fighter. Certainly he lacked the killer instinct himself and
admitted as much, or rather, denied possession of it: 'I found no
joy in knocking people unconscious or battering their faces. The
lust for battle and massacre were missing.' And it was here that
Tunney was poised at last on the brink of the great philosophical
revelation that would sweep him to the championship. Tunney
concluded that 'the killer instinct was really founded in fear, and
that the killer of the ring raged with ruthless brutality because
deep down he was afraid.' From here it was only a short step to
'deep down he was afraid of me',[8] and from that point Dempsey,
like Johnson and Willard before him, was a doomed man.

Tunney noticed one other thing in the Carpentier fight. In the
second round the Frenchman had momentarily reversed the
roles of victim and executioner by hitting Dempsey hard on the
jaw with a perfect right hook. This was the moment which Shaw
had described, in terms of Dempsey's luck, as 'like that of the

batsman who skies the ball into the hands of mid-on, and sees it slip through his fingers'.[9] Tunney, however, was not so impressed, and actually felt that the stroke of luck had been Carpentier's in delivering the blow, rather than Dempsey's in surviving it:

> I was in a position to see the punch clearly and note how Carpentier delivered it. He drew back his right like a pitcher with a baseball. The punch was telegraphed all over the place. Yet it landed on a vulnerable spot. How anybody could be hit with a punch launched like that was mystifying to one who understands boxing. It was a vivid demonstration that the champion could be hit with a right.[10]

Notice how Tunney the supreme rationalist is unable to conceive the possibility of a clumsy punch ever finding its target, how he admits bewilderment that the powers of the intellect should be thus deceived, even for the split second that it takes for a punch to reach its destination. It was a bewilderment Tunney was to experience at least once more in his boxing life, as we shall see.

Tunney knew that in order to defeat Dempsey he needed speed, skill, and courage, all of which he possessed, and a little more weight, a deficiency which time would adjust. He needed the belief he was the better man, and now he had that too, ever since his revelation that all killers are cowards at heart. There remained that right-hand punch to unsettle the champion as Carpentier had unsettled him. This Tunney did not have. He had always been recognised as a relatively light hitter, not because he was unable to punch his weight, but because when he did so his hands were too brittle to take the strain. And so Tunney, the good Shavian, having learned by now that the Life Force can make a weak muscle strong if only the mind appreciates the urgency of the need, took himself off to Canada for the winter to chop trees, strengthening the resistance of his hands through constant use of the axe, the comedy being heightened by the fact that all this time the boxing world, oblivious of Tunney's grandiose schemes, continued smugly on its way, unaware that a man who was the very negation of all it stood for was about to snatch its most coveted prize.

In retrospect it is rather surprising that Tunney should have continued to draw so many jeers. Nobody apart from Greb had ever got the better of him. He advanced to take the World Light-Heavyweight Championship which Carpentier had once flung away in such profligate fashion against poor Siki, at which point the Shavian context of his rise begins to become confused. On 24 July 1924, in New York City, Tunney knocked out Carpentier in the fifteenth round, and it was after this triumph, of the new Cashel over the old, that Shaw became convinced that Tunney was destined to bring Dempsey down. When he told Tunney as much, the boxer was highly flattered and asked Shaw for his reasons. 'Because', Shaw is supposed to have replied, thinking back no doubt to Paquito and the old days in Panton Street, 'of the way you ride punches', to which Tunney made the most astonishing response in the history of boxing: 'I learned that trick from Cashel Byron'.[11]

The romance was out in the open at last. With that one breathtaking remark, Tunney was staking his claim as the first prizefighter in history to train by a philosophic concept, although it is doubtful whether even he could quite have appreciated the degree to which the situation had by now matured into high comedy. There was Dempsey, stalking the ring like a hungry tiger, punching all and sundry into a pulp, and there was his quietly relentless challenger, reading the classics, modelling himself at least in part on a Victorian pugilist who had never existed, and telling himself that Dempsey was surely fated to play Paradise to his Byron. An astounding scenario, with no conceivable impediment to its acceptance as the most bizarre combination of art and sport in the modern era.

Except that it isn't true. The reported exchange between Shaw and Tunney on the theme of Byron's efficacy as a practical model comes from a memoir composed by Blanche Patch, one of those Shavian biographers who shares with St John Ervine the unfortunate belief that the biographer is more interesting than his subject. As Shaw's secretary from 1920 until his death thirty years later, Miss Patch was ideally placed to observe the nature of Shaw's friendships, and that a conversational exchange between Shaw and Tunney approximating to her version did take place seems highly probable. What is wrong with the story is that it makes Byron an accessory *before* the fact of Tunney's triumph instead of after it. The distinction is profound, because it was only after the event that Tunney appears to have succumbed here and there to the temptation to use his renown as the fighting ratiocinator as a means of entrée into literature, telling the panjandrums of that eccentric principality what he thought they would like to hear instead of what he had to tell them. Miss Patch's location of the Shaw–Tunney exchange cannot possibly be the right one, because at the time he was challenging for Dempsey's crown Tunney had never been introduced to Shaw. It was only later, in the summer of 1928, after the curious anti-climax of his farewell contest against an indifferent performer called Tom Heeney, that Tunney was summoned to the presence.

But although Miss Patch's reporting is not strictly accurate, it might just as well have been. Events proved Shaw and Tunney to be right on all counts. When the champion finally stepped into the ring with his unusual challenger, in Philadelphia on 23 September 1926, it was Dempsey who showed signs of nervousness, while Tunney, who had been discovered by delighted reporters reading *The Way of All Flesh* on the eve of the contest, was in just the right mood to deal with father-figures. The contest was the most widely-publicised and the most fulsomely reported in the history of pugilism. Seven years before, when Dempsey had, in the expressive phrase of Ring Lardner, 'made big Jess sit down seven times in one round',[12] the gate receipts had amounted to just under half a million dollars. The first Dempsey–Tunney fight drew 130,000 people who paid nearly two million dollars for the privilege of witnessing – what?

It has often been forgotten that although in terms of professional precedence Dempsey was very much the senior figure and the undisputed star of the show, in fact the two men were perfectly balanced opponents. Tunney was slightly the younger, having been born on 25 May 1898, a year after Dempsey, but in all other details the two fighters were very nearly mirror-images. When they stepped into the ring at Philadelphia, Dempsey had had 77 professional contests,

Tunney 73. Both men stood six feet one inch; Tunney weighed 192 pounds, Dempsey 191. Both men had a reach of 77 inches, both had a fist of 11¼ inches, both had a chest measuring 42 inches. And yet no two opponents have ever been more utterly dissimilar in temperament, in attitude, in style. The gulf between the two types of which each man was the apogee was perhaps even wider than the one dividing Corbett and Sullivan. Dempsey was a man's man, a fighter's fighter. What he did was comprehensible even to the most uninformed rubberneck at the back of the cheap seats; he hit people very hard very often until they fell down; he was afraid of no man, and a great many men were very much afraid of him. He was the All-American hero, the straight-dealing, hard-punching, uncomplicated sporting idol of a continent. When Ring Lardner attended the 1921 Disarmament Conference and made a joke to that effect, he was echoing the sentiments of every red-blooded American male; having suggested that it might not be a bad idea if all the battleships in the world were sunk and all the guns and bombs thrown away, Lardner observed, 'That would leave every nation in the same position, namely without nothing to fight with except their fists. And we have got Dempsey.'[13] Even the most illiterate individual knew, without quite knowing how he knew, that in Dempsey and Tunney two antipathetic American types were squaring off. In a story called *Broadway Complex*, Damon Runyon[14] used this essential difference between the champion and his challenger as a short-cut for defining the personality of one Cecil Earl, a saxophonist who suddenly takes to hitting people:

> Well, the next time I see Cecil he comes into Mindy's again, and this time it seems he is Jack Dempsey, and while ordinarily nobody will mind him being Jack Dempsey, or even Gene Tunney, although he is not the type for Gene Tunney, Cecil takes to throwing left hooks at citizens' chins.

And so the last stage of Tunney's five-year-plan was executed with godlike detachment. The obscure ex-Marine who had watched so carefully when Dempsey put Carpentier away in four rounds, was at last in Carpentier's place; this is his description of what then happened:

The bell rang! The fight was on!

Dempsey cautiously advanced to meet me in the centre of the ring and, after a little fiddling, he started a left hook, which I leaned outside of. We clinched and were broken by the referee. Again Dempsey had a left hook, this time a little wider than the first. Again I slipped it by leaning outside. We clinched again. There was little in-fighting. Dempsey was warming now to the business of defending his championship. I was cautiously waiting the chance in accordance with my plan.

After some more fiddling and a feint by me, Dempsey responded with another left hook, which was a little wider and longer than the last. This time I *stepped* outside.

In the front row sat Mike Trant, of the Chicago Police Department, Dempsey's bodyguard. Mike did not like me – he had read in the newspapers that much of my spare time had been given to books. That, in Mike's opinion, was a proof of weakness.

'Come on, Jack', he bellowed, 'knock the big sissy into my lap.'[15] Strong words. But, alas, Mike was immediately ejected from the stadium by a small tenor-voiced usher.

With my back to the ropes, I slipped and blocked five or six blows that Jack threw in my direction as he followed me. Neither of us had yet landed a clean blow. Both had landed several light blows in the clinches. The referee was between us now. I circled around the referee to the centre of the ring, and Dempsey, following on his toes, leaned slightly forward as though teetering off balance. I sensed he was thinking that he would have to lengthen the left hook in order to nail me as I stepped back when he led it.

My object in stepping outside and backing up was to make the champion believe I was nervous and afraid. This was different from the brazenness of my statements before the fight. A new psychology altogether. I hoped by making him think that I was scared of him, he would get a little anxious to hit me and finish the job. I wanted him to become a little over-confident.

We were out in the centre of the ring now. The moment had arrived for me to come out of my shell and attempt to win the fight. I felt comfortable as I dug my right heel into the canvas for a firm foothold. I feinted him once, he blinked. I feinted him again. Thinking that I was again going to step outside of his lead, he took an extra hitch for more length as he started his left hook. As it came, I stepped in, instead of out, and with everything I had in my right hand hit Jack on the cheekbone. Shucks, too high for a knockout! His knees sagged, and in the short exchange that followed he was very unsteady and dazed. He later said that if I had followed up this advantage I should have won the fight in the first round. I did not follow up my advantage, but Jack had not been ten years in the ring for nothing. He covered.

That first blow won the fight for me. Jack was very ineffective after that. He hit me but one hard blow during the whole contest; it was a terrific left hook in the sixth round, landing on my Adam's apple. The cartilage was pushed into my throat and lacerated the mucous membrane on the side. I coughed blood and was hoarse for several days.

When the decision was rendered at the end of the tenth round, Jack, with the assistance of Gene Normile, Philadelphia Jack O'Brien, and another handler, was helped to the centre of the ring to shake hands with his conqueror. It was a splendid gesture, and his muttered message of 'All right, Gene! Good luck!' was most touching. He was on the verge of collapse.

The fight attracted the largest crowd that ever attended a sports event up to that time; 145,000 came from all corners of the globe. After the excitement in the dressing-room subsided, I went to a small hotel and had several pots of tea. At the end of a few hours conversation, I went to bed quite weary. I was soon asleep.

Upon awakening in the morning, I wondered if the proceedings of the night before had been a dream. It was hard to believe that I was the world's heavyweight champion. My thoughts went back to the early days in France; to the later struggle in getting started after my discharge from military service. I thought of the first time I met Jack Dempsey, coming across the Hudson on a Jersey Central ferryboat. He was gracious, kindly, and mirthful. I was a young unknown kid, just starting. Though there were only eleven months difference in our ages, it seemed like the king and the page-boy. He was generous, democratic, and invincible. He looked the part of the great champion he was. The consciousness of his position did not keep him from sitting with the unknown beginner during the twenty minutes it took to cross the river. That was the first impression I had of Jack Dempsey, and the most lasting. I pictured him as he was led from his corner, battered, bruised, and blind from his own blood to the centre of the ring to congratulate his conqueror. What a contrast!

I thought that one day a young pugilist would dethrone me as I had Dempsey. I felt how sincere would be my gratitude if, on the following day, when all the shouts and cheers were for my conqueror, he would take a few minutes out to drop in to see me. I decided that, though the world might have started forgetting the king that was, I would drop in some time during the day to pay my respects to the fellow that had been so thoughtful and considerate to the kid on the ferryboat one day back in 1920. He had still one championship that had not been at stake at the Sesquicentennial Stadium. He was still that champion to me.

When I told my desire to a friend, he said, 'What a great newspaper story that will make!'

'No, unless it can be done quietly, it won't be done at all', I remarked. Sometime after lunch, I went to the Adelphi Hotel, where Dempsey's party made its headquarters. I was ushered up to a suite of rooms. After passing through four or five doors. I found myself in a large sitting-room. In it was Gene Normile, dishevelled and weeping, in a silk dressing-gown. He was in his bare feet. Before him was a half-empty bottle of Scotch whisky. Tommy Laird, a San Francisco newspaper man, and Jerry the Greek, Dempsey's trainer, were the only others I knew. I was not in the room two minutes before I experienced for the first time the resentment that some of the experts and followers of boxing felt over my defeat of Dempsey.

Jerry, in his broken English, kept saying, 'You canna licka the chump'. He continued to repeat this until Gene Normile made it plain to Jerry that he would not have 'a guest of his insulted in such a way'. Poor Jerry was heart-broken over Dempsey's defeat. Normile sat there, a pathetic figure in contrast with the contented, witty fellow whom I had first met in California who, upon telling me that Wills had no chance to get a match with Dempsey, said, 'I put the sacks in on the spade' (meaning that he had eliminated Wills as far as consideration from Dempsey went).

There was great confusion in the room. Somebody had gone to another part of the hotel to inform Dempsey that I had stepped in to see him. The messenger came back and asked me to follow him. I climbed a flight of stairs, walked through a long hall with several turns, and was led into a room that was empty. I was advised to sit down. Dempsey would be in presently. In about five minutes Jack came into the room from the hall. He looked the worse for wear. Unless my face after the first Greb match was as bad looking a sight as his, I have never seen its equal. He seemed heartbroken over the loss of his title. Hearing from me that he had hit me some hard blows, he seemed to cheer up a bit.

As I was leaving, Jack said wearily: 'Gene, your troubles are just beginning, whether you know it or not. Every time you turn round you'll find a process-server.'

I took my leave with the thought that I had never known a more gracious loser. I was soon to learn that Dempsey was right. Not to stint myself with regard to troubles, I made mistake after mistake. I seemed to enjoy making them. At one time I had four lawsuits against me aggregating 2,150,000 dollars.

The first three, two blackmailers and a bootlegger, left the jurisdiction of the state after instituting proceedings. The fourth, a bookmaker, went to trial, and after hearing evidence for ten days the jury returned a verdict in my favour in twenty minutes.

A good lawyer is more important to a champion nowadays than all the managers. I am convinced that had the law firm of Chadbourne, Stanchfield and Levy not taken over my affairs, at the behest of Dudley Field Malone, who had to return to his European practice, the parasites would have left me penniless.

The following day, at a luncheon in my first contact with Metropolitan newspaper men after the fight, I made the error of criticising their attitude toward my victory in a smarty-smarty manner. This may have been justified, but it certainly was unwise. Practically overnight I became the most unpopular of all the heavyweight champions. Had I been at all diplomatic, this friction with the newspaper men might have been avoided. Moreover, looking back from this distance I could have been a more gracious winner. I goaded and gloated. I richly deserved what I got. There seems to be a curious attitude in public psychology with regard to champions. Most of the champions become unpopular. None to my knowledge, however, ever received the almost general disapproval as rapidly as I did. This was new to me.

I got my first real demonstration of it in Madison Square Garden about two weeks after winning the championship. The Metropolitan Boxing Writers' Association presented belts to both Dempsey and me emblematic of the world's heavyweight championship on this occasion.

They had not been able to make the presentation to Dempsey while he was champion because of his ineligibility in the State of New York which forbade his getting into a ring anywhere in the state.

Dempsey, who exactly six weeks earlier was actually booed out of Madison Square Garden because of Harry Wills' presence, now as an ex-champion was cheered. I, his conqueror, was jeered. Before I left the ring I had planned a psychological defence for all future jeers. Climbing through the ropes, I was unable to suppress a smile.

I had determined that for the next booing I should get fifty cents of every dollar the booers paid for the privilege. In the future there would be no free boos. I never entered a boxing ring again until I retired unless I was given fifty per cent of the gate receipts! I broke this rule once or twice away from New York.

Those first few months of crown-wearing developed a martyr complex. I imagined myself as Atlas with the worries of the world on my back. Fortunately, I gradually began to see the ridiculousness of this attitude. I was lending too much

importance to the new position. Justifiable ridicule helped me
to see light.[16]

Tunney's admission of hubris, and his subsequent rejection
of his own behaviour, although it smacks rather of the histrionics of a converted sinner at a Revivalist meeting, would
certainly appear to have some basis in fact, for less than six
weeks after his ordeal at Madison Square Garden, he was
actually belittling the very father-figure of his philosophic
ascent, Shaw himself. In the aftermath of Tunney's sensational
victory, the entrepreneurs of America quickly adjusted to the
new facts of life. It was obvious to most of them that although an
unorthodox character in the boxing context, Tunney was, in his
own way, just as marketable a commodity as Dempsey, and in
one respect much more so. For when a man can talk as politely
and think as clearly and read as fluently as the new champion
evidently could, there is no reason why you should not attempt
the conversion from pugilist to thespian. After all, there was the
memorable precedent of Jim Corbett. With such thoughts in
mind one of the intellectual giants of the emergent motion
picture industry, one Jesse L. Lasky, decided that the property,
*Cashel Byron's Profession* was there; the actor, Gene Tunney, was
there; the author, Bernard Shaw was there. All that was required
was for Jesse L. Lasky to bring the interested parties together
and a box-office bonanza would be assured. At which point
Tunney of all people laughed Lasky – and Shaw – out of court.
In the *New York Sun*, 20 November 1926, there appeared the
following account of negotiations:

> Gene Tunney might be prevailed upon to play Cashel Byron
> in the proposed film version of George Bernard Shaw's *Cashel
> Byron's Profession* – provided the scenario did not follow too
> closely the text of the book.
>     'The character of Cashel Byron is badly drawn', said the
> heavyweight champion, 'and the story is silly. Frankly, I had
> not read the book until there was some talk of my making the
> picture, and I was very much disappointed in it.' The scene
> was Tunney's suite at the Hotel Breslin; the time, yesterday.
> The interview was prompted by the sight of a copy of the book
> in question on Gene's dressing table, coupled with a

recollection of the recent news that Jesse L. Lasky had cabled an offer of 75,000 dollars to Shaw for the motion picture rights to the novel. Lasky set forth that he intended to star Tunney in the film and Shaw countered with a suggestion that, if his price of 100,000 dollars be met by Lasky, the role of the villian in the piece be assigned to Jack Dempsey.

'When Shaw conceived the idea of writing a novel around a boxer, he had a splendid opportunity but he missed it', Gene continued. 'In the beginning of the book there is a promise of fine things to come, but the promise is not fulfilled. Shaw understands neither the temperament nor the psychology of the professional boxer, with the result that Byron is made to appear as no more than a blundering vulgarian. There are no gentlemanly traits about him, save a dash of chivalry. He scarcely is a character to excite the admiration of anyone and that the girl in the book, reared in an atmosphere of culture and refinement, should fall in love with a man whose only appeal was a magnificent body, is absurd.

I regard Shaw as the possessor of one of the greatest minds among living men – possibly the greatest – and *Cashel Byron's Profession* must be viewed only as a product of his immature years. He would be incapable of writing such a book today. I certainly would not lend myself to the filming of the book as it is written. I would insist that the scenario merely be based on the story, as is done in many film versions of famous works. Under such an arrangement, Byron would be a stronger, finer character and the story would proceed along more rational lines.

Having been challenged by the champion, Shaw promptly entered the ring and ended the contest in the first round. His official biographer, Archibald Henderson, writes:

Shaw blandly replied that he shared Tunney's disapprobation of *Cashel Byron's Profession*, which was undoubtedly an immature work; confessed that Tunney doubtless knew more about present-day prizefighting than he did; and urged Tunney to go ahead and rewrite the book, if he thought he could improve it.[17]

Lasky's project faded away, and Tunney's response to Shaw's whirlwind assault has never been revealed. But while it is interesting that in criticising the novel Tunney was inadvertently disclosing that he had hardly grasped its central proposition at all, and while it is downright comical that he of all fighters should believe that well-bred young ladies are not susceptible to the appeal of rippling biceps, there is something much more fascinating about the interview in the *New York Sun*, the confession that 'frankly, I had not read the book until there was some talk of my making the picture'. In the light of Tunney's brilliant performance as an autodidact, his interest in Shaw, his assiduous determination to do his cultural homework, and his preoccupation with the social status of the modern prizefighter, it seems almost unbelievable that he should have reached the watershed of November 1926 before reading Shaw's novel.

There is one other tiny fragment of evidence to suggest that just possibly Tunney's tendency to dissemble in the face of literary distinction may have been as considerable as the deadly accuracy of his perceptions regarding Dempsey's strategic vulnerabilities. Another, quite independent witness has disclosed an incident involving Tunney and a literary lion which suddenly lights the stage of the Cashel Byron drama. The American writer Garson Kanin, in recounting various aspects of his friendship with Somerset Maugham, reports a conversation in which Maugham describes the compliment to his writing which he treasures the most:

'A compliment that stays in my mind is the one paid to me by your Gene Tunney. He told me – I can't remember where – probably when I was staying with Billy Phelps. William Lyon Phelps, wasn't it? While I was staying with him in – ?'

'Probably New Haven,' I suggest.

'Yes, I suppose it was. And Mr Tunney came to call one day and surprised me by telling me that when he was in training for his fight with Jack Dempsey the only book he read was *Of Human Bondage*. He won the fight, didn't he?'

'Yes.'

'That's what makes it a compliment, don't you see? If he'd lost it wouldn't have been a compliment at all.'[18]

The disclosure suddenly reveals the vista of a priceless literary comedy, with Tunney the pugilistic suppliant at the court of cultural respectability, wandering through the snuggeries of Bohemia even as Cashel Byron once wandered through the drawing rooms of Belgravia, and telling the same tale wherever he goes, amending only its central detail in accordance with the identity of the great man he is telling it to. It is a picture, not altogether displeasing to those who feel sometimes that perhaps the twentieth century is inclined not to pay its respects to its most gifted literary creators, of Tunney hunting down H. G. Wells and telling him that the road to victory over Dempsey was paved with the heroism of Mr Polly in his routing of Uncle Jim; of confessing to Arnold Bennett that the triumphs in Philadelphia and Chicago were inspired by the impudence of Denry Machin; of confiding to Conan Doyle, who in 1909 had graciously declined the offer to referee the fight between James J. Jeffries and Jack Johnson, that the downfall of Dempsey had been effected by an alliance between the forces of Sherlock Holmes' ratiocination and Rodney Stone's physical fitness. The possibilities are endless, and it is a pity that Tunney has never hinted as to their extent.

However faulty Blanche Patch's memory may have been, it is at least certain that by the time Dempsey went into training for his comeback attempt, Tunney was by now thoroughly conversant with the plot and dialectics of *Cashel Byron's Profession*. On 21 July 1927 Dempsey knocked out a heavyweight called Jack Sharkey and settled down for his final preparations. Tunney presumably went on reading. As for Shaw, he was involved in a pugilistic controversy yet again, this time with the tiddlers of the middleweight division. Earlier that month the world champion Mickey Walker had come to London to give a spectacular beating to the local challenger, Tommy Milligan. Walker was the very embodiment of pugnacity, a man so incensed at being knocked out one night by Harry Greb that after the fight he followed his conqueror to a night club, caught up with him in the car park, waited till Greb had his overcoat half-off, and then in his own expressive words, 'I let him have it'.[19] It was this propensity to playfulness which had inspired the sporting press to nickname Walker 'The Toy Bulldog'. So far as

poor Milligan was concerned, Walker might just as well have
been a real bulldog for all the chance he had of holding off
Walker's violent attacks. Milligan's defeat was followed by
considerable uproar from assorted armchair warriors who had
never themselves thrown a punch in anger, among them Sir Hall
Caine, who had been disgusted, not by the sight of the carnage
(he had not attended the contest), but by reading the reports in
the newspapers the following day. On 10 July 1927 the *Sunday
News* went and asked Shaw what he thought of it all:

At the outset let me say that I am entirely in sympathy with
Hall Caine. On his information he was right. And in so far as
the spectators of the fight (of whom I was not one) may have
seen it as his informant described it, his objection to it is quite
valid.

But I can reassure him on one point. The cruelty of the
business is imaginary. I do not mean that the combatants do
not hurt each other. But they suffer nothing that is not in the
day's work of a hard-trained athlete in any sport. No
reasonably hardy youth has ever been deterred from boxing
by the pain it involves, or, what is worse, the exhaustion.

The two scullers who rowed themselves clean out at Henley
the other day must have been in far worse plight than either
Mr Milligan or Mr Walker when they shook hands after the
count-out.

Most boxers if offered an oar in the University boatrace
would probably decline on the ground that they prefer a less
arduous form of sport in which, whenever the strain becomes
too great, they can always repose on the floor for nine
seconds, besides having compulsory rests every three
minutes. Mr Walker may, for all I know, disapprove of
football as savage and dangerous: certainly he could make
out a very good case for that view. The knock-out, for which
all pugilists strive nowadays, far from being painful, is the
most perfect known anaesthetic, and leaves none of the
unpleasant after-results of chloroform.

To the greener spectators who have never had a turn with
the gloves, it may seem that the combatants are raining
smashing blows on one another; but the percentage of these

punches that gets really home is known only to the combatants, and is always very small.

Nobody who has not tried has any idea of how hard it is to plant an effective hit on a boxer, though I have seen two men without any knowledge of the game attack'one another ferociously in the street, and in thirty seconds pulp one another into a condition that would scare Messrs Dempsey, Tunney and Carpentier into the nearest monastery. No doubt sensation hunters who pay £10 to see something terrible like to believe that something terrible is happening; and the showman who takes the £10 naturally does not try to cure their delusion; but if they knew how little the combatants are the worse for all the punching, they would demand their money back.

Therefore, I beg Hall Caine not to waste his sympathy. If he and I, when we were Mr Milligan's age, could have got half as well paid for our successes as he for his defeat, we should have thought ourselves on velvet. The Puritan who objected to bear-baiting in Sackerson's time was on firmer ground when he said that it was not the pain to the bear but the pleasure to the spectators that was damnable.

If the spectators believe that what they are witnessing is not a trial of skill between two athletes who have no quarrel with one another and bear no malice, but a savage encounter like a dog fight, then beyond question the spectacle is demoralising. And if journalists who know nothing about boxing write dog fight descriptions of the contest, they spread the evil. I therefore suggest that Commander Kenworthy be asked to introduce a Bill making it a punishable offence for a newspaper to order or publish any description of a prize fight until they have sent for a professional boxer and made the writer spar a bye with him, and obtain from a couple of competent judges a certificate that he at least knows his right hand from his left.

As to the organisers of the spectacles, I should urge them to confine their engagements to really accomplished boxers, bearing in mind that there is nothing so tedious as second-rate boxing, and that as to mere slogging exhibitions, which have neither the brutal realism of a genuine fight nor the

interest of a skilled game, I can guarantee them to reduce Sir
Hall Caine to a condition of such deadly boredom that even
disgust would be a relief.

What killed the ring again and again in the nineteenth
century was not the brutality of the fighters (for the spectacle
of Sayers bunging up Heenan's eyes as Nat Langham had
bunged up his own, cannot have been so very dreadful), but
the appalling dullness of most of the fights, complicated by
the blackguardism of pugilistic business at that time, which
went to the length of poisoning poor Heenan.

As to the illiteracy of the ring, it is not safe to count on it
nowadays. Pugilism is unquestionably a literary taste; the
wonder is that Sir Hall Caine has never acquired it. There is
something in it that appeals irresistibly to the romantic
coward that is in all of us. Even the boxers themselves wield
the pen today. Mr Norman Clark, an ex-welterweight
champion and a well-known boxing referee, has written not
only a treatise on boxing but a popular exposition of the
Kantian philosophy. Carpentier's autobiographical sketches
are so vivacious and individual that it is impossible to believe
that they are manufactured by his press agent. And Mr Gene
Tunney, who was very nearly lured into engaging himself to
appear in a film based on a boxing novel of my own, saved
himself at the eleventh hour by reading the novel, and
showing himself a sound critic by promptly pointing out that
it was quite unsuited for the purpose.

These literary pugilists are the only ones that can keep an
audience awake when they are boxing. The American boxer
of today feeds the newspapers with articles not only on his
punch, but his psychology. He will presently be expected to
have a University degree, carrying strings of letters after his
name, followed by a list of the books he has written.

To sum up, I do not think Mr Cochran need share Sir Hall
Caine's humane concern about the sufferings of Mr Milligan;
but I strongly advise him to consider, in view of the fact that
the best and cheapest view of a glove fight is from a
comfortable fauteuil in a picture house, whether the ring is
not likely to be pitched in a studio in future, instead of in the
midst of a vast collection of people who have more money

than brains, and can never in the nature of things get the sanguinary sort of value they pay their ten-pound notes for.

Shaw's gentle lampoon of the literary-pugilist type, of which Tunney, for all Shaw's pretence to the contrary, was the sole representative, may have helped the new champion to curb the propensities of his own rampant ego, but what Tunney never seems to have realised is that no matter how humbly he might have conducted himself after the toppling of Dempsey, he would still have felt the same cold wind of hostility. His victory had been followed by national uproar, although at this distance of time it is perhaps difficult to grasp the sheer enormity of what he had done. In overthrowing the great Dempsey, he had contradicted the myth of an entire generation, and nobody ever really forgave him for it. In bars across America drunks sat sprawled in the small hours, staring down into empty glasses commiserating with themselves for the irretrievably lost youth which the passing of Dempsey seemed to symbolise. All those breezy philistines in the tales of Ring Lardner, with their quaint habit of dating the flowering of their own manhood from the day when Dempsey had sent big Jess to the cleaners, gaped at the awesome sight of Jack on the wrong end of the punches and thought, perhaps for the first time in their lives, of the approach of middle age. Just as Corbett before him, in dethroning Sullivan, had politely ushered into history all those harmless braggarts whose hand, they said, had once shaken the hand of John L., Tunney had debased the coinage of hero-worship.

As for his own public image, Tunney, always slightly contemptuous of the Dempseyesque lineaments of the sporting folk hero, had hardly bothered with it at all, adhering instead to the naïve belief that so long as he won his contests with skill and courage, people would admire him. The result was, as it slowly dawned upon him, that he was destined to become the least-loved of all the great prizefighters of the modern epoch. Gradually he came to see the nature of the blasphemy he had perpetrated. The 1920s in America were the years of sporting giantism, years when grown men shed sentimental tears at the mere contemplation of Bobby Jones's putter, when a college football star like Red Grange, having been raised up by news of a petition nominating him for Congress even though he was under age, could be brought down again by an audience with President Coolidge, when heroes like Dempsey and Babe Ruth were inflated by manic publicity into superhuman symbols for whom the normal laws of survival had no application. For any one of these idols to have revealed human frailties was unthinkable, and so besotted did their followers become, that there grew up a general current of opinion which insisted that the man who excels in sport can excel in anything. And now that one of the gods had been brought down, the crash reverberated across the continent.

It is an interesting illustration of the indomitable illogicality of this blind folk-worship that Dempsey, who had once been the object of some extremely unkind publicity through his failure for one reason or another to get himself into the armed forces during the First World War, should have been deified by the nation, while his conqueror, who had served dutifully in the Marines, was rejected by the same public. And yet there was something understandable about this judgement. The instincts of the mob were sound after all. Tunney's bearing and conduct hinted strongly at a deep-seated belief in his own superiority. The public sensed this and reacted accordingly. It respected his courage and admired his professionalism, but it was not sorry to see him go. As the most acute American boxing writer of the period put it:

> The fighter who dethrones a pugilant hero has a hard struggle to win popular acceptance thereafter, as readers of Pierce Egan have reason to know. The microcosm is a worshipper of demigods, like the larger world around it. Gene Tunney is belittled to this day, particularly by fans who never saw him, simply because he whipped Jack Dempsey.[20]

At the time of the fall the boxing world recoiled in stunned horror. It had seen Dempsey reduced to shambling impotence in Philadelphia. At the end of the ten rounds Tunney had emerged an easy points winner, and many expert witnesses felt that had the fight been scheduled for twelve rounds instead of ten, then Dempsey, impaled time and again on the end of Tunney's left jab, must surely have been counted out. It hardly needs saying that among the experts who felt this was Tunney himself.

But the sporting brain, and the soul which influences its judgement, are irrational things. In spite of the onesidedness of the contest in Philadelphia, the boxing fraternity refused to believe what it had seen. There must have been some awful cosmic error. The great Dempsey outwitted, outpunched, outfought? It was not possible. Ask Willard, and Firpo and all the rest of them. It simply was not possible. Something had gone seriously wrong with the working of the universe that night, something which only a return contest could rectify. The second Dempsey–Tunney fight was arranged to take place in Chicago, a year less a day after the first one; shrewd psychologists looking for straws in the wind no doubt took note of the nonchalance with which the new champion agreed to give Dempsey another chance.

The second Dempsey–Tunney fight remains the most famous in the history of professional boxing. 145,000 people paid more than two and a half million dollars to watch it. Two thirds of them, in the outermost seats, did not know who had won when the fight was over. Forty million Americans listened to a blow-by-blow commentary over the radio; during the controversial seventh round, five of those listeners dropped dead from heart failure. But the fight has become famous for quite a different reason. What happened was that for a split second Paradise got on top. For the first six rounds Tunney swept elegantly into a huge points lead. And then Dempsey, probably in desperation, lashed out and knocked Tunney down. In that moment when Tunney went tumbling, the recent past of both men crowded into the ring, and because Tunney's past was the better assimilated, the more profoundly understood, it was Dempsey who was fated to defeat. Had he only remembered the outcry after his destruction of Willard eight years before, perhaps he might have thwarted the Life Force after all. But the rule obliging a fighter to retire to a neutral corner while the referee is counting over his fallen opponent was antipathetic to everything Dempsey stood for. He was a killer or he was nothing, and when the prey was sighted primeval instincts took control. In his excitement Dempsey persisted in standing over the fallen Tunney. The referee rightly refused to begin counting until the ex-champion had removed himself and by then five seconds had passed, vital seconds in which Tunney was able to gather his scrambled wits.

But while Dempsey was losing the battle with his own temperament, Tunney was winning his. Lying on the ring floor this extraordinary man quietly cogitated on the novelty of his predicament. It is often forgotten that this was the first time in his life that Tunney had ever been knocked off his feet in the ring. All his professional life he had regarded the problem of what to do once he arrived there simply as one more hypothetical question to be answered like any other, and he had finally reached the conclusion that if ever he were knocked down, he would stay down for as long as possible. A hotblooded hero, a Dempsey, might leap to his feet immediately to show everyone he was not hurt. But Tunney sat there while the crowd howled themselves into hysteria, and coldly reasoned that once your opponent has obliged you to take a rest, it would be foolish not to extend that rest for as long as the rules permit. So he stayed down, watching Dempsey and the referee performing their frantic choreography.

Tunney has always insisted that at the count of 'Two', that is to say, after he had been down for seven seconds, his head cleared and left him perfectly capable of rising and continuing to outbox Dempsey. But why should he? As he remarked later, 'I'd take the full count, of course. Nobody but a fool fails to do that.'[1] In any case, even knocked off his feet, Tunney had not the slightest doubt that he was the better man. This was no more than a momentary embarrassment which could not possibly affect the outcome; Tunney wasted precious little time thinking about it. For there was something else troubling him as he sat there, another emotion altogether, which was preoccupying him to the point of distraction; his own bewilderment, the same bewilderment that had so shaken him seven years before when he had watched Carpentier hit Dempsey with that haymaker right hand. How had he arrived at this unprecedented juncture in his affairs, sitting there while Dempsey and the referee pushed and shoved each other around? How had such a disgraceful event come about? How on earth had Dempsey actually managed to hit him?

To me the mystery has always been how Dempsey contrived to hit me as he did. In a swirl of action, a wild mix-up with things happening fast, Jack might have nailed the most perfect boxer that ever blocked or side-stepped a punch, he was that swift and accurate a hitter. But what happened to me did not occur in any dizzy confusion of flying fists. In an ordinary exchange Dempsey simply stepped in and hit me with a left hook.

Had Tunney been taking a breather when the catastrophe happened? Was he feeling weary? Had his strength been sapped by the force of Dempsey's attacks? On the contrary:

It was in the seventh round. I had been outboxing Jack all the way. He hadn't hurt me, hadn't hit me with any effect. I wasn't dazed or tired. I was sparring in my best form, when he lashed out.

Writing in retrospect of this awful moment of truth, Tunney works himself into a paroxysm of self-loathing:

For any boxer of skill to be hit with a left swing in a commonplace manoeuvre of sparring is sheer disgrace. It was Dempsey's most effective blow, and I knew how to evade it, side-step or jab him with a left and beat him to the punch.

Tunney now tries to explain to himself how this thing happened, looking wherever he can for the rational explanation which he believes lies behind every event in the universe, or at least inside the boxing ring:

I didn't see the left coming. So far as I was concerned, it came out of nowhere. That embarrassed me more than anything else, not to mention the damage done. It was a blow to pride as well as to the jaw. I was vain of my eyesight. My vision in the ring was always excellent. I used to think I could see a punch coming almost before it started. If there was anything I could rely on, it was my sharpness of eye – and I had utterly failed to see that left swing.

Or, as Cashel Byron had put it long ago to Lydia Carew, 'I know what a man is going to do before he rightly knows himself. The power this gave me, civilised me.'[2] But Byron's system had never gone wrong; Tunney's has, and there must be a solution of this mystery. Finally it occurs to him:

The only explanation I have ever been able to think of is that in a training bout I had sustained an injury to my right eye. A sparring partner had poked me in the eye with thumb extended. I was rendered completely blind for an instant, and after some medical treatment was left with astigmatism which could easily have caused a blind spot, creating an area in which there was no vision. Our relative positions, when Dempsey hit me, must have been such that the left swing came up into the blind spot, and I never saw it.[3]

Having settled the matter to his own satisfaction, conveniently ignoring in the process the fact that the blind spot is a natural optical phenomenon present in all human beings, fit or otherwise, Tunney goes on to other things, leaving his readers to recall that after the pregnant seconds of the Long Count, he rose as the referee intoned 'Nine' and outboxed Dempsey with ridiculous ease for the rest of the contest, leaving him almost helpless at the final bell, 'sticking it out with stubborn courage'.

After one more fight Tunney retired undefeated – like Byron – and although there was no estate for him to inherit, he had actually gone one better. In the last three years of his ring career he had earned a total of 1,742,282 dollars, and now, at last, he was able to enter the last act of the drama. He began by giving a course of lectures on Shakespeare at Yale University, went for a walking trip in Europe with Thornton Wilder, married a young gentlewoman from Greenwich, Connecticut, and, after a honeymoon away from America, issued a prepared statement with which a great many professional boxers of the period would have been hard put to understand, let alone find time to disagree with:

It is hard to realise as our ship passes through the Narrows that fifteen months have elapsed since the *Mauretania* was carrying me in the other direction. During those fifteen months Mrs Tunney and I have visited many countries and have met some very interesting people. We thoroughly enjoyed our travels, but find the greatest joy of all in again being home with our people, and friends.

The echo of a rumor at home that I am contemplating returning to the boxing game to defend the heavyweight championship reached me in Italy. This is in no sense true, for I have permanently ended my public career. My great work now is to live quietly and simply, for this manner of living brings me most happiness.[4]

Tunney was to prove as good as his word, attempting to intervene neither in the protracted quadrille of mediocrity which the boxing authorities were obliged to stage in order to settle the issue of the succession, nor in the endless post mortems on the two Dempsey fights on which the profession embarked. But if Tunney remained aloof, most other people could not resist the temptation to savour again in retrospect the sensational events surrounding the World Heavyweight Championship of 1926–7.

At this point there enters the last of the philosopher-athletes to embroil himself in the melodrama, Norman Clark, a distinguished ex-amateur welterweight champion and, at the time of Tunney's retirement. a certified referee and secretary of the British Boxing Board of Control. Clark, as Shaw had reminded Sir Hall Cain, was the author of a book of Kantian philosophy, and also wrote another work entitled *How to Box*, a work whose sentiments place their author unmistakably on the side of the thinking boxer against the natural puncher. Some of Clark's analogies are slightly alarming, as for instance his attempt to prove that boxing is a reasonable process:

> As Socrates once said, on seeing a young man daily struggling to develop himself into a Hercules: 'What's the good of it? If you become the strongest man on earth, you won't be any stronger than a bullock, and what's the good of that?' Thus, the only manner in which man can make himself athletically superior to the beast is by conscious physical control and more all-round adaptability of instinct, and the true test of any sport is how far it requires this. Thus, cricket and boxing are high-class, rowing and running low-class: nothing is clearer.

On the contrary, nothing is less clear than that a Paavo Nurmi or a Herb Elliot is 'low-class' compared to any other athlete, but Clark, in a gallant attempt to prove his point, flirts recklessly with the muse of zoology when he asks:

> Could we train any 9-stone ape or aboriginal to outbox Jim

Driscoll? In all these things it is athletic adaptability to some special mode of athletics that consists of continuous change; and in such work as this we find the human organism, matched weight for weight with anything in the animal world, would be more than able to hold its own.

Gracefully sidestepping the problem of whether it would be possible to train a 9-stone Jim Driscoll to outrun Paavo Nurmi, or even a small dog, Clark continues:

The process by which it would do it is mind, and whether this would be a greatly conscious mind, as in the case of C. B. Fry, or simply a wonderful mode of natural adaptability, as in the case of Sam Langford, makes little difference.

Clark further believes that boxing is

the best all-round exercise and cleverest of sports, and considered in its highest aspects, as a test of speed, skill and stamina between two clever exponents, is one of the prettiest, most strenuous and graceful athletic spectacles.

There is one other reflection of Clark's of particular relevance in the context of any discussion of the relative merits of Dempsey and Tunney. In rejecting the conventional idea of the fighting instinct as 'a ludicrous blood passion that makes men see red, swell purple, and generally fill the air with blood and thunder', Clark nominates instead the theory of the calm at the centre of the whirlwind, and defines it quite beautifully as 'the intense determination of the highly strung man – a determination that increases rather than diminishes under punishment.' Who is the exemplar of this type?:

'A Frenchman made of ice', someone once called Carpentier, and the phrase covers all essential in the boxer's psychology.[5]

Clearly Clark is the kind of man who will warm to the technical control of a Gene Tunney, while remaining undaunted by the prospect of a dialectical duel with a Bernard Shaw. In the New York *Evening Post* for Saturday 27 April 1929, there appeared the following description by Clark of his visit to 10 Adelphi Terrace:

The room was very tastefully furnished. The pictures were mostly landscapes by Sartoris, with one by Flandrin. There were portraits of Descartes, Einstein, Schopenhauer, Nietzsche, Strindberg, with a stack of photographs which, on being turned over like a pack of cards, proved to be portraits of Rodin, Wells, and Shaw himself, with several caricatures. But I had not the time or the presence of mind to examine the things at all carefully. Suddenly the door swung open and a tall, very upright man bounded in, all eyes and fluffy beard and so full of pleasant vitality that his entrance seemed like pulling up the blinds on a sunny spring morning.

'Ah, here we are!' he exclaimed, his eyes still dancing as he shook hands briskly. 'You have made a mistake in coming to see me.' I was about to stammer an apology, but he waved me into a settee, and settling himself into his chair, added, 'In the theatre there must always be a certain amount of give and take, you know. What would become of your great boxing shows if the spectators knew how few blows were getting home, and what limited damage they really did? Well, it's the same in my profession. You should always avoid seeing the artist, if possible.' Then he lay back in his chair, wreathed in the kindliest smiles, and I thought of Max Beerbohm's 'Magnetic! He has the power of infecting others with the delight he takes in himself.'

But despite his vivacity and easy charm, Shaw struck me as somewhat shy; or, more accurately, he was conscious of my shyness, and this had much the same effect on him as when you address him as 'Sir'. He therefore took refuge in a flood of conversation, in which he showed that he had read all the letters and writings I had sent him, and remembered them quite well. 'You say in your article on my *Cashel Byron's Profession*,' he started, evidently choosing the subject to put me at my ease, 'that I am wrong when I say that pugilistic genius is no more remarkable than respiration or, say, the bees building their hive. Well, why am I wrong? The boxer's assets are ability to judge and time blows, and select almost instantaneously the right move at the right time, and this is just as instinctive as the processes I mention. No doubt the ability is rarer: there are a thousand men who can breathe to every one who can effectually knock another down. But this does not alter the essential nature of the process, as you show clearly when you talk about "having a man guessing", meaning, in effect, that you have him beaten because his conscious mind is arresting his subconscious.'

Then after a pause he added, 'It is not very different with other types of ability. Give me an arithmetical sum to do, and after filling a slate with figures for half an hour I will give you the wrong answer, but give it to a born mathematician and he will solve it as quickly and surely as Shakespeare or myself would find ideal words to express some particularly subtle thought or feeling. The main characteristics of any specific ability are that it comes easy to those who possess it, and is remarkable in proportion to the number of creatures who do not possess it.'

'But are not different types of ability of different standards?' I suggested.

'Ah, that's a different question,' said Shaw. 'Broadly, values of specific types of ability may be judged in three ways – their rarity, their commercial value and how they stand in the evolutionary scale. Jack Johnson's profession when it carried no money with it used to be regarded as the lowest profession; but if money alone is the test it should now be logically superior to mine or the Astronomer Royal's. Yet from the evolutionary standpoint, the Astronomer Royal and myself may perhaps be pardoned if we claim superiority over Jack Johnson.'

'And what of utility?' I asked.

'More difficult still,' Shaw replied. "The shipbuilder doubtless feels he is of more use than an astronomer, but without the latter his ships could not be navigated, while without me people would not know what to think of themselves.'

I asked Shaw if he ever went to boxing contests nowadays.

'Oh, very rarely,' he replied with a smile. 'Before I wrote *Cashel Byron* I used to frequent the old Queensberry contests at Lillie Bridge and the early boxing association contests at the old St James's Hall, which grew out of them, with a poet friend of mine, who, like all poets, had an incorrigible passion for fighting. The chief arenas then', Shaw explained, 'were Bob Habbijam's school of arms and Bill Richardson's Blue Anchor (immortalised in my *Admirable Bashville*); but I never went to these places. The National Sporting Club did not then exist, and I have never witnessed a fight in it. The most brilliant boxer of that day was Jack Burke; but he was killed in a bicycle accident. It was an exhibition spar of his that suggested the exploits of Cashel Byron.'[6]

'Then there would be Ned Donnelly, the royal professor,' I suggested, 'who, when commanded to appear before the king, immediately bought a new top hat and frock coat.'

'I knew him,' said Shaw. 'He taught all my friends. Ned Skene, in *Cashel Byron's Profession*, owes something to him.'

'And the greatest Birmingham amateurs, Tom Hill and Anthony Diamond.'

'Diamond? Yes; I remember him well,' said Shaw. And he then told me that there was a formidable amateur, brother of a well-known scholar and publicist who competed in the Queensberry heavyweight championship one year and had a walkover. He then entered for the Association championship at St James's Hall. On that occasion Diamond, having already won several lightweight championships, was due to box in the middles but found someone boxing he did not want to meet, so jumped up into the heavies and was drawn against the Queensberry giant.

'The big man hadn't a chance. Being a gentleman, he wouldn't make a bull rush and commit murder; and Diamond was so much too quick for him that it was a relief to everyone when one of his gloves came off and had to be replaced.' Diamond won the competition easily and impressed G.B.S. as being among the best boxers he had ever seen. I suggested that an exhibition like that perhaps made him feel boxing was rather a brutal sport.

'Oh, boxing is rarely more distressing than running a mile or rowing in a boat race,' Shaw answered. 'It was the bloody-minded newspaper reporters who gave that impression, just as it was the people who clamour against the cruelty of the ring who are incidentally the best propagandists for its box office. A bruise soon healed and the jaw knockout, far from being painful, was the most perfect form of anaesthetic. No; I gave up going to boxing because I found the second-rate boxing one usually sees so tedious; whilst as to mere slugging exhibitions, which have neither the brutal realism of a genuine fight nor the interest of a skilled game, these reduced me to such a condition of deadly boredom that even disgust would have been a relief.'

Shaw, however, was persuaded to recall the glimpses in 1918, when Carpentier met Beckett at the Holborn Stadium, and apparently was much struck with the Frenchman. Writing me shortly afterwards, he said, 'I am gratified to find that your estimate of Beckett as being centrally a sensible chap (and not fitted for fighting), tallied with mine. Carpentier is a genius *hors concours*, not comparable with boxers like Mitchell, because he is not really in the same street with them. The transfiguration which takes place when he stands up to fight is amazing; he becomes a being of a different order. A great boxer would rise to him and say, "Here at last is the sort of antagonist I want." An ordinary boxer would be frightened out of his wits. Joe the Sensible did not concern himself either way. Carpentier's second lead was like the kick of a thoroughbred horse in the face; Beckett shook his head violently to convince himself it was still on his shoulders and not halfway down Holborn. If the fourth blow, a straight right, had not got on the fatal spot anything might have happened, for it looked as if Beckett could simply wear out Carpentier's fists with his head and then pummel his way to the end or even bring off a knockout on his own account. As it was, Beckett as a boxer did not exist. He might as well have been a punching ball.'

Carpentier evidently revived Shaw's interest in boxing, for he has since followed – on the film – the careers of Dempsey and Tunney. The latter visited him at his town house when in London quite recently, and the pair had a long talk together. Shortly afterward I happened to meet Shaw in the street, and he described to me how favourably Tunney had impressed him, and also gave his opinion of him as a boxer. It occurred to me that this would make an excellent addition to my interview; so I wrote it up as well as I could remember it, and sent it to Shaw with a request that I might be allowed to publish it.

But Shaw, apparently, insists on protecting his guests from any nice things he says about them; and he will not on any account have words put into his mouth, even when, in broad effect, they represent what he said. In due course there came the following letter:

4, Whitehall Court,
London, S.W.1.
21st February, 1929.

Dear Norman Clark,

It is quite out of the question for me to give to the press anything that passes between me and my private guests, or to criticise them in public in any way.

Besides, you have not got the hang of Tunney at all. On the evidence of the films I should say that he is an extraordinarily difficult man to hit. Carpentier's rights looked as fatal as ever, but as they produced absolutely no effect they cannot have got home. Tunney never crouches, always has his head as far back as it will go, and has a peculiar biff that stalls off every attempt to rush him. He systematically gets away and makes his opponent miss until disappointment and exhaustion have brought him down to a condition of definite inferiority. When Dempsey, after these get-aways, had him against the ropes and managed to get his arms round him for his terrible rabbit punch, Tunney simply held him until the referee interposed, in spite of every arm-breaking trick that Dempsey knew. His confidence in himself and his system amounts to something like contempt for his most famous adversaries: reputations cannot frighten him: personalities cannot hypnotise him: he does not need to be a brilliant boxer like Carpentier or a terror like Dempsey; he wins by mental and moral superiority combined with plenty of strength, an inaccessible head, and that very disheartening biff that sickened Dempsey when he rushed for an apparently certain victory after the count in the seventh round. With Tunney's character Carpentier could have beaten Dempsey. Carpentier never looked like a baby in Dempsey's hands though he was smashed in the first ten seconds, but Dempsey, in the first fight with Tunney, after the first two rounds, did look like a schoolboy larking with an instructor. I never said to you that Tunney was the only big man who could box. I don't know that he can box better than you can. In an exhibition spar with soft gloves Carpentier could outshine him. He does not knock out his opponents; he wears them out. In short, he is neither the smartest boxer nor the hardest puncher of his time; but he certainly is the most remarkable character, and it's by character that he has won. You might say that he wins because he has the good sense to win. Fifty years ago he would have had too much good sense to be in the ring, but today no other profession could have done as much for him.

There! You see it's no use trying to report me unless you take it down in shorthand. An attempt to paraphrase me only ends in twaddle.

Faithfully,
G.B.S.

I much appreciated Shaw's kind and interesting letter. But I cannot allow what I wrote to be described as twaddle; and if he persists I shall disqualify him. In effect, his letter neatly endorses what I said; namely that Tunney is essentially orthodox in his methods, and (regarding Carpentier as scarcely a heavyweight) the only big man since Jack Johnson who can really box. Of course, I quite agree with G.B.S. when he says, 'I don't know that Tunney can box any better than you could'; that was to be expected. But to follow this with the statement that Carpentier would outshine Tunney with soft gloves is not only to make an unjustifiable assumption, but to cast an uncalled-for reflection on me. I refuse to say any more on the matter. Shaw is evidently trying to create mischief among three great pugilists. He was very keen to protect Tunney from me; now, it seems, I have to protect Tunney from him.

Tunney kept his own counsel, then and later. Instead of debating his own status with those who could never affect it one way or the other, he cultivated the Shavian connection.

The prolonged exhibition spar between Gene Tunney and Bernard Shaw began in the late summer of 1928 when Tunney, having dispatched Heeney and gone into sporting retirement, arrived in London to be guest of honour at a dinner arranged by Sir Harry Preston, whom Tunney described as 'a sort of unofficial host for sporting England'. In his account of the affair, decorously withheld until the year after Shaw's death, Tunney claims a familiarity with the Shavian canon mildly surprising in view of his reported failure to encounter *Cashel Byron's Profession* until the last year of his boxing career. Either he had spent the bulk of 1927 and 1928 catching up with the plays, or his earlier acquaintance with them had not led him on to the novels. Whatever the condition of his Shavian scholarship, there is no question that Tunney was intrigued at the inclusion of Shaw's name among the forty dinner-guests:

> Among those who had been invited was George Bernard Shaw; that beguiled me particularly. I had seen and read Shaw's plays, and I knew of his interest in boxing. He had sparred a good deal in his youth, and certainly few eminent men of letters could approach his knowledge of the ring. Furthermore, we had once before exchanged comments in a way that greatly stimulated my desire to meet him. In a newspaper interview I had expressed a low opinion of his novel about a prizefighter, *Cashel Byron's Profession*; when another reporter passed my words on to Shaw he remarked: 'If Tunney said those things, he must have good taste. I'd like to meet the young man.'[1]

But on the night of the dinner Shaw was on the French Riviera, and sent Tunney a note expressing his regret at not being present. Tunney replied and Shaw responded with another letter. The correspondence was under way:

31st Agusut, 1928

Dear Mr Tunney,

On Tuesday next I leave here and change to Hôtel La Résidence, Geneva, Switzerland. I shall stay there until the middle of the month. I must return home about the 15th.

If you are still on this side of the Atlantic then, give me a hail, and I will fix up a meeting if you are not by that time tired of literary people. Not a word of this to any living soul or we shall be dogged by cameras, microphones and journalists. I take it that we are both desirous of complete privacy.

You might drop me a line to Geneva as to your movements. I do not know where you are, so am addressing this to the American Express Co; which is usually a sure fire for visitors from America.[2]

But Tunney was unable to extend his visit long enough to await Shaw's return from the continent. Four months later, however, he returned with Mrs Tunney to London, after holidaying in the Adriatic island of Brioni. From Brioni he wrote to Shaw telling him of his coming visit to London to present a trophy to the Royal Marines on behalf of the United States Marine Corps. On his arrival in London in December, Tunney found a note from Mrs Shaw advising him of a luncheon arranged for the following day:

It was at this luncheon that we met for the first time. The luncheon was an extremely pleasant one, and in the course of it we described Brioni to the Shaws with considerable enthusiasm. Later, they made a few enquiries of their own, and wrote to Brioni for reservations; when we returned from a Mediterranean trip we discovered to our surprise that they were registered at the hotel.

We also found on our arrival that an enterprising distiller in Zara had sent me a case of cordials. Practical jokes have always been a failing of mine, and the cordials provoked me to play a trick on G.B.S. Knowing him to be a confirmed teetotaller, I sent the case of cordials to him under an assumed name, just to see what he would reply. With it, I enclosed a note in broken English, professing my great devotion and expressing doubts at the reports that so great a man abstained from alcoholic beverages. Because it seemed more appropriate to the comedy, and since I was certain that Shaw wouldn't check, I pretended the case contained fine wine. This was Shaw's response:

24th April, 1929

I appreciate your kind intention in sending me a case of wine, but I must return it unopened, as I drink nothing but water. May I add that as I am here on a holiday I prefer to leave my public character behind me, and to be treated as far as possible as a quite private and unknown individual.[3]

In spite of Tunney's perverse sense of humour, his family and Shaw's spent some weeks together at Brioni, during which time Mrs Tunney fell ill, recovered, and, after the Shaws had gone home, suffered a relapse:

30th May, 1929.

My dear Gene,

We got a fright about you on the way from Spoleto to Venice. Just before we left Pola the captain said – quoting an Italian paper – that Mrs Tunney had had a relapse. We both felt that we must jump off at Brioni, to offer moral support if nothing more solidly useful. But the captain then added that in the masterly hands of the Italian doctors from Trieste and Rovigno a complete cure had been effected and an 'out of danger' bulletin issued.

On this we decided to continue our voyage; but as there was on board, bound for Brioni, a pleasant old bird named Sinton, who slaps the whole world on the back and fears not any man, I gave him a card for you, knowing that he would slap you on the back anyhow and introduce himself as Sinclair Lewis's Dodsworth.

On the *Morosini* an Italian colonel was so interested in you that I told him in my best Italian that the secret of success as a pugilist is – on your authority – to be afraid of being hit on the head. He and the whole captain's table – we were at dinner – immediately explained to me most kindly that my Italian is not correct, as I said exactly the reverse of what I meant, which was of course, that the heroic Tunney was totally indifferent to the most terrific punches on his frontispizio. However, on my declining to accept this construction, and pointing out to the colonel that if you were hit on the head you were knocked out, whereas if you hit the other fellow on the head you were victorious, he became thoughtful and said that this had not occurred to him before, and that it was true and original!

The Danieli is palatial but frightfully exposed to noise. After three nights of it we can sleep through anything. We shall stay another week anyhow. Our love to Polly.[4]

Shaw delighted in Tunney's company, using him as a kind of walking allegory of his own theories about the Distribution of Income:

I have two friends: Dean Inge and Gene Tunney. What auctioneer is going to value their relative worth in pounds or dollars? At present Gene can buy Dean Inge up ten times over without overdrawing his bank account. Is that distribution an ideal one?[5]

Something else which appealed to Shaw's sense of irony was, as in *Cashel Byron*, the paradox of a famous athlete eclipsing in renown the world's greatest thinkers and artists:

I was staying on an island off the Adriatic with Gene Tunney, the boxer, and Richard Strauss, the composer. When all three of us walked together all eyes turned our way, but when Strauss and I walked alone, nobody took any notice.[6]

Being Shaw, he could not resist the afterthought, 'Very few people have an eye for greatness.' But Tunney served a more practical purpose, for he appears to have been very nearly the only man alive who could persuade Shaw to stop working:

Three years after the victory over Dempsey, the Shaws and the Tunneys brightened for one another a gloomy holiday which the four of them happened to be taking in Istria. 'Tunney has just blown in,' G.B.S. told me on a postcard announcing their arrival. 'We are both very well and getting a real rest,' added Charlotte. 'The island is dull, but that is good for us! Mrs Tunney has been very ill and given us a great fright but we think she will be all right now.' They both got bored with the cold and rain; even G.B.S., now seventy-five, complained, which was unusual for him, of having to walk a mere eighth of a mile, in the teeth of the 'bitter bora', from their quarters to the dining-room. 'There is nobody here that we know,' he told me, 'except Gene Tunney. A settled melancholy, peculiar to the place perhaps, devours us.' There seemed to be nothing for it but to dash off another play; but Gene came to the rescue. 'Mr Tunney is a most wonderful help,' Mrs Shaw commented, gratefully. 'He takes Mr Shaw off to the polo ground, or the golf course, or sailing, or something, and so keeps him from writing, which is splendid.' Through the years they remained in touch with one another: on the day after Shaw's ninety-third birthday Gene went down to Ayot and told him round by round of Mills' fight against Lesnevich the night before. He was astonished that the old gentleman knew as much about each of them as he did, astonished too to find him so hale, 'as clear as a bell', in his nineties. Ayot looked like becoming a Mecca for boxing men: Joe Louis too was eager, perhaps not unaccompanied by a press photographer, to make the pilgrimage.[7]

In 1930 the ghost of Cashel Byron was raised yet again. The idea of a moving picture adaptation had never quite died, and now it was floated once more, in the vastly differing circumstances of an industry swept into confusion by the practicality of adding sound to pictures. Naturally it was Tunney whom Hollywood approached, but Tunney had no interest in the project, although 'I felt I ought to transmit the proposal to the author. The reply was most interesting, since it included Shaw's own opinion of the characters in the book, as well as the surprising information that at one time he had played with the idea of writing a film expressly for me.'[8] Shaw's response to the overture also reveals that all those years ago, when James J. Corbett had skittered through the role on

Broadway, Shaw was perfectly well aware of what had been done to the book:

Easter Sunday, 1930.

My dear Gene,

The Cashel Byron proposals are only blind snatches at your publicity and mine by people who don't know the book and couldn't judge it if they did. There is not a single really likeable character in it: Cashel, though honest and super-competent professionally, is selfish and limited; the lady is a prig and a bluestocking; his relations with his egotistical actress-mother are odious; the other girl is humiliated by her poverty and has to marry a man she doesn't respect; and the only real hero in the plot is the footman Bashville; in fact I made him the titular hero when I had to dramatize the novel in a burlesque to keep Corbett's travesty out of London.

In the Corbett version, which I read and never saw, Cashel was played off – so I was told – as the Long Lost Heir of a noble family. That is just the sort of game they would have to play with C.B's P. to make it what they call sympathetic; but the result would not be a success; or, if it were, it would be so unlike the book that they might just as well change the names as well as the natures of the characters and put it up as a new and original scenario by Young Kipling Snooks. They would spoil it by putting a championship fight in it. Now you are one of the few men on earth who cannot be filmed in a sham fight, because you have been filmed in no less than three real ones of the first order; and a stage one after that would be unbearable.

At Brioni I amused myself one evening by inventing quite an amusing boxing film for you; but it was a movie; and since then the advent of the talkies has upset everything. I could not produce genuine American dialogue even if I had time, which will not occur for many months, as I am working to distraction preparing a complete collected edition of my works for America, and when that is through a new play to succeed *The Apple Cart* is pressingly wanted.

I think Charlotte has written to Polly. Whether or no, give

her my love; and come, both of you, to see us when you next
land on these shores, first thing.[9]

Having squashed the Cashel Byron idea, Shaw soon after
found himself obliged to squash another. Tunney had decided
to become an author himself, and began work on an account of
his boxing career. In time the American publishers, Houghton-
Mifflin, sold British rights to Jonathan Cape, who naturally felt
that a preface by Shaw would immeasurably increase the book's
commercial attraction. The request was passed back to Tunney,
who conveyed it to Shaw, knowing instinctively that in refusing
the request, the arch-dialectician would surely give a brilliant
exhibition. Tunney was proved correct, and commented later,
'His reply was a masterpiece, both for the finesse with which he
rejected a request that was really too much, and for the shrewd
criticism of my book. The letter is a classic of its kind.'[10]

My dear Gene,

I have read the book. Have you ever read the autobiographies
of George Fox, the founder of the Quakers, and Samuel
Wesley, the founder of the Methodists? They are very
remarkable books about very remarkable men (especially
George, who was a magnificent fellow); and as such they must
be read. But there is one difficulty about reading them
without skipping. The daily work of George and Samuel was
to sail into every town they met on their journeys and literally
raise hell (and incidentally heaven) in it. George sometimes
tried to pass peacefully through: but it was no use: before he
could get away the church bells were sure to ring; and then, as
he says, 'they struck on my heart'; and back he went to 'the
steeple house' all out, and let them have it all in. Even Charles
II saw as plainly as Cromwell that in some sort the spirit of
God was in the man.

Wesley left the steeple house alone, but took on everyone
outside it, from drunken bullies and blackguards to Beau
Brummell, one down and t'other come on, in his fights for
salvation. So far, it is all very exciting.

But you are finally forced to confess that the sameness of
their experiences makes you feel after a while that you are not

getting any further. Only a small percentage of the meetings differ from the rest by some exceptional incident or the appearance of some interesting historical character. You brighten up when Fox is imprisoned, and are relieved when he discovered osteopathy by resetting a broken neck in America and thereby restoring a dead planter to life. Wesley becomes so unreadable that you skip to Beau Brummell.

Now you may ask what the devil all this has to do with your biography. Well, just as one prayer meeting is very like another, one fight is very like another. Just as at a certain point in Wesley's biography I wanted to skip to Beau Brummell, there was a point in yours at which I wanted to skip to Dempsey. Your appalling industry as a boxer involved an unconscionable number of fights with opponents who never succeeded in making themselves interesting to the general public as Carpentier did and as Dempsey did mainly by beating Carpentier.

And you greatly underrate the interest taken in Carpentier. You see him only when he was like a pithed cockerel after he made the fatal mistake of clinching with Dempsey in the very first exchange and being rabbit punched. If he had studied Dempsey and fought him as you fought him, he would probably have beaten him easily on points and possibly knocked him out, although his terrible right hand punch may not have been what it once was. Up to the moment when you knocked him out, he seemed to be putting up a much better fight against you than Dempsey did (though I suspect the film I saw was cut), though he was obviously not up to your weight and reach. You do not see him as Europe saw him; and you even speak of him as 'the little Frenchman' though he was quite big enough for anybody and was very well built for boxing.

Now as you know most about it, I have no doubt that your values as between Carpentier, Dempsey, and the less popular boxers who gave you more trouble, are quite right – for the moments at which you fought them. By all appearances Dempsey was overtrained when he first met you, and just right when he met Carpentier. Carpentier had married and gone comparatively soft when he met Dempsey, and seemed like a lightweight giving an exhibition spar against you, just as Dempsey with his fiddling and feinting looked like a schoolboy fooling with an instructor. But you know – in fact you say so in the book – what an amazing difference there is between the figure cut by one and the same boxer when he has his opponent easily in hand and when it is the other way about. Your valuation of C and D is not the same as that of the public that remembers their victories. All you know about them is that you took their measure and wiped the floor with them. You came, you saw, you overcame. By doing so you inevitably belittled them, and have taken less credit for your victories than a completely objective historian would give you.

This is the only criticism I have to make; and it is in the nature of the case and could not have been avoided. The book will also suffer a little in general readability for being less an autobiography than a professional record. Charlotte, who is much interested in you, and not in the least interested in boxing, declares that she cannot understand a word of it, and, I suspect, deplores your misspent and violent youth. But at your age an autobiography is impossible: there are too many of your contemporaries alive. By the way, I should get a lawyer friend if you have one, to read the MS. carefully for libels. You are rich enough to be a mark.

As to a preface, whenever a publisher suggests that, sock him in the solar plexus. Of course he wants to trap my circulation on top of yours; but when you want a publisher for your next book on the strength of this one they will all declare that your first book does not count as it was the Shaw preface that sold it. It is the greatest insult an author can be offered to send for another author to help. Your publicity is greater than mine – you may remember that at Brioni, when I was talking to Richard Strauss, nobody troubled about us until you joined us; and then the cameras came with a rush – but if a publisher intimated to me that he would not touch a book of mine unless it had a preface by Gene Tunney, I should summon the last scrap of my failing strength and jump on him until we both were dead. I must stop now: the village post is departing. Our love to Polly.[11]

Having been rebuffed in their request for a preface, the publishers saw instantly that in the form which it took, the rebuff was more delicious than any preface could ever be, and asked permission to use it for promotional purposes. Tunney having refused to co-operate, the publishers turned to Shaw himself, with results which Shaw describes in a postcard to the Tunneys written in December 1932, pertaining to the coming invasion of the United States:

> We start for our cruise around the globe on the 15th. It is now the night of the 12th; and I have about three months work to get through before we embark. We shall just touch San Francisco, where W. R. Hearst will fly me to Los Angeles with a night at his ranch on the way. Then through the canal to the Atlantic, where we touch New York at noon on the 11th April and recoil at noon next day. I shall no doubt have to allow myself to be exploited a bit during that 24 hours, if only to insult America in a broadcast.
>
> I have told Cape he may use anything he likes of mine, subject to your consent, for publicity. It's bringing coals to Newcastle; but I have no objection on earth; my reservation was as to a preface, for the reasons given. Our love to both of you. Is Polly quite well again?[12]

As the years passed, the Tunneys and Shaws made it a practice to meet whenever the logistics of their respective careers permitted. In this way Tunney came to know a succession of creative artists he might otherwise never have encountered, including H. G. Wells, Sir John Lavery and John Collier. The ex-champion's pursuit of culture was no less relentless than his old pursuit of Dempsey. He worked hard at it, although he soon found that not all the world's literary lions were quite so amenable as Shaw, Maugham and Wilder. In effect Tunney was having to cope with the identical prejudices which had so rankled with Cashel Byron in his quest for Lydia Carew. There was Max Beerbohm, for instance, who seems to have proceeded on the assumption that so long as he belittled his own pretensions, this somehow gave him the licence to belittle everyone else's. Max had no time at all for the careful correctitude of Tunney's responses to beauty. After meeting the ex-champion at Shaw's home, Beerbohm told a friend:

'G.B.S., you know, loved prizefighters,' he said. 'He had a deep regard for prizefighters. One night, he invited me to Adelphi Terrace to meet a great countryman of yours in that field – Mr Tunney. Charming man, delightful man. Not at all what you would have expected. I mean, you would never have guessed his profession from his conversation. It was so literary, you know. The windows of G.B.S.'s flat looked out over the river, and the sun was setting. Do you know' – Max leaned forward – 'Mr Tunney took me by the arm and led me to the windows and compelled my attention to the beauties of the sunset? I had never – no, I think I had *never* before met anyone so militantly aesthetic. I felt I could not reach his level, I could not match his appreciation. When he left, I felt he must have an impression of me as somewhat soulless.'

Max didn't want me to have this impression. He leaned forward just a little more and made a confidential comment to me on the incident. When Max reached the climax of a story, the little pauses, the little intakes of breath, were not hesitations, they were the beautifully timed dynamics of crescendo. 'You know,' he said, 'I cannot be considered a coarse person . . . and yet . . . you know . . . I had to strain every nerve . . . to meet . . . *that* sensitivity.'[13]

Beerbohm's account of the meeting with Tunney is at least as comic as Beerbohm intended it to be, although not quite for the reasons Beerbohm intended. The real joke raised by his conduct on being presented to Tunney is that many years before, in his capacity as dramatic critic of the *Saturday Review*, a post which Shaw had relinquished to him three years before, and for which he somehow contrived to reconcile a distaste for the duties involved with a retention of them for twelve years, Beerbohm had reviewed the publication by Grant Richards of *Cashel Byron's Profession* at six shillings. In the course of the review he made several dogmatic pronouncements about the nature of prizefighters whose wit and sagacity are compromised only by the small detail that they are all utterly wrong:

Take Cashel himself. Mr Shaw means to present him as a very stupid young man with a genius for pugilism. But soon he turns out to be a very clever young man, with a genius for introspection and ratiocinatory exposition. These powers are not incompatible with a genius for prizefighting. But quite incompatible with it are physical cowardice and lack of any sentiment for the art practised. Mr Shaw makes Cashel a coward, and lets him abandon prizefighting without a pang at the first opportunity, in order to prove his thesis that prizefighting is a mere mechanical business in which neither sentiment nor courage is involved. As usual he goes further than the truth. It is untrue that prizefighters are heroes and artists and nothing else, as the public regards them. But it is equally untrue that you can use your fists (gloved or ungloved) without courage, or that any man with supreme natural ability can care nothing for the channel in which it exclusively runs. Thus Cashel does not credibly exist for us: he is the victim of a thesis. Besides, he is Mr Shaw.[14]

There is some poetic justice in the fact that thirty years later, Beerbohm should have found himself confronted by the living refutation of all his arguments; predictably, having been confronted by it, he chose to ignore it. Beerbohm had no experience of either prizefighting or the fighting temperament, otherwise he would have known that the cowardly boxer, so far from being an impossibly Shavian paradox, is a commonplace inside the profession, and that to retire when you have saved enough money is less evidence of cowardice than of an instinct for self-preservation. As Tunney had carried out in real life every one of the impossible things whose feasibility Beerbohm had denied in Shaw's fiction, the spectacle of the cynic being led to a sunset by the votary and instructed in the art of looking out of a window is more amusing than Beerbohm's essay. At any rate, one hopes that Tunney was not too discouraged by Beerbohm's conduct. But then there were always the considerable compensations of the Shavian connection; when asked once by a baffled biographer why he persisted so loyally with the Tunney relationship, Shaw replied, 'To keep my feet on solid ground.'[15]

On 5 September 1936, Shaw wrote to Tunney from Malvern inviting him to come to London, after which, Tunney says, 'the letters grew fewer. For one thing, I came to know how much correspondence he had to take care of personally, and I sympathised with his burden. I never wrote a letter to Shaw that he did not answer, and eventually I began to feel that I had no right to intrude on his time.' Tunney then goes on to say a curious thing. On the entry of the United States into the Second World War, he had become a naval officer; being familiar with Shaw's militant pacifism, he had felt reluctant to contact him. 'Then, in 1946, I heard from him again quite suddenly.'[16]

4th December, 1946.

My dear Gene,

I have just picked up your address from a letter you wrote to the Bakon Yeast Man, Curt Fresnel, about H. G. Wells; and I feel I must give you a hail to show that I have not forgotten our old happy contacts.

As I am abominably old, having overstayed my reasonable time so long as to have passed my 90th birthday, you may write me off as a deader. I have only some scraps of wit left and shall soon forget the alphabet and the multiplication table and be unable to walk more than a hundred yards without two sticks. Still I am alive enough to drop you a line.

Charlotte died in 1943. Among her portraits of famous friends was yours. I hear that you and your lady are prosperous and well, and have three sons and a daughter. Keep them off the stage and out of the ring if you can.

I have just received a most barbarously written biography of Harry Greb, which describes him vividly as the foulest fighter on earth, who instructed you so thoroughly in all the tricks of the trade that he never afterwards had a chance against you. All his opponents seem to have liked him though he never fought them fairly.

Is Joe Louis the wonder they say he is?

I tried to see H. G. Wells in his last year; but his baroness put me off every time. We were very good friends; he had Greb's art of keeping all of them, though in controversy or under criticism he made Greb appear an angel in comparison. On paper he died in despair; but I cannot believe that his gaiety ever deserted him. He and I ended as Great Men, and you began as one. Have you found congenial work? But I must stop asking questions, as you must not bother to answer until you have nothing better to do: and meanwhile I shall take silence to be a friendly wave of the hand.[17]

Shaw's last letter to Tunney, written in the summer of 1948, coincided with the visit to London of Joe Louis:

Dear Gene,

It may amuse you to hear that when Joe L. arrived here it was announced that the only people he wished to visit were myself and Winston Churchill. The whole British press made a rush for me (probably also for Churchill) to learn the date and place and hour and minute of the visit. I said I had not heard from Mr Louis; but two comparatively unknown persons like myself and Mr Churchill could not but feel flattered by a visit from a world-famous head of his profession.

This redoubled the clamour for the date. I repeated that I had not heard from the champion; but that he and Mrs Louis would be welcome in my house after his tour, when there could be no question of advertising ourselves. It would be strictly private: no photographers, no reporters, no interviewing, only we three for the pleasure of meeting one another.

And that was the last I heard of it. I have no reason to believe that J.L. knew about the stunt at all, or had ever heard of me or of Winston. I am told that the tour was a failure, and am not surprised; for exhibition spars in soft gloves draw no gates here: they are out-of-date and forgotten; and our sporting crowds know nothing about boxing. What they pay for is bashing. Louis got his 100,000 dollars (reputed) for nothing.

I hope you are all well at home, as I hold you in affectionate remembrance. I am damnably old [92] and ought to be dead.[18]

Long before the dying fall of these last exchanges, the process of Life imitating Art had become complete, as this extra-ordinary evolutionary comedy came to its denouement. Shaw the writer had once taken up boxing, and it remained only for Tunney the boxer to take up writing. This he had done in 1932 with *A Man Must Fight* and in 1941 with *Arms for the Living*. In his first book Tunney tells the only really interesting story he knows, the two fights with Dempsey and their unusual background. At first the reader is carried gently along on a complacent tide of self-justifying reminiscence. The author may be no prose master, but he is at least sufficiently aware of literary style to know he does not possess any. He conducts his narrative clearly and with no fuss, doubtless confident in the knowledge that he is telling a tale which no other man alive could possibly know, or knowing it, could muster the technique to tell it.

Or almost no other man. In following Tunney's account of his own boxing fortunes at their climacteric in Philadelphia, it is as well to remember that Tunney was not the first Cashel Byron, and that an ancient predecessor had once told his own version of the eternal conflict with Paradise:

'Time' was called, and the first round was on.

Now, I knew that the most dangerous thing I could do was to let Sullivan work me into a corner when I was a little tired or dazed, so I made up my mind that I would let him do this while I was still fresh. Then I could find out what he intended doing when he got me there. In a fight, you know, when a man has you where he wants you, he is going to deliver the best goods he has.

From the beginning of the round Sullivan was aggressive – wanted to eat me up right away. He came straight for me and I backed and backed, finally into a corner. While I was there I observed him setting himself for a right-hand swing, first slapping himself on the thigh with his left hand – a sort of trick to balance himself for a terrific swing with his right. But before he let the blow go, just at the right instant, I sidestepped out of the corner and was back in the middle of the ring again, Sullivan hot after me.

I allowed him to back me into all four corners, and he thought he was engineering all this, that it was his own work that was cornering me. But I had learned what I wanted to know – just where to put my head to escape his blow if he should get me cornered and perhaps dazed. He had shown his hand to me.

In the second round he was still backing me around the ring. I hadn't even struck at him yet, and the audience on my right hissed me for running away and began to call me 'Sprinter'. Now I could see at a glance that Sullivan was not quite near enough to hit me, so suddenly I turned my side to him, waved both hands to the audience and called out, 'Wait a while! You'll see a fight.'

At the end of the round I went to my corner and said to Brady and Delaney, 'Why I can whip this fellow slugging!'

At this there was a panic in my corner, all of them starting to whine and plead with me.

'You said you were going to take your time,' they said. 'What are you going to take any chances for?'

'All right,' I replied, to comfort them. 'But I'll take one good punch at him in this round, anyway.'

So far Sullivan hadn't reached me with anything but glancing blows, and it was my intention, when the third round started, to hit him my first punch, and I felt that it *must* be a good one! If my first punch didn't hurt him, he was going to lose all respect for my hitting ability. So, with mind thoroughly made up, I allowed him to back me once more into a corner. But although this time I didn't intend to slip out, by my actions I indicated that I was going to, just as I had before. As we stood there, fiddling, he crowding almost on top of me, I glanced, as I had always done before, first to the left, then to the right, as if looking for some way to get out of this corner. He, following my eye and thinking I wanted to make a getaway, determined that he wouldn't let me out this time!

For once he failed to slap himself on the thigh with his left hand, but he had his right hand all ready for the swing as he was gradually crawling up on me. Then, just as he finally set himself to let go a vicious right I beat him to it and loosed a left-hand for his face with all the power I had behind it. His head went back and I followed it up with a couple of other punches and slugged him back over the ring and into his corner. When the round was over his nose was broken.

At once there was pandemonium in the audience! All over the house, men stood on their chairs, coats off, swinging them in the air. You could have heard the yells clear to the Mississippi River!

But the uproar only made Sullivan the more determined. He came out of his corner in the fourth round like a roaring lion, with an uglier scowl than ever, and bleeding considerably at the nose. I felt sure now that I would beat him, so made up my mind that, though it would take a little longer, I would play safe.

From that time I started doing things the audience were seeing for the first time, judging from the way they talked about the fight afterwards. I would work a left-hand on the nose, then a hook into the stomach, a hook up on the jaw again, a great variety of blows, in fact; using all the time such quick side-stepping and footwork that the audience seemed to be delighted and a little bewildered, as was also Mr Sullivan. That is, bewildered, for I don't think he was delighted.

In the twelfth round we clinched, and, with the referee's order, 'Break away', I dropped my arms, when Sullivan let go a terrific right-hand swing from which I just barely got away; as it was it just grazed the top of my head. Some in the audience began to shout 'Foul!' but I smiled and shook my head, to tell them, 'I don't want it that way.'

So the next eight rounds continued much in the fashion of toreador and the bull, Sullivan making his mad rushes and flailing away with his arms; rarely landing on me, but as determined as ever. Meanwhile I was using all the tricks in my boxing repertoire, which was an entirely new one for that day and an assortment that impressed the audience. Then I noticed that he was beginning to puff and was slowing down a little.

When we came up for the twenty-first round it looked as if the fight would last ten or fifteen rounds longer. Right away I went up to him, feinted with my left and hit him with a left-hand hook alongside the jaw pretty hard, and I saw his eyes roll. . . . Summoning all the reserve force I had left I let my guns go, right and left, with all the dynamite Nature had given me, and Sullivan stood dazed and rocking. So I set myself for an instant, put just a little more in a right and hit him alongside the jaw. And he fell helpless on the ground, on his stomach, and rolled over on his back! The referee, his seconds, and mine picked him up and put him in his corner; and the audience went wild.[19]

Tunney stage-manages his own retrospective triumph rather more modestly than Corbett, sounding almost bored, even boring, as he moved from incident to incident. But then a most peculiar thing begins to happen. Through the decorous neutral tints of Tunney's prose there starts to shine the lurid light of mysticism, or of coincidence at the very least. The reader begins to experience the unsettling sensation that he has read all this before, somewhere else, in a totally different context, in another world. The first faint shadow of speculative surprise flickers for a moment with that proud boast of Tunney's that 'my vision in the ring was always excellent. I used to think I could see a punch coming almost before it started',[20] the remark which seems to echo with freakish accuracy another proud boast made by another heavyweight in a world that neither Tunney nor any other flesh-and-blood pugilist could ever have known; but the conclusions implied by that echo seem to be so fantastical as to be hardly thinkable. And yet now that identical sensation is becoming too marked to ignore, of something, or somewhere, being revisited. The time and place are different, and the sensibility directing the story is fresh and original enough, but still there is an unmistakable feeling of having been here before. It becomes strongest when Tunney arrives at the climax of his story. He is describing his emotions as the first Dempsey fight begins:

When we finally got into the ring things went so much according to plan that they were almost unexciting to me.

We read on, still uncertain as to the source of our confusion. Tunney tells of that surprise right hand punch which rocked Dempsey's body and upset the fine balance of his fighting brain:

I feinted Dempsey a couple of times and then lashed out with the right hand punch, the hardest blow I have ever deliberately struck. . . . He was shaken, dazed. His strength, speed and accuracy were reduced.[21]

Where has all this happened before? And then we remember. The closing pages of *Cashel Byron's Profession*. It is almost as though Tunney were working from Shaw's text. Byron, in preparing to begin his fight with the brutal Paradise:

> . . . stepped through the ropes languidly, and rejecting the proffered assistance of a couple of officious friends, drew on a boxing glove fastidiously, like an exquisite preparing for a fashionable promenade.

Then, in the opening moments of the contest, Paradise rushes at Byron:

> There was a sound like the pop of a champagne cork, after which Cashel was seen undisturbed in the middle of the ring, and Paradise flung against the ropes and trying to grin at his discomfiture, shewed his white teeth through a mask of blood.[22]

What Tunney appears to be doing is to recast his own image in the Shavian mould, which, of course, he had a perfect right to do if he so desired. But it is tempting to wonder whether Shaw, who said that he cultivated Tunney's friendship 'to keep my feet on solid ground',[23] ever quite realised that Dempsey had been defeated by the Life Force disguised as Cashel Byron, that Ned Donnelly had fought his greatest fight in Philadelphia fifty years after welcoming Shaw into the gymnasium in Panton Street, and that James Joseph Eugene Tunney was the most vivid and certainly the most realistic character in the entire Shavian canon.

Whatever the degree of Shaw's own awareness of this unique situation, and however much Tunney's respect for Byron's defensive technique was retrospective, there was not the remotest chance that Shaw might be able to explain to literary friends the bizarre complexities of the Byron–Shaw–Tunney triangle. Instead, Shaw's occasional eccentricities as a fight fan inside the literary and dramatic world remained a mystery to those who had never been initiated into it. There was once an occasion, at a reception held for Shaw by Sir Barry Jackson, when the guest of honour scandalised the company by abruptly disappearing without a word of explanation. It seemed like a studied insult, especially as Shaw had apparently taken good care to cover his tracks once he left the reception. Certainly it proved impossible to find him.

But there was one place where none of his welcoming committee thought of looking. Had they scoured the back stalls of a Birmingham cinema, they would have found their guest of honour sitting there in the dark watching the flickering images of the second Dempsey–Tunney fight, remembering perhaps the days with Donnelly and Beatty, Panton Street and the tourney at Lillie Bridge, and at the same time contemplating the miraculous spectacle of Life imitating Art.

# NOTES

References to Shaw's Correspondence are to Dan H. Laurence's *Bernard Shaw: Collected Letters*, two volumes, Max Reinhardt, 1965 and 1972; e.g. CL, Vol. One, p. 26. In all references to *Cashel Byron's Profession*, the Constable edition of 1932 has been used, as it contains material later appended by Shaw. All other works referred to are listed in the Bibliography.

*Introduction*

1 The two pioneer Fabians must have made the most piquant pair of opponents in the history of boxing; Shaw, who rejected outward appearances while preserving the strictest moral principles, and the frock-coated, monocled Bland, who respected the externals while rejecting the moral principles, fathering a succession of illegitimate children on whom Edith showered as much motherly solicitude as if they had been her own. To Edith (1858–1924), whose most famous books include *The Railway Children, The Treasure Seekers* and *The Phoenix and the Carpet*, the sparring matches must have been like championship fights with herself as the crown; for while she adored her philandering husband, she was also one of that sad battalion of modernistic young women who fell madly in love with Shaw, without ever extracting from him the slightest hint of reciprocal passion. In a poem she wrote of his 'maddening white face', and Hesketh Pearson quotes her as describing Shaw as 'one of the most fascinating men I ever met'. Bland, however, having taken Shaw's sexual measure, was urbane enough not to be jealous of him. See *Bernard Shaw, His Life and Personality* by Hesketh Pearson, pp. 116–17.

2 The phrase is Shaw's own, and one of his favourites in describing that aspect of himself which was so adept at attracting spectacular publicity. Comically abusive descriptions of the chimera G.B.S. are scattered through his autobiographical writings and whether his stage managing of the ostrich was real or retrospective, there is no question that he came in the end to admire his creation with the unselfconscious relish of the true artist.

PART ONE

*Chapter 1*

1 CL, Vol. One, p. 19.

2 See *Self-Defence or the Art of Boxing* by Professor Ned Donnelly.

3 See *A Note on Modern Prizefighting* appended to *Cashel Byron's Profession*. Donnelly used Langham's name to add prestige to his own, and was well-advised to do so; for Langham, a farm labourer from Hinckley, Leicestershire, won a great reputation as the only man ever to defeat the great Tom Sayers of St Pancras. Among those who would have been impressed by Donnelly's connections with Langham was Shaw himself, who referred to the Langham–Sayers contest many years later, in an interview published in the *Sunday News*, 10 July 1927 (p. 157 above). See also *The Great Prize Fight* by Alan Lloyd, p. 55.

4 CL, Vol. Two, p. 120.

5 *Bernard Shaw, An Autobiography*, ed. Weintraub, Vol. One, pp. 97–8.

6 CL, Vol. One, p. 20.

7 George's role as an evangeliser for the gospel of Socialism was prodigious. Shaw wrote: 'When I was swept into the Great Socialist Revival of 1883, I found that five-sixths of those who were swept in with me had been converted by Henry George.' As for the part George played in indirectly leading Shaw to *Das Kapital*: 'I read his *Progress and Poverty*, and went to a meeting of Hyndman's Marxist Democratic Federation, where I rose and protested against its drawing a red herring across the trail blazed by George. I was contemptuously dismissed as a novice who had not read the great first volume of Marx's *Capital*. I promptly read it, and returned to announce my complete conversion by it. Immediately contempt changed to awe; for Hyndman's disciples had not read the book themselves.' See *Bernard Shaw, An Autobiography*, ed. Weintraub, Vol. One, pp. 113–14. Also *Sixteen Self-Sketches* by Shaw, p. 58.

8 CL, Vol. One, p. 49.

9 Ibid., pp. 49–52.

10 See Preface to *Cashel Byron's Profession*, p. 1.

11 CL, Vol. One, p. 60.

12 Ibid., p. 161.

13 Ibid., p. 202.

14 See *Bernard Shaw, An Autobiography*, ed. Weintraub, Vol. One, p. 301.

15 CL, Vol. Two, p. 481.

16 See *Salt and his Circle* by Stephen Winsten. Preface by Shaw, p. 10.

17 CL, Vol. One, pp. 425–8.

18 See *Shaw, His Life and Personality* by Pearson, p. 106.

19 Preface to *Cashel Byron's Profession*, p. x.

20 CL, Vol. One, p. 113.

21 Ibid., p. 111.

22 Ibid., pp. 113–14.

23 See *Shaw, Man of the Century* by Henderson, Vol. One, p. 118.

24 Ibid., p. 119.

25 Ibid., pp. 118–19.

26 See *History of the English People in the Nineteenth Century*, Vol. Six, by Elie Halevy, p. 48.

27 See *The Rise and Fall of the Man of Letters* by John Gross, pp. 99–112.

28 See *Victorian England – Portrait of an Age* by G. M. Young, p. 162.

29 CL, Vol. One, p. 388.

30 See *Days With Bernard Shaw* by Stephen Winsten, p. 178.

31 See *Shaw, Man of the Century* by Henderson, Vol. One, p. 111.

32 CL, Vol. One, pp. 30–1.

33 See *Shaw, Man of the Century* by Henderson, Vol. One, p. 111.

34 Ibid., p. 111.

35 CL, Vol. One, pp. 31–2.

36 See *Shaw, Man of the Century* by Henderson, Vol. One, p. 116.

37 The *Star* was founded in 1888 with T. P. O'Connor (Tay Pay) as its first editor. O'Connor soon saw that Shaw's political tracts were too outrageous to publish and told Shaw so. According to Shaw: 'He was too good-natured to sack me, and I did not want to throw away my job; so I got him out of his difficulty by asking him to let me have two columns a week for a feuilleton on music. He was glad to get rid of my politics on these terms; but he stipulated that – musical criticism being known to him only as unreadable and unintelligible jargon – I should, for God's sake, not write about Bach in B minor. I was quite alive to that danger; in fact I had made my proposal because I believed I could make musical criticism readable even by the deaf. Besides, my terms were moderate: Two guineas a week.' But when Shaw left the *Star*, it was because his terms had grown slightly less moderate. As Tay Pay wrote in his valedictory: 'The larger salary of a weekly organ of the classes has proved too much for the virtues even of a Fabian.' See *Bernard Shaw, An Autobiography*, ed. Weintraub, Vol. One, p. 218.

38 CL, Vol. One, p. 185.

39 Ibid., p. 242.

40 Ibid., p. 336.

41 See *Days With Bernard Shaw* by Winsten, p. 83 and pp. 172–3.

42 Flinging abuse at Morley's *Life of Gladstone* became for a time a popular literary diversion. Frank Swinnerton described Morley as 'a most influential buzzer' and referred to his authorship thus: 'author of the monument under which Gladstone was long buried'. Arnold Bennett wrote of 'the calamities of tedium' produced by biographers like Morley, and added later 'Nobody, after reading Morley, could construct for himself a portrait of the man Gladstone. The book is inhuman.' Even Gladstone's son Herbert had to admit that 'Morley's pages do not present, for those who did not know Mr Gladstone, a true and complete view of his personality.' See *Background With Chorus* by Frank Swinnerton, p. 87, also *The Evening Standard Years* by Arnold Bennett, p. 156 and p. 324.

*Chapter 2*

1 See Preface to *Cashel Byron's Profession*, p. vii.
2 Ibid., pp. vii–viii.
3 Ibid., p. viii.
4 See *Bernard Shaw, His Life and Personality* by Pearson, p. 113.
5 See *Shaw, Man of the Century* by Henderson, Vol. One, p. 126.
6 See *Bernard Shaw, His Life and Personality* by Pearson, p. 113.
7 Ibid., pp. 113–14.
8 Years later, long after Mrs Besant had forsaken the gods of Utopian Socialism for the nebulosities of Madame Blavatsky, Shaw wrote that 'the chief fault of her extraordinary qualities was that she was fiercely proud. I tried, by means of elaborate little comedies, to disgust her with beneficence and to make her laugh at her pride; but the treatment was not, as far as I know, very successful.' See *Shaw, Man of the Century* by Henderson, Vol. One, p. 126.
9 See *Bernard Shaw, His Life and Personality* by Pearson, p. 114.
10 See *Days With Bernard Shaw* by Winsten, p. 111.
11 See *Bernard Shaw, An Autobiography*, ed. Weintraub, Vol. One, p. 98.
12 CL, Vol. One, p. 260.
13 Ibid., p. 550.
14 See *Shaw, Man of the Century* by Henderson, Vol. One, pp. 127–8.
15 Charles Aubrey Smith (Cambridge, Sussex and England) (1863–1948). Captained Arthur Shrewsbury's side to Australia 1887–8; captained first-ever English touring side to South Africa 1888–9. His eccentric bowling action earned him his nickname 'Round-the-Corner' Smith. Later he became Hollywood's symbolic English gentleman, playing in such un-Shavian dramas as *Tarzan the Ape-Man*, *The Life of a Bengal Lancer*, *China Seas* and *The Prisoner of Zenda*.
16 See *Days With Bernard Shaw* by Winsten, p. 156.
17 See Preface to *Cashel Byron's Profession*, p. x.
18 Although Sullivan is usually listed as the first World Heavyweight Champion under Queensberry rules, and although it is true he did defend his title in glove contests, the victory over Paddy Ryan which won him the title was a bare-knuckle fight. Corbett was the first World Heavyweight Champion to win *and* lose the title wearing gloves.

*Chapter 3*

1 See *What Do You Know About Boxing?* by W. Buchanan-Taylor, p. 115.
2 Ibid., p. 114.
3 Dixon's play proved surprisingly durable. In 1909 a veteran producer called George Brennan began making a silent movie out of it, and got as far as the end of the first reel. But the man who eventually succeeded in giving Dixon's melodrama a kind of immortality was D. W. Griffith, who came to an arrangement with Dixon in 1915 and committed the Reverend's excesses to celluloid. See *The Real Tinsel* by Rosenberg and Silverstein, pp. 324–5.

4 O'Brien was not quite the blushing violet which the incident in the hotel suggests. Edmund Wilson quotes the following anecdote concerning O'Brien's famous victory over Fitzsimmons: 'O'Brien knocked out Fitzsimmons – but Fitzsimmons was old then. Jack found out that Fitzsimmons' mother and father were in the poor-house in Ballarat, Australia, and when the fight began he said, "Yuh know where I'm going to send yuh? I'm going to send yuh right back to Ballarat to join your old man and your old woman in the poor-house".' See *The Twenties* by Edmund Wilson, p. 272.

## Chapter 4

1 See Preface to *Cashel Byron's Profession*, p. x.
2 See *Bernard Shaw, An Autobiography*, ed. Weintraub, Vol. One, p. 102.
3 See *Bernard Shaw, His Life and Personality* by Hesketh Pearson, p. 59.
4 See *The Shavian Playground* by Margery Morgan, pp. 15–20.
5 Ibid., pp. 15–20.
6 See 'A Note on Modern Prizefighting', appended to *Cashel Byron's Profession*.

## PART TWO

### Chapter 1

1 Whether Dempsey was also above reproach as an artist is a different matter. The shambling figure of Luis Angel Firpo stands across the path of the theory, a great ursine impediment to the idea that Dempsey was an incomparable virtuoso. Can a man be a virtuoso who trades punches on terms of desperate equality with a brave amateur? The answer is yes, because the lapse of concentration for one-tenth part of one second can turn the greatest champion into the greatest booby. Even so, the untidy night's entertainment provided by Dempsey and Firpo has never fitted very well into the mosaic of the Dempsey legend, as A. J. Liebling, one of the most perceptive of all boxing writers, has noted: 'Firpo was so crude that Marciano would be a Fancy Dan in comparison. He could be hit with only one hand – his right – he hadn't the faintest idea of what to do in close, and he never cared much for the business anyway. He knocked Jack McAuliffe out, and then, in a later "elimination" bout, stopped poor old Willard. He subsequently became a legend by going one-and-a-half sensational rounds with Dempsey, in a time that is now represented to us as the golden age of pugilism.' See *The Sweet Science* by A. J. Liebling, p. 256.
2 It is said that Sullivan insisted on the use of gloves because after his bare-knuckle defence against Jake Kilrain in 1889, he had been plagued by so many legal actions arising out of his breach of state laws. Sullivan claimed to be out of pocket for the Kilrain bout by 18,670 dollars.

### Chapter 2

1 CL, Vol. One, p. 137.
2 Ibid., p. 150.

3  Ibid., pp. 140–1.
4  Ibid., p. 144. The poem referred to was Beatty's *Quia Multum Amavi* which appeared in *Today*, February 1886.
5  Ibid., pp. 150–1.
6  Ibid., p. 152.
7  Ibid., p. 160.
8  Ibid., p. 163.
9  Ibid., pp. 169–70.
10 Ibid., p. 250.
11 Ibid., p. 388.
12 CL, Vol. Two, pp. 59–62.
13 CL, Vol. Two, p. 120.
14 Ibid., pp. 465–8.
15 See *Days With Bernard Shaw* by Stephen Winsten, p. 54.
16 CL, Vol. One, p. 173.
17 Ibid., p. 375.
18 Ibid., pp. 559–60.
19 See note 2 to Preface above.

*Chapter 3*

1  Orson and Valentine were two diametrically opposed characters in a popular pantomime of the period. The role of the ugly Orson was sometimes played by retired prizefighters, whose professional obligations had moulded their features into the required shape.
2  See Shaw's *London Music*, entry of 17 January 1890.
3  See *The Statesman*, 13 December 1919.
4  See *Very Ordinary Sportsman* by J. P. Mallalieu, p. 155.
5  Ibid., p. 157.

*Chapter 4*

1  See *Very Ordinary Sportsman* by J. P. Mallalieu, p. 154.
2  In the Shavian context, it is vitally important to keep in mind the fact that Carpentier, far from retiring after the Siki débâcle, continued practising his profession for some years, and still had in front of him one of the most fascinating stylistic battles of his career, the one in which the failed Cashel Byron fought the flourishing one.
3  See 'Battling Siki of Senegal' by Richard West, *The Spectator*, 22 November 1975.

*Chapter 5*

1  See *The Aspirin Age*, ed. Isabel Leighton, pp. 170–1.
2  Ibid., p. 169.
3  Ibid., p. 163.
4  Ibid., p. 162.

5 See *The Noble Art* compiled by T. B. Shepherd, p. 25.
6 See *The Little Nugget* by P. G. Wodehouse, p. 75.
7 See *The Noble Art*, ed. T. B. Shepherd, pp. 214–15.
8 See *The Aspirin Age*, ed. Isabel Leighton, p. 168.
9 See Shaw report on Dempsey–Carpentier fight, *Observer*, 11 September 1921.
10 See *The Aspirin Age*, ed. Isabel Leighton, p. 166.
11 See *Thirty Years With G.B.S.* by Blanche Patch, p. 153.
12 See *The Portable Ring Lardner*, p. 214.
13 Ibid., p. 609.
14 Runyon was one of millions of sporting gentlemen who assumed cultural curiosity to be incompatible with the fighting temperament. In a story called *Bred for Battle*, Thunderbolt Mulrooney, only child of a slugger who married the sister of one of his toughest rivals, refuses to lay a glove on his opponents. It is finally revealed that Thunderbolt is the illegitimate son of a stoop-shouldered aesthete who plays the zither. See *Take It Easy* by Damon Runyon.
15 Tunney had long since become inured to strong words. For some years he had been weathering the storm of abuse which the boxing fraternity, of which Dempsey's bodyguard was a perfect representative, was always inclined to fling at a man known to do something as girlish as think two consecutive thoughts. One witness told the critic Edmund Wilson that 'somebody began a fight with the gentleman Tunney by saying "Yuh oughtn'ta be a prizefighter, yuh fuck – yuh oughta be a bootblack."' See *The Twenties* by Edmund Wilson, p. 272.
16 See *The Boxing Companion*, ed. Denzil Batchelor, p. 263. The mention of Harry Wills is a reference to the fact that Wills, who campaigned throughout the 1920s for a shot at Dempsey's title, never did manage to tempt the champion into the ring with him. Whether Dempsey was dubious of his ability to defeat Wills, whether it was the machinations of adherents like Normile that frustrated the challenge, or whether there was an unspoken agreement among the boxing fraternity that the risk of being saddled with another black champion as arrogant as Jack Johnson was too awful to contemplate, nobody has ever been sure. It is part of the sentimental legend of boxing that a contract was actually signed between Dempsey and Wills, but was never implemented; it was eventually buried under the coping-stone of the new Madison Square Garden.
17 See *Bernard Shaw, Man of the Century* by Archibald Henderson, Vol. One, note to p. 102.
18 See *Remembering Mr Maugham* by Garson Kanin, p. 193.
19 See *The Boxing Companion*, ed. Denzil Batchelor, pp. 229–33.
20 See *The Sweet Science* by A. J. Liebling, p. 196.

Chapter 6

1 See *The Aspirin Age*, ed. Isabel Leighton, p. 175.
2 See *Cashel Byron's Profession* (p. 74 above).

3 See *The Aspirin Age*, ed. Isabel Leighton, pp. 173–4.
4 See *Only Yesterday* by Frederick Lewis Allen, p. 149.
5 See *The Noble Art* compiled by T. B. Shepherd, pp. 12–13.
6 Before we leave Burke for the last time and abandon him to his fate in the pages of *Cashel Byron's Profession*, it is only fair to note that in addition to so casually catching the literary fancy of the young Shaw, Jack Burke remains in the record books for another, rather more technical achievement, which will now never be surpassed. On 6 April 1893, Burke went to New Orleans to fight a rival lightweight called Andy Bowen, only to discover that he and his opponent were so perfectly matched that any hope of a decision was remote. The spectators arrived early, watched the contest for a few hours before going off to get some dinner. When they returned, Burke and Bowen were still fighting. It is said that local vaudevillians watched the opening rounds, left for their various theatres to play their parts, and then came back to find Burke and Bowen just beginning to warm up. At daybreak, after seven hours and ten minutes of scrapping spread over 110 rounds, Bowen stumbled from exhaustion and the referee declared 'No Contest'. Bowen was later killed in mid-contest, but Burke, who never did much in the ring after the marathon at New Orleans, partnered his wife in a boxing act in vaudeville. He died in 1913.

## Chapter 7

1 See *Colliers Magazine*, 23 June 1951.
2 Ibid.
3 Ibid.
4 Ibid.
5 See *Bernard Shaw, His Life and Personality* by Pearson, p. 355.
6 See *Days With Bernard Shaw* by Stephen Winsten, p. 115.
7 See *Thirty Years with G.B.S.* by Blanche Patch, p. 154.
8 See *Colliers Magazine*, 23 June 1951.
9 Ibid.
10 Ibid.
11 Ibid.
12 Ibid.
13 See *Conversations With Max* by S. N. Behrman, pp. 179–80.
14 See *Saturday Review*, 2 November 1901.
15 See *Shaw's Corner* by Stephen Winsten, p. 195.
16 See *Colliers Magazine*, 23 June 1951.
17 Ibid.
18 Ibid.
19 See *The American Reader*, ed. Paul M. Angle, pp. 414–17.
20 See p. 165 above.
21 See *The Aspirin Age*, ed. Isabel Leighton, pp. 162–78.
22 From *Cashel Byron's Profession*, Ch. 10.
23 See note 15 to Part 2, Chapter 7 above.

# THE WORLD HEAVYWEIGHT
# CHAMPIONSHIP: 1892–1928

1892: 7 September. James J. Corbett defeated John L. Sullivan in 21 rounds at New Orleans, Louisiana.

1897: 17 March. Robert Fitzsimmons defeated Corbett in 14 rounds at Carson City, Nevada.

1899: 9 June. James J. Jeffries defeated Fitzsimmons in 11 rounds at Coney Island, New York.

1900: 11 May. Jeffries defeated Corbett in 23 rounds at Coney Island, New York.

1902: 25 July. Jeffries defeated Fitzsimmons in 8 rounds at San Francisco, California.

1903: 14 August. Jeffries defeated Corbett in 10 rounds at San Francisco, California.

1905: James J. Jeffries retired.

1906: 23 February. Tommy Burns defeated Marvin Hart over 20 rounds at Los Angeles, California.

1908: 25 December. Jack Johnson defeated Tommy Burns in 14 rounds at Sydney, Australia.

1910: 4 July. Johnson defeated Jeffries in 14 rounds at Sydney, Australia.

1915: 5 April. Jess Willard defeated Johnson in 26 rounds at Havana, Cuba.

1919: 4 July. Jack Dempsey defeated Willard in 3 rounds at Toledo. Ohio.

1920: 6 August. Dempsey defeated Billy Miske in 3 rounds at Benton Harbour, Michigan.

1920: 14 December. Dempsey defeated Bill Brennan in 12 rounds at New York City, N.Y.

1921: 2 July. Dempsey defeated Georges Carpentier in 4 rounds at Jersey City, New Jersey.

1923: 4 July. Dempsey defeated Tom Gibbons over 15 rounds at Shelby, Montana.

1923: 14 September. Dempsey defeated Luis Angel Firpo in 2 rounds at New York City, N.Y.

1926: 23 September. Gene Tunney defeated Dempsey over 10 rounds at Philadelphia, Pennsylvania.

1927: 22 September. Tunney defeated Dempsey over 10 rounds at Chicago, Illinois.

1928: 23 July. Tunney defeated Tom Heeney in 11 rounds at New York City, N.Y.

1928: Tunney retired.

# BIBLIOGRAPHY

Allen, Frederick Lewis. *Only Yesterday*. Bantam, New York, 1958.
Angle, Paul M. (ed). *The American Reader*. Rand McNally, Chicago, 1958.
Batchelor, Denzil (ed.). *The Boxing Companion*. Eyre and Spottiswoode, London, 1964.
Beerbohm, Max. *Around Theatres*. Hart-Davis, London, 1953.
Behrman, S. N. *Conversations With Max*. Hamish Hamilton, London, 1960.
Bennett, Arnold. *The Evening Standard Years*. Chatto and Windus, London, 1974.
Buchanan-Taylor, W. *What Do You Know About Boxing?* Heath Cranton, London, 1947.
Corbett, James J. *The Roar of the Crowd*, Doubleday, Garden City, New York, 1926.
Donnelly, Ned. *Self-Defence or the Art of Boxing*. Wyman, London, 1897.
Dreiser, Theodore, *A Book About Myself*. Constable, London, 1897.
Gross, John. *The Rise and Fall of the Man of Letters*. Weidenfeld and Nicolson, London, 1969.
Halevy, Elie. *History of the English People in the 19th Century*. Ernest Benn, London, 1934.
Henderson, Archibald. *Bernard Shaw, Man of the Century*. Da Capo Press, New York, 1956.
Kanin, Garson. *Remembering Mr Maugham*. Athenaeum-Bantam, New York, 1966.
Lardner, Ring. *The Portable Ring Lardner*. Viking, New York, 1946.
Laurence, Dan H. (ed). *Bernard Shaw: Collected Letters*, Vol. One, 1965; Vol. Two, 1972. Max Reinhardt, London.
Liebling, A. J. *The Sweet Science*. Gollancz, London, 1956.
Leighton, Isabel (ed). *The Aspirin Age*. Penguin, Harmondsworth, 1964.
Lloyd, Alan. *The Great Prize Fight*. Cassell, London, 1977.
Magnus, Philip. *Gladstone*. John Murray, London, 1954.
Mallalieu, J. P. *Very Ordinary Sportsman*. Routledge and Kegan Paul, London, 1957.
Moore, Doris Langley. *E. Nesbit*. Ernest Benn, London, 1933.
Morgan, Margery, M. *The Shavian Playground*. Methuen, London, 1972.
Patch, Blanche. *Thirty Years with G.B.S.* Gollancz, London, 1951.
Pearson, Hesketh. *Bernard Shaw, His Life and Personality*. Collins, London, 1942.

Runyon, Damon. 'Bred For Battle', from *Runyon on Broadway*. Constable, London, 1950.

Shaw, George Bernard, *Heartbreak House*. Constable, London, 1919.

—— *The Admirable Bashville*. Constable, London, 1926.

—— *The Intelligent Woman's Guide*. Constable, London, 1928.

—— *Immaturity*. Constable, London, 1931.

—— *Cashel Byron's Profession*. Constable, London, 1932.

—— *An Unsocial Socialist*. Constable, London, 1932.

—— Introduction to *Great Expectations* by Charles Dickens. Hamish Hamilton Novel Library Edition, London, 1947.

—— *Sixteen Self-Sketches*. Constable, London, 1949.

—— *London Music*. Constable, London, 1937.

Shepherd, T. B. (ed). *The Noble Art*. Hollis and Carter, London, 1950.

Swinnerton, Frank. *Background With Chorus*. Hutchinson, London, 1956.

Tunney, Gene. *A Man Must Fight*. Jonathan Cape, London, 1932.

—— *Arms for Living*. Longmans, London, 1941.

Weintraub, Stanley (ed.). *Bernard Shaw, An Autobiography 1856–1898*. Max Reinhardt, London, 1969.

Wilson, Edmund. *The Twenties*. Macmillan, London, 1975.

Winsten, Stephen. *Days with Bernard Shaw*. Hutchinson, London, 1951.

—— *Salt and His Circle*. Hutchinson, London, 1951.

—— *Shaw's Corner*. Hutchinson, London, 1952.

Wodehouse, P. G. *The Little Nugget*. Penguin, Harmondsworth, 1975.

Young, G. M. *Victorian England – Portrait of an Age*. O.U.P., Oxford, 1936.

# INDEX

New York stage, 48–57
*New York Sun*, 153, 155; and *Cashel Byron's Profession*, 58–60
*Night's Lodging, A* (Gorky), 51
Normile, Gene, 149–51, 201
Nurmi, Paavo, 167, 168

O'Brien, Jack, 66–9, 149, 198
*Observer, The* 114
O'Connor, T. P., 35–6, 197
*Of Human Bondage* (Maugham), 155
Oliphant, Laurence, 31
*Our Corner* magazine, 20, 21, 41; serialises Shaw's rejected fiction, 20, 43–4
*Our Mutual Friend*, 31

*Pall Mall Gazette*, 15, 31–5
Palmer, Pedlar, 82
Panton Street gymnasium, 3–5, 82, 96, 99, 101, 143, 145, 193, 194
'Paquito', *see* Beatty, Pakenham
Patch, Blanche, 145–6, 156
Patterson, Jenny, 89–90
Payne-Townshend, Charlotte, *see* Shaw, Charlotte
Pearson, Hesketh, 44, 71, 195
*Peter Pan* (Barrie), 51
Phelps, William Lyon, 155
Pitt, William, 133
Poincaré, Raymond, 127
Preston, Sir Harry, 175
*Prince Otto* (Stevenson), 21
*Professor's Love Story, The* (Barrie), 51

Queensberry, Marquess of, and Queensberry Rules, 5, 83, 96

Richards, Grant, 46, 185
Richardson, Bill, and the Blue Anchor, 71
Rickards, Tex, 114
Ricketts, Charles, 37
Robertson, John M., and Shaw's early novels, 20–1, 23, 41; on *Cashel Byron's Profession*, 21–2, 44
Rousseau, Jean-Jacques, 35
Royal Library of Dublin, Shaw presents manuscripts to, 26
Rubinstein, Arthur, 55
Runciman, James, 46
Runciman, John F., 46
Runyon, Damon, 147, 201
Ruskin, John, 17, 34
Russell, Bertrand, 97
Ruth, Babe, 161
Ryan, Paddy, 57, 198

Saint Louis, Senegal, 122, 123
*Salome* (Wilde), 51

Salt, Henry, 31
*Saturday Review*, 41, 185
*Saturday Review* (American), 46
Sayers, Tom, 108–9, 159, 196
Scott, Clement, 49
Scott, Sir Walter, 14, 19, 27
Senegal and the Senegalese, 122–4, 127–30, 132, 135
Sharkey, Jack, 156
*Shaving of Shagpat, The* (Meredith), 31
Shaw, Charlotte (née Payne-Townshend) (wife of G.B.S.), 36, 172, 179, 180, 183, 187
Shaw, George Bernard: *Cashel Byron's Profession*, see separate entry; early novels, 3, 20–1, 37–41, 43, 45–8; and Ned Donnelly, 3–7, 82, 99, 171; and Pakenham Beatty, 5–7, 86–98; and Socialism 8, 18–19, 26–7, 39–41, 43; vegetarianism, 8; and Ethel Southam, 9–11; on effective narrative fiction, 9–10; and publishers' rejections, 23–6, 28, 29, 34–5, 37; and John Morley, 28–9, 31–7, writes for *The Star*, 35–6; *The Admirable Bashville*, 39, 46–8, 93, 180; and Annie Besant, 41–4; and the New York press, 51–6, 58–66; *Notes on Modern Prizefighting*, 75–6; and the Life Force, xii, 80, 143; and Life imitating Art, 80; no interest in boxing for many years, 81–3, 97–8; *nom-de-plume* of L. O. Streeter, 87–8; essay on Carpentier's fight with Beckett, 98–112; predicts result of Carpentier v. Dempsey, 102, 110, 111; on betting and boxing, 107–8, 120, 131; plea on behalf of prizefighting, 109, 111–12; sees film of Dempsey–Carpentier fight, 114; report on the film, 114–20, 143–4; on American in-fighting, 117–20; comments on Siki–Carpentier fight, 127–30; and allegations of skulduggery over the fight, 130–4; watches film of second Dempsey–Tunney fight, 194; apocryphal story of Shaw and Tunney, 145–6; and proposal for Tunney to play Cashel Byron, 153–5; on the Milligan–Walker fight, 156–60; and Norman Clark, 168–74; views on Tunney, 172–4, 178–9; correspondence with Tunney, 175–8, 180–4, 187–8; meets Tunney, 172, 176–7; at Brioni with him, 176–8, 183; holiday in Istria, 178–9; declines to write preface to Tunney's book, 181–3
Shaw, George Carr, father of G.B.S., 87–8
Shaw, Lucinda, mother of G.B.S., 10, 47, 92